DATE DUE

MY 21 '97			
OC 16 '97			
NO 18 '97			
DE 19 97			
DE 17 98			
MY 24 99			
AP 24 00			
OC 14 00			

DEMCO 38-296

FINANCIAL STATEMENT ANALYSIS

Second Edition

WILEY FRONTIERS IN FINANCE
Edited by Edward I. Altman

Damodaran on Valuation: Security Analysis for Investment and Corporate Finance
Aswath Damodaran (Book/Disk set also available)

Study Guide for Damodaran on Valuation: Security Analysis for Investment and Corporate Finance
Aswath Damodaran

Valuation: Measuring and Managing the Value of Companies, Second Edition
Tom Copeland, Tim Koller, and Jack Murrin (Book/Disk set also available)

Financial Statement Analysis, Second Edition
Martin S. Fridson

Style Investing: Unique Insight Into Asset Allocation
Richard Bernstein

The Stock Market, 6th Edition
Richard J. Teweles, Edward S. Bradley, and Ted M. Teweles

Fixed Income Securities: Tools for Today's Markets
Bruce Tuckman

Financial Statement Analysis

A Practitioner's Guide, Second Edition

Martin S. Fridson

John Wiley & Sons, Inc.

New York • Chichester • Brisbane • Toronto • Singapore

In memory of my father, Harry Yale Fridson
who introduced me to accounting, economics, and logic, as well as
the fourth discipline essential to the creation of this book—hard work!

This text is printed on acid-free paper.

Copyright © 1995 by Martin S. Fridson
Published by John Wiley & Sons, Inc.

All rights reserved. Published simultaneously in Canada.

Reproduction or translation of any part of this work beyond
that permitted by Section 107 or 108 of the 1976 United
States Copyright Act without the permission of the copyright
owner is unlawful. Requests for permission or further
information should be addressed to the Permissions Department,
John Wiley & Sons, Inc.

This publication is designed to provide accurate and authoritative
information in regard to the subject matter covered. It is sold
with the understanding that the publisher is not engaged in
rendering legal, accounting, or other professional services. If
legal advice or other expert assistance is required, the services
of a competent professional person should be sought.

Library of Congress Cataloging-in-Publication Data:

Fridson, Martin S.
    Financial statement analysis : a practitioner's guide / Martin S.
Fridson.—2nd ed.
        p.   cm.—(Wiley Frontiers in Finance)
    Includes bibliographical references and index.
    ISBN 0-471-08553-7
    1. Financial statements.   2. Ratio analysis.   I. Title.
    II. Series.
    HF5681.B2F772   1995
    657'.3—dc20   94-31659

Printed in the United States of America

10 9 8 7 6 5 4 3 2

PREFACE TO SECOND EDITION

This new edition of *Financial Statement Analysis,* like its predecessor, seeks to equip its readers for practical challenges of contemporary business. Once again, the intention is to acquaint readers who have already acquired basic accounting skills with the complications that arise in applying textbook-derived knowledge to the real world of extending credit and investing in securities. Although only a few years have passed since publication of the first edition, a swiftly changing environment has necessitated extensive revisions and additions.

For one thing, fraudulent financial reporting has grabbed more and more headlines as the 1990s have unfolded. This is not to say, necessarily, that misrepresentation is more prevalent than in the past. Perhaps investigative journalists are more effective than formerly in ferreting out chicanery. However that may be, today's financial analysts will profit by closer scrutiny of the audit process, an area of increased focus in the present edition. Instead of merely reciting the particulars of notorious frauds, I have highlighted danger signals that may help readers avoid victimization in future scams.

A second important financial trend of the past few years is the reduced popularity of highly leveraged transactions. Even before the first edition of *Financial Statement Analysis* was completed, credit problems began to develop at a few excessively debt-laden companies. The difficulties received some mention then. This new edition, however, views the phenomenon from a superior vantage point by following the emergence from bankruptcy of many of the prominent overleveraged buyouts.

Various transformations in the business world have prompted refinements in several recommended analytical methods. For example, assessment of electric utilities must now take into account a greatly increased regulatory emphasis on competition. Inevitably, too, the new edition contains an altered mix of illustrative industries and companies, reflecting changes in growth, risk, and profitability.

In the constantly evolving field of financial reporting, analysts armed only with formal accounting knowledge are seriously handicapped. They may expend considerable time and energy attempting to determine precisely how a new development will "work out on the books." Before long, however, they will discover that the details disclosed in the press release are probably insufficient to generate a completely accurate pro forma estimate of the next period's stated asset values and net income. The exercise is usually beside the point, in any event, for investors and lenders are typically more interested to know (and to know quickly) whether the news *materially* affects the criteria by which they evaluate the company.

Answering this question has less to do with the technicalities of accounting adjustments than with the impact on future cash flow. It is on the latter that this book focuses, drawing its illustrations from a practitioner's experience with hundreds of issuers over several business cycles.

As for the plan of *Financial Statement Analysis,* readers should not feel compelled to tackle its chapters in numerical sequence; yet there is a logical intent underlying the arrangement of the material. To understand why quarterly and annual reports often seem to conceal more than they reveal, analysts must first discard the premise that financial statements simply represent corporations' attempts to offer unbiased portraits of themselves to interested parties. In Part One, I discuss the complex motivations of issuing firms and of their managers—which do not necessarily coincide—as well as the additional distortions sometimes produced by the organizational context in which the analyst operates.

Part Two takes a hard look at the information that appears on the basic financial statements—as well as the information that is left out. Under close scrutiny, terms such as "value" and "income" begin to look muddier than they appear when considered in the abstract. Even "cash flow," a concept commonly thought to be redeemingly clarifying, is not entirely invulnerable to stratagems designed to manipulate the perceptions of investors and creditors.

Having observed in Part One how the battle for analysts' hearts and minds is fought from the issuer's side, then having learned from Part Two the range of ploys available to management, the reader should by now have imbibed the healthy skepticism necessary for reaching sound conclusions through a structured approach. In Part Three, for both credit and equity evaluation, forward-looking analysis is emphasized over seductive but ultimately unsatisfying retrospection. Tips for maximizing the accuracy of forecasts are included, and a critical eye is cast on standard financial ratios, however widely accepted they may be. The final chapter underscores the need for modifying one's analytical techniques when the economic characteristics of companies (or government entities) refuse to conform to familiar models.

One last pointer for readers of *Financial Statement Analysis* is that I have attempted, insofar as possible, to make each chapter self-contained. Carrying this policy to the extreme, however, would result in certain terms being defined repeatedly, which would severely impede the narrative. Accordingly, a Glossary is included in the volume so that readers can easily learn the meaning of an unfamiliar term regardless of where in the text they may encounter it. For the most part, rudimentary accounting concepts are not defined in the Glossary since, as mentioned earlier, the book's level of discussion presumes a general acquaintance with such material.

ACKNOWLEDGMENTS

Mukesh Agarwal
John K. Bace
Mitchell P. Bartlett
Richard J. Byrne
Richard Cagney
Sanford M. Cohen
Margarita Declet
Sylvan Feldstein
David S. Fitton
Thomas J. Flynn III
Igor S. Fuksman
Ryan J. Gelrod
Kenneth R. Goldberg
Evelyn F. Harris
Avi Katz
Rebecca Keim
James F. Kenney
Les B. Levi
Michael Marocco

John W. Mattis
Krishna Memani
Ann Mame Mullan
Kingman Penniman
Richard A. Rolnick
Clare D. Schiedermayer
Elaine Sisman
Charles Snow
Vladimir Stadnyk
Scott L. Thomas
John Tinker
Sharyl C. Van Winkle
David M. Waill
Steven R. Waite
Douglas Watson
Burton Weinstein
Stephen W. Weiss
Mark D. Zand

CONTENTS

Part One

**READING BETWEEN
THE LINES**

1

THE ADVERSARIAL NATURE OF FINANCIAL REPORTING

FINANCIAL STATEMENT ANALYSIS is an essential skill in a variety of occupations, including investment management, corporate finance, commercial lending, and the extension of credit. For individuals engaged in such activities—or who analyze financial data in connection with their personal investment decisions—there are two distinct approaches to the task.

The first is to follow a prescribed routine, filling in boxes with standard financial ratios, calculated according to precise and inflexible definitions. It may take little more effort or mental exertion than this to satisfy the formal requirements of many positions in the field of financial analysis. Operating in a purely mechanical manner will not provide much of a professional challenge, nor will a rote completion of all of the "proper" standard analytical steps ensure a useful—or even a nonharmful—result, but some individuals will view these problems as only minor drawbacks.

This book is aimed at the analyst who will adopt the second and more rewarding alternative, namely the relentless pursuit of accurate financial profiles of the entities being analyzed. Tenacity is essential because financial statements often conceal more than they reveal. To the analyst who pursues this proactive approach, producing a standard spreadsheet on a company is a means rather than an end. Investors derive but little satisfaction from the knowledge that an untimely stock purchase recommendation was supported by the longest row of figures available in the software package. Genuinely valuable analysis begins *after* all the usual questions have been answered. Indeed, a superior analyst adds value by raising questions that are not even on the checklist.

Some readers may not immediately concede the necessity of going beyond—even, in certain cases, of discarding—an analytical structure that puts all companies on a uniform, objective scale. Comparability, after all, is a cornerstone of generally accepted accounting principles (GAAP). It might therefore seem to follow that financial statements prepared in accordance with GAAP necessarily produce fair and useful comparisons. Moreover, corporations that issue financial statements would appear to have a natural interest in utilizing formats that facilitate convenient, cookie-cutter analysis. After all, these companies spend heavily to disseminate information about themselves. They employ investor-relations managers, they communicate with existing and potential shareholders via interim financial reports and press releases, and they dispatch senior management to periodic meetings with securities analysts. If companies desire so earnestly to make themselves and their financial results known to investors, they should be eager to make it easy for analysts to monitor their progress . . . or so it would seem.

In truth, the two foregoing assumptions—the objectivity of GAAP-based financial statements and the desire of corporations to facilitate accurate analysis—misconstrue the motives that frequently underlie financial reporting. Corporations have substantial incentives to exploit the fact that accounting principles are neither fixed for all time nor so precise as to be open to only a single interpretation. Analysts who appreciate the magnitude of the economic stakes, as well as the latitude available under the accounting rules, will see that a verdict derived by passively calculating standard ratios may prove dangerously naive.

To be more specific, a corporation exists for the benefit of its shareholders, not for the purpose of educating the public about its financial condition. From this standpoint, the best kind of financial statement is not one that represents the company's condition most fully and most fairly, but rather one that results in the highest possible price for the company's stock. The Securities and Exchange Commission (SEC) and the Financial Accounting Standards Board prohibit companies from going too far in the latter direction, but these regulators refrain from advising corporations exactly how far they may go. Opinions are bound to vary regarding the ethical aspects of the problem, such as the extent to which a company is obligated to divulge bad news that may harm the perception (and the price) of its stock. Some corporations will inevitably gravitate toward the standard of disclosure that if nobody happens to ask about a specific event, then declining to volunteer the information does not constitute a lie. (The SEC says that a company must disclose the information if it is material but does not define materiality with any great precision.)

Woolworth shed light on the corporate perspective on financial reporting when it launched an internal investigation of alleged accounting irregularities on March 30, 1994. After initiating the probe, the variety store operator revised the slim profits it reported in the first two quarters of fiscal 1993 to losses.

According to a special committee formed for the investigation, Woolworth's outside auditor said that during the period in question, the company's management had pushed repeatedly for reporting "another good quarter." Several employees told the committee that it was a "tradition" to show a profit, no matter how small, in every three-month period. The chief financial officer of Woolworth's Kinney Shoe subsidiary claimed that he was ordered to improve the unit's reported earnings, regardless of how the adjustment was achieved. Similarly, the controller of Woolworth Canada said that he was instructed to send headquarters financial results that bore little resemblance to actual performance. The controller indicated further that he was told to offset the disparity by underreporting later results.[1]

An unbroken record of positive earnings was sure to enhance the image of Woolworth's stock. If the streak could be sustained only by doing violence to the underlying financial realities, however, conflicts with sound reporting practices were bound to arise. While the investigators found no evidence that any company officer had sought personal gain, they concluded that senior management had "failed to create an environment in which it was clear to employees at all levels that inaccurate financial reporting would not be tolerated."

Is the Woolworth case an isolated example of management trying to improve appearances by transforming losses into nominal profits? A research team led by Harvard economist Richard Zeckhauser has compiled evidence that such practices are in fact widespread.[2]

Suppose that the earnings reported by a large sample of corporations simply reflected the many random, often uncontrollable factors that

[1]Patrick M. Reilly, "Woolworth Executives Faulted in Probe, but Lavin Reinstated as Chief Executive," *The Wall Street Journal* (May 19, 1994); and Stephanie Strom, "Woolworth's Treasurer Blew Whistle," *New York Times* (May 20, 1994).
[2]Richard Zeckhauser, Jayendu Patel, Francois Degeorge, and John Pratt, "Reported and Predicted Earnings: An Empirical Investigation Using Prospect Theory." Project for David Dreman Foundation (1994).

influence profits. By the rules of probability, the companies in aggregate would report modest year-over-year increases in quarterly profits about as often as they reported modest declines. Instead, the authors find that corporations post small increases far more frequently than they post small declines. The strong implication is that when companies are in danger of showing slightly negative earnings comparisons, they locate enough discretionary items to squeeze out marginally improved results.

On the other hand, if a corporation has suffered too big a profit decline to overcome in a particular quarter, it has an incentive to "take a big bath." The reasoning is that investors will not be much more disturbed by a 30% drop in earnings than by a 20% drop. Therefore, the company may find it expedient to accelerate certain future expenses into the current quarter, thereby ensuring positive reporting earnings in the next period.

The study by Zeckhauser and his associates corroborates the "big bath" hypothesis by showing that large earnings declines are more common than large increases. The overall impression is that corporations regard financial reporting as a technique for propping up stock prices, rather than a means of disseminating objective information.[3]

Once a corporation's managers accept the premise that financial statements are instruments for maximizing shareholder wealth, they will soon see that the potential for enhancing value is considerable. The company can realize these benefits in three ways—by obtaining lower-cost capital, by creating higher earnings expectations than it could if it were instead to prepare its financial statements strictly according to the principle of keeping the public fully and accurately informed, and by downplaying contingent liabilities that threaten the firm's value.

MINIMIZING COST OF CAPITAL

The first variable that a company may try to control through its reporting policy—cost of capital—is partly a function of its perceived riskiness, that is, of the relative probability that the company will fail on its obligations. To the extent that a firm can reduce investors' and lenders' perceptions of its riskiness, it can lower the rate it must pay to obtain financing. Note that to achieve the savings, it is not necessary to reduce the *actual* risk, but only the *perceived* risk.

[3]Ibid.

The flexibility of present accounting standards affords numerous opportunities for a company to lower outsiders' perceptions of its riskiness without making the sacrifices necessary to bring reality into line with those perceptions. For example, the company can transform certain liabilities into off-balance-sheet—hence less visible—items. It can "smooth" its earnings through discretionary decisions about when to book income and expenses, thereby projecting the image of a stable company that is unlikely to lose its ability to service debt, even in a severe business downturn. Additionally, a company can delay the establishment of reserves for expected asset write-offs. This ploy enables the firm to report a larger cushion of equity below its debts than a conservative valuation would produce.

A few of these deceptions may be uncovered by alert financial analysts, but if on the whole the subterfuges succeed, the rewards can be vast. An interest-cost savings of one-half of a percentage point on $1 billion of borrowings equates to $5 million (pretax) per year. If the company is in a 34% tax bracket and its stock trades at 15 times earnings, the payoff for risk-concealing financial statements is $49.5 million in the cumulative value of its shares.

Bearing in mind their fiduciary duty to shareholders, some corporate managers will go so far as to ask themselves whether they are acting responsibly if they do *not* take advantage of opportunities of this magnitude. Carrying the logic one step further, a company might feel honor-bound to increase its riskiness (and therefore its potential returns, since the two are positively related) as long as the change is likely to go unrecognized by readers of its financial statements. If this stratagem succeeds, lenders will have unwittingly taken on greater risk without extracting compensation from the borrower, a circumstance that represents a net economic gain to the borrower. How can a corporate management committed to maximizing shareholder wealth justify passing up a free benefit, legally obtained?

Admittedly, this discussion states the case rather baldly, but analysts should harbor no illusions about the premises under which many issuers of financial statements operate. Some companies, to be sure, strike a balance at a point nearer to the ideal of fair and reasonable disclosure than the preceding scenario suggests. Of these, some are undoubtedly motivated as much by honor and integrity as by enlightened self-interest. By the same token, there are others that take all the leeway available and not always for the high-minded reasons of fiduciary duty alluded to previously. For example, narrowly construed self-interest often drives managers to manipulate financial reporting in order to earn bonuses tied to quantitative targets. Whatever the underlying motives, however, managements' determined efforts to change perceptions without changing realities can lead unwary financial analysts to incorrect and costly conclusions.

MAXIMIZING GROWTH EXPECTATIONS

The second approach to maximizing share price through financial reporting decisions involves the artificial boosting of earnings expectations. In comparison with the opportunities available in this area, the benefits of manipulating cost of capital are minor. Indeed, an entrepreneur-manager may find it impossible to resist the temptation to stretch the rules to the limit if analysts' earnings projections will thereby increase.

Instead of a company that is large enough to support a billion dollars in debt, as in the previous example, imagine a smaller company that is currently reporting annual net earnings of $20 million. Assume that five years from now, when its growth has leveled off somewhat, the company will be valued at 15 times earnings. Further assume that the company will pay no dividends over the next five years and that investors in growth stocks currently seek returns of 25% (before considering capital gains taxes).

These assumptions permit the analyst to place an aggregate value on the company's shares, given one final and essential input, namely, the expected growth rate of earnings. Suppose earnings have been growing at a 30% annual rate and appear likely to continue increasing at the same rate over the next five years. At the end of that period, earnings (rounded) will be $74 million annually. Applying a multiple of 15 times to that figure produces a valuation at the end of the fifth year of $1.114 billion. Investors seeking a 25% rate of return will pay $365 million today for that future value.

These figures are likely to be pleasing to a founder/chief executive officer who owns, for sake of illustration, 20% of the company's shares. The successful entrepreneur is worth $73 million on paper—quite possibly up from zero just a few years ago. At the same time, the newly minted multimillionaire is a captive of the market's expectations.

If for some reason investors conclude that the company's potential for increasing its earnings has declined from 30% to 25% per annum—still a level well above average for U.S. corporations—the value of its shares will decline from $365 million to $300 million, keeping previous assumptions intact. Overnight, the long-struggling founder will see the value of his personal stake plummet by $13 million. Financial analysts may shed few tears for him—he is still worth $60 million on paper, after all—yet if they were in his shoes, how many would take a $13 million loss with perfect equanimity? Most would be sorely tempted, at the least, to avoid reporting such losses via every means available to them under GAAP.

That all-too-human response is the one typically evidenced by owner-managers who face falling growth expectations. Many, perhaps most, have no intention to deceive. It is simply that the entrepreneur is by nature a self-assured optimist. A successful entrepreneur, moreover, has had this optimism vindicated. Having taken his company from nothing to $20 million of earnings against overwhelming odds, he believes he can lick whatever short-term problems have arisen. He is confident that he can get the business back onto a 30% growth curve, and perhaps he is right. One thing is certain—if he were not the sort who believed he could beat the odds one more time, he would never have built a company worth $300 million.

Financial analysts, however, must assess the facts more objectively and recognize that the situation in which the company finds itself is not unique, but on the contrary, quite common. Almost invariably, companies try to dispel the impression that their growth is decelerating, since that perception can be so costly to them.

Simple mathematics, however, tends to make false prophets of companies that extrapolate high growth rates indefinitely into the future. Moreover, once the underlying growth rate begins to level off (see Exhibit 1–1), restoring it to the historical rate requires overcoming several powerful limitations.

Limits to Continued Growth

Saturation.   Sales of a hot new consumer product can grow at astronomical rates for a time. Eventually, however, everybody who cares to will own one (or two, or some other finite number that the consumer believes is enough). At that point, potential sales will be limited to replacement sales plus growth in population, that is, the increase in the number of potential purchasers.

Entry of Competition.   Rare is the company with a product that cannot either be copied or encroached on by a "knockoff" that is similar enough

EXHIBIT 1–1   The Inevitability of Deceleration

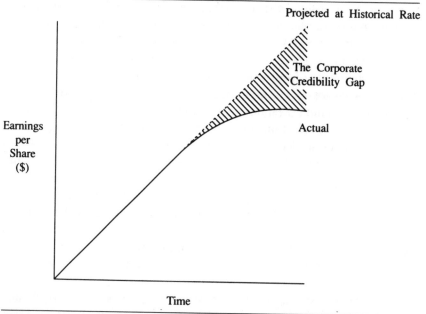

Shifting investors' perceptions upward through the Corporate Credibility Gap between actual and management-projected growth is a potentially valuable but inherently difficult undertaking for a company. Liberal financial reporting practices can make the task somewhat easier. In this light, analysts should read financial statements with a skeptical eye.

to tap the same demand yet different enough to fall outside the bounds of patent and trademark protection. Likewise, service businesses that achieve phenomenal growth rates will almost certainly attract direct competitors, since methods of doing business are generally not patentable.

Increasing Base.   A company that sells 10 million units in Year 1 can register a 40% increase by selling just 4 million additional units in Year 2. If growth continues at the same rate, however, the company will have to generate 59 million new unit sales to achieve a 40% gain in Year 10.

   Arithmetically, it is possible for volume to increase indefinitely in absolute terms, but a rate of growth far in excess of the Gross National Product's annual increase is nearly impossible to sustain over very long periods. By definition, a product that experiences higher-than-GNP growth captures a larger percentage of GNP each year. As the numbers get larger, it becomes increasingly difficult to switch consumers' spending patterns to accommodate continued high growth of a particular product.

Market Share Constraints.   A company may for a time avoid the limits imposed by the growth of its market and of the overall economy by expanding sales at the expense of its competitors. Even when growth is achieved by market share gains rather than by expanding the overall demand for a product, however, the firm must eventually bump up against a ceiling on further growth at a constant rate. For example, suppose a producer with a 10% share of market is currently growing at 25% a year while total demand for the product is expanding at only 5% annually. By Year 14, this supergrowth company will require a 115% market share to maintain its rate of increase. (Long before confronting this mathematical impossibility, the firm's growth will likely be curtailed by the antitrust authorities.)

Basic economics and compound-interest tables, then, assure the analyst that all growth stories end, a cruel fact that must eventually be reflected in stock prices. Financial reports, however, frequently tell a different story that defies common sense yet almost has to be told, given the stakes. Users of financial statements should acquaint themselves with the most frequently heard corporate versions of "Jack and the Beanstalk," in which earnings—in contradiction to a popular saw—do grow to the sky.

Commonly Heard Rationalizations for Declining Growth

"Our Year-over-Year Comparisons Were Distorted."   Recognizing the sensitivity of investors to any slowdown in growth, companies faced with earnings deceleration commonly resort to certain standard arguments to persuade investors that the true, underlying profit trend is still rising at its historical rate (see Exhibit 1–2). Freak weather conditions may be blamed for supposedly anomalous, below-trendline earnings. Alternatively, the company may allege that shipments were delayed (never canceled, merely delayed) because of temporary production problems caused, ironically, by the company's explosive growth. (What appeared to be a negative for the stock price, in other words, was actually a positive. Orders were coming in faster than the company could fill them—a high-class problem indeed.) However plausible these explanations may sound, the analyst should bear in mind that for many companies in the past, short-term "distortions" have proven to be advance signals of earnings slowdowns.

EXHIBIT 1–2   "Our Year-over-Year Comparisons Were Distorted"

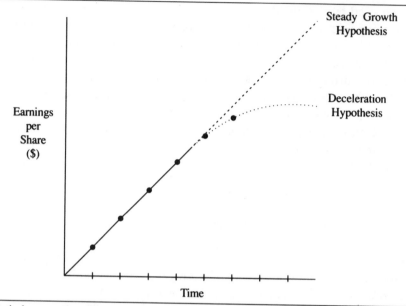

Is the latest earnings figure an outlier or does it signal the start of a slowdown in growth? Nobody will know for certain until more time has elapsed, but the company will probably propound the former hypothesis as forcefully as it can.

"New Products Will Get Growth Back on Track."   Sometimes, a company's claim that its obviously mature product lines will resume their former growth path becomes untenable. In such instances, it is a good idea for management to have a new product or two to show off. Even if the products are still in development, some investors who strongly wish to believe in the company will remain steadfast in their faith that earnings will continue growing at the historical rate. (Such hopes probably rise as a function of owning stock on margin at a cost well above the current market.) A hardheaded analyst, though, will wait to be convinced, bearing in mind that new products have a high failure rate.

"We're Diversifying Away from Mature Markets."   If a growth-minded company's entire industry has reached a point of slowdown, it may have few alternatives to redeploying its earnings into faster-growing businesses. Hunger for growth, along with the quest for cyclical balance, is a prime motivation for the corporate strategy of diversification.

Diversification reached its zenith of popularity during the 1960s. At that time, relatively little evidence had accumulated on the question of whether it was possible to achieve satisfactory financial performance by acquiring quality companies in businesses that were widely perceived as growth industries. Many corporations subsequently found that in view of the large earnings multiples that had to be paid to acquire coveted growth companies, they were unable to generate satisfactory returns on investment on their diversification initiatives. To do so would have necessitated achieving extraordinary earnings acceleration. This was particularly difficult for managers who had no particular expertise in the businesses they were acquiring. Still worse was the predicament of a corporation that paid a big premium for a so-so competitor in a "hot" industry. After all, the number of industry leaders available for acquisition is by definition limited.

By the 1980s, the stock market had rendered its verdict—widely diversified "conglomerates" generally traded at cheaper prices than their constituent companies would have sold for in aggregate had they been listed separately. Based on this experience, analysts should adopt a "show-me" attitude toward a story of renewed growth through acquisition. It is often nothing more than a variant of the myth of above-average growth forever.

Thinking of growth stories as myths, by the way, is an excellent device for recognizing their rationally refutable elements each time they appear in a new guise. Like all good myths, eternal growth at superior rates is a tale that everyone wants to believe, even though logic says it cannot be true. Furthermore, it appears to share with the greatest myths the quality of universality.

A Growth Story from the United Kingdom

The British economy provided an especially interesting version of the hypergrowth story when specialty retailing boomed during the late 1980s.[4] As often happens, promoters and bankers got carried away with a sound concept, namely, a chain of stores focused exclusively on merchandising a narrow but potentially very profitable product line. Buoyed by a vibrant retailing environment, public offerings of such companies as Sock Shop and Tie Rack were heavily oversubscribed. Sock Shop, initially priced at

[4]Maggie Urry, "When a Niche Becomes a Tomb," *Financial Times* (February 24, 1990).

31.5 times earnings, flew up to a multiple of more than 50.[5] In the euphoria, entrepreneurs even launched (and eventually folded) a venture called Tooth Booth, which specialized in toothbrushes, toothpaste, and mouthwash.

Sock Shop's February 1990 filing under the United Kingdom's Insolvency Act signaled the specialty retailing market's transition from boom to bust. The company's particular problems stemmed largely from an ill-fated expansion into the United States. More generally, though, the specialty retailers fell victim to a perennially overlooked risk that threatens any successful growth company—competitive response. To begin with, the specialty retailers' concepts were easily copied. Moreover, the niche stores had prospered by aggressively and creatively merchandising product lines that had previously been neglected by general merchandise retailers. Once the department stores awoke to the threat, they were able to recapture sales by paying closer attention to items formerly consigned to inconspicuous spots on the floor. With their far greater financial resources and more broadly diversified revenue bases, the department stores fared much better than the specialty retailers.

Goliath triumphing over David is not the sentimental ending most people hope for, which is precisely why financial analysts must view growth stories with a jaundiced eye. Speculators who pushed up the shares of Sock Shop may, in their sympathy for its founders, have focused inadequately on its propensity to enter into high-cost leases on its stores. A closer investigation of the balance sheet would have disclosed that a portion of Sock Shop's assets were "premiums" paid to obtain leases, which were capitalized in accordance with U.K. accounting practices. The value of these assets became questionable when a softening retail environment dampened the demand for tiny shops best suited to such exceedingly narrow concepts as underwear (Knickerbox) and ladies' shirtwaists (Blouse House).

DOWNPLAYING CONTINGENCIES

A final way in which disclosure can be molded to suit the issuer's interests is by downplaying the significance of contingent liabilities that may in fact have a decisive influence on the value of the firm. In this era of class

---

[5]Kevin Goldstein-Jackson, "Finding Profit from a Loss," *Financial Times* (February 24, 1990).

action suits and massive environmental hazards, the entire net worth of even a multi-billion-dollar corporation may be at risk in a particular type of litigation. Understandably, an issuer of financial statements would rather not have securities analysts focusing on such matters.

At one time, analysts tended to shunt aside claims that ostensibly threatened major corporations with bankruptcy. They observed that massive lawsuits were often settled for small fractions of the original claims. Furthermore, the outcome of a lawsuit often hinged on facts that emerged only when the case finally came to trial (which by definition never happened if the suit was settled out of court). Considering also the susceptibility of juries to emotional appeals, securities analysts of bygone days found it extremely difficult to incorporate legal risks into earnings forecasts based primarily on macro- and microeconomic variables. At most, a contingency that was in reality capable of wiping out a corporation's equity became a "soft" factor influencing the multiple assigned to a company's earnings.

Manville Corporation's 1982 bankruptcy marked a watershed in the way analysts have viewed legal contingencies. To their credit, specialists in the building-products sector had been asking detailed questions about Manville's exposure to asbestos-related personal injury suits for a long time before the company filed under Chapter 11 of the Bankruptcy Code. Still, when the company announced on August 26, 1982, that it was seeking protection from its creditors, the calamity seemed sudden to many investors. Manville's stock plunged by 35% on the day following its filing.

In part, the surprise element was a function of disclosure. The company's last quarterly report to the Securities and Exchange Commission prior to its bankruptcy had implied a total cost of settling asbestos-related claims of about $350 million, less than half of Manville's $830 million of shareholders' equity. On August 26, Manville put the potential damages at no less than $2 billion.

For analysts, the Manville episode drove home the point that the inconceivable—a bankruptcy at an otherwise financially sound company, brought on solely by legal claims—had become a nightmarish reality. The impact was heightened because the problem had lain dormant for many years. Manville was bankrupted by lawsuits arising from diseases contracted decades earlier through contact with its products.

The Manville bankruptcy, along with others discussed in Chapter 6, greatly raised analysts' awareness of legal risks, but the impact on corporations facing similar contingencies has been less dramatic. Even though disaster scenarios seem less far-fetched nowadays, analysts can still be lulled by companies' matter-of-fact responses to questions about claims asserted against them.

Thinking about it from the issuer's standpoint, one can imagine a number of reasons why the investor-relations officer's account of a major legal contingency is likely to be considerably less dire than the economic reality. On a conscious level, the company's managers have a clear interest in downplaying (to the extent their legal counsel will permit) risk factors that may depress the value of their stock and options. Furthermore, as participants in a highly contentious lawsuit, the executives are unlikely to be able to testify passionately on their company's behalf while simultaneously remaining objective enough to concede that the plaintiffs' claims are not entirely unfounded and might, in fact, prevail. (Indeed, any such public admission could compromise the corporation's case, so candid disclosures may not be a viable option.) Finally, it would hardly represent aberrant behavior if, on a subconscious level, management were to deny the real possibility of a company-wrecking judgment. It must be psychologically very difficult for managers to acknowledge that their company faces financial failure for reasons seemingly outside their control, even though they may have compiled an excellent record of earnings growth and maintained a conservative balance sheet.

Given all the thoughts that run through the minds of corporate managers when a huge contingent liability surfaces, it is beside the point for an analyst to think, "These are honorable people. They would not lie to me about such a thing." There is no deliberate dishonesty on the part of individuals who cannot admit to themselves that the unthinkable has suddenly become thinkable. Even managers who are quite willing to face the facts, moreover, may assess the situation unreliably. After all, they have probably never worked for a company with a comparable problem and have little basis for estimating the likelihood that the worst-case scenario will be fulfilled. Analysts who have seen other corporations in similar predicaments are better off relying on their own judgment. At a minimum, analysts should speak to a few plaintiffs, who are likely to be as strongly convinced as the defendants are that justice is on their side. In all probability, as well, the plaintiffs will be able to present arguments that sound plausible—otherwise, they would not find it economically advisable to pursue their case—even though the corporation's managers, for their part, argue with equally strong logic that the claims against them will never stand up in court.

THE IMPORTANCE OF BEING SKEPTICAL

By now, the reader presumably understands why this chapter is entitled "The Adversarial Nature of Financial Reporting." The issuer of financial statements has been portrayed in an unflattering light, invariably choosing the accounting option that will tend to prop up its stock price, rather than generously assisting the analyst in deriving an accurate picture of its financial condition. Instead of sharing in the optimism that drives all great business enterprises, the analyst is advised to maintain an attitude of skepticism bordering on distrust. Some readers may feel they are not cut out to be financial analysts if the job consists of constant naysaying, of posing embarrassing questions, and of being a perennial thorn in the side of companies that want to win friends among investors, customers, and suppliers.

Although pursuing relentless antagonism can indeed be an unpleasant way to go through life, the relationship depicted here between issuers and users of financial statements implies no such acrimony. Rather, analysts should view the issuers as "adversaries" only in the sense that they regard the opposing team in a pickup basketball game as such. On the court, the competition can be intense—that adds to the fun—but afterward, everyone can go out for pizza and have a swell time together. In short, financial analysts and investor-relations officers can view their work with the detachment of litigators who engage in every legal form of shin-kicking out of sheer desire to win the case, not because the litigants' claims necessarily have intrinsic merit.

Too often, the analyses of accounting practices published in the financial press recount the give-and-take of financial reporting and analysis in a highly moralistic tone. Typically, the author exposes a tricky presentation of the numbers and reproaches the company for greed and chicanery. Viewing the production of financial statements as an epic struggle between good and evil may suit a crusading journalist, but a financial analyst may not feel so comfortable riding about on a high horse. An alternative is to learn to understand the gamesmanship of financial reporting, perhaps even to appreciate on some level the cleverness of issuers who repeatedly devise new stratagems for leading investors off the track. Outright fraud, surely, should not be countenanced, but disclosure that improves on economic realities without violating the law requires truly impressive ingenuity.

At the very least, regarding the interaction between issuer and analyst as a sort of game, rather than as a morality play, makes it easier to view the action from the other side. Just as a chess master anticipates an opponent's future moves, analysts who wish to excel should consider which gambits they themselves might use if they were sitting in the issuer's seat.

"Oh no!" some readers must be thinking at this point. "First the author tells me that I must not simply plug numbers into a standardized spreadsheet. Now I have to engage in role-playing exercises to try to figure out what sorts of tricks will be embedded in the statements before they even come out. I thought this book was supposed to make my job easier, not more complicated."

In truth, my goal is to make the reader a better analyst, and if I could achieve that end by providing shortcuts, I would not hesitate to do so. The institutional setting in which financial reporting occurs, however, necessitates the recommendation of many steps that go beyond the conventional calculation of financial ratios. Without the extra vigilance advocated in these pages, the analyst's efforts will be undermined by a system biased toward producing simple answers to complex questions, minimizing flak from individuals who have the effrontery to refuse to accept reported financial data at face value, and giving issuers the benefit of the doubt.

This systematic bias is inherent in selling stocks. Within the universe of investors are many large, sophisticated financial institutions that utilize the best available techniques of analysis to select securities for their portfolios. Also among the buyers of stocks are individuals who, not being trained in financial statement analysis, are poorly equipped to evaluate annual and quarterly earnings reports. Both types of investors are important sources of financing for industry, and both benefit over the long term from the returns that accrue to capital in a market economy. The two groups cannot be sold stocks in the same way, however.

What sells best to individual investors, who are, in most cases, not experts in financial analysis, is a "story." Sometimes the story tells of a new product with seemingly unlimited sales potential. Another kind of story portrays the recommended stock as a "play" on some current economic trend, such as declining interest rates or a step-up in defense spending. Some stories lie in the realm of rumor, particularly those that relate to possible corporate takeovers. Salient characteristics of most stories involving common stocks are the promise of spectacular gains, superficially sound logic, and a paucity of quantitative verification.

No great harm is done when an analyst's stock purchase recommendation, backed up by a thorough study of the issuer's financial statements, is translated into soft, qualitative terms for laypersons' benefit. Not infrequently, though, a story originates among stockbrokers or even in the executive offices of the issuer itself. In such an instance, the zeal with which the story is disseminated may depend more on its narrative appeal than on the solidity of the supporting analysis.

Although the fondness for stories shown by individual investors does little to nurture serious financial analysis, the environment created by institutional investors is likewise far from ideal. The best investment organizations conduct rigorous and imaginative research, but many others operate in the mechanical fashion derided earlier in this chapter. They reduce financial statement analysis to the bare bones of forecasting earnings per share, assuming in effect that any stock found to be fairly priced on that basis can be viewed as having a sufficient investment rationale. Much Wall Street research, regrettably, caters to these institutions' tunnel vision, sacrificing analytical comprehensiveness to the operational objective of maintaining up-to-the-minute earnings estimates on vast numbers of companies.

An investment firm, moreover, is not the only kind of workplace that can constrain the serious analyst of financial statements. The credit departments of manufacturers and wholesalers have their own set of institutional hazards.

Consider, to begin with, the very term "credit approval process." As the name implies, the vendor's bias is toward extending rather than refusing credit. Up to a point, this is as it should be. In Exhibit 1–3, "neutral" Cutoff Point A, where half of all applicants are approved and half are refused, represents an unnecessarily high credit standard. Any company employing it would turn away many potential customers that posed almost no threat of delinquency. Even Cutoff Point B, which allows more

EXHIBIT 1–3   The Bias toward Favorable Credit Evaluations

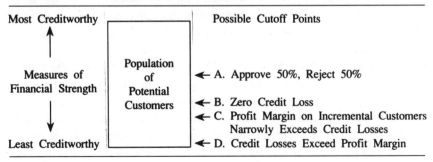

business to be written but produces no credit losses, is less than optimal. A profit-maximizing credit manager aims for Cutoff Point C, where losses on receivables occur but are slightly more than offset by the profits derived from incremental customers.

To achieve this optimal result, a credit analyst must approve a certain number of accounts that will eventually fail to pay. In effect, the analyst is required to make "mistakes" that could be avoided by obeying the conclusions reached through the careful examination of applicants' financial statements.

This is all quite rational and in no way inconsistent with thorough analysis, so long as the objective is to maximize profits. There is always a danger, however, that the firm will seek to maximize sales at the expense of profits, that is, to bias the system even further, to Cutoff Point D in Exhibit 1–3. If the firm's salespeople are paid on commission and their compensation is not somehow linked to the collection experience of their customers, they may exert pressure on credit analysts to approve applicants whose financial statements cry out for rejection.

A similar tension between the desire to book revenues and the need to make sound credit decisions exists in commercial lending. At a bank or a financial company, an analyst of financial statements may be confronted by special pleading on behalf of a loyal, long-established client that is under allegedly temporary strain. In another instance in which the analyst finds a company's financial measures to be substandard, the lending officer may argue that the loan ought to be approved because the proposed borrower, although young and struggling at present, has the potential to grow into a major client. Requests for exceptions to the normal credit policies are likely to grow in number and in fervor during periods of slack demand for loans.

When considering pleas of mitigating circumstances, the analyst should certainly take into account all the relevant credit factors, including qualitative ones not reflected in the financial statements. At the same time, though, the analyst must remember that *all* credit factors include negative as well as positive considerations. Companies in the "temporarily" impaired and the startup categories have a higher-than-average propensity to default on their loans. The analyst should render the fairest possible credit judgment, without considering in the first instance the business opportunity represented by the proposed loan. It may be rational for the lending institution to make a loan—at a hefty spread—to a well-below-prime-quality borrower, but that decision is separate from an assessment of the credit. Unfortunately, lending institutions sometimes lose sight of the distinction. They consequently delude themselves into thinking that they are obtaining large spreads for lending to highly creditworthy borrowers. Even worse, they may succumb to competitive pressure and end up lending to high-risk companies on terms as favorable as those they offer to decidedly less risky ones.

CONCLUSION

A primary objective of this chapter has been to supply an essential ingredient that is missing in many discussions of financial statement analysis. Accounting rules, cash flows, and analytical techniques are all critical, but a complete picture must include what goes on in the minds of corporate managers and analysts, as well as the dynamics of the organizations in which they work. Neglecting these factors will lead to false assumptions about the intent underlying communications between issuers and investors. Moreover, analysts can suffer through lack of awareness of the pressures applied on them, often in subtle ways, from their own co-workers. If one's conclusions are deemed "wrong," it is important to know whether that judgment reflects analytical shortcomings or a failure to conform to a higher-level decision that uninvested funds must be "put to work" or that loan volume must be increased.

To be sure, the subject of motivations has not heretofore been entirely overlooked in the literature. Not uncommonly, issuers are depicted as profit-maximizing firms, inclined to overstate their earnings if they can do so legally and if they believe it will boost their equity market valuation. This model lags behind the portrait of the firm now prevalent in other branches of finance.[6] Instead of a monolithic organization that consistently pursues the clear-cut objective of share price maximization, the firm is now viewed more realistically as an aggregation of individuals with diverse motivations.

Using this more complex model of the firm, an analyst can answer an otherwise puzzling riddle concerning corporate reporting. Overstating earnings would appear to be a self-defeating strategy in the long term, since it has a tendency to catch up with the perpetrator. Suppose, for example, a firm reports depreciation over a longer period than can be

---

[6]See, for example, Michael C. Jensen and William H. Meckling, "Theory of the Firm: Managerial Behavior, Agency Costs and Ownership Structure," *Journal of Financial Economics* (1976:3), pp. 305–60.

justified in light of the rate of technological change in its industry's manufacturing methods. When the time comes to replace the existing equipment, the firm will face a choice between two unattractive options. It can penalize reported earnings by writing off the remaining undepreciated balance on equipment that is obsolete and hence of little value in the resale market. Alternatively, the firm can delay the necessary purchase of more up-to-date equipment, thereby losing ground competitively and reducing future earnings. Would the company not have been better off to have refrained from overstating its earnings in the first place, an act that probably cost it some measure of credibility among investors?

If the analyst considers the matter from the standpoint of management, however, a possible solution to the riddle emerges. The day of reckoning, when the firm must "pay back" the reported earnings "borrowed" via underdepreciation, may be beyond the planning horizon of senior management. A chief executive officer who intends to retire in five years, and who will be compensated in the interim according to a formula based on reported earnings growth, may have no reluctance to exaggerate current results at the expense of future years' operations. The long-term interests of the firm's owners, in other words, may not be consistent with the short-term interests of their agents, the salaried managers.

Plainly, analysts cannot be expected to read minds or to divine the true motives of management in every case. There is a benefit, however, in simply being cognizant of objectives other than the ones presupposed by the exposition found in introductory accounting texts. If nothing else, the awareness that management may have something up its sleeve will encourage readers to trust their instincts when some aspect of a company's disclosure simply does not ring true. In a given instance, management may judge that its best chance of minimizing analysts' criticism of an obviously disastrous corporate decision lies in stubbornly defending the decision and refusing to change course. Even though the chief executive officer may be able to pull it off with a straight face, however, the blunder remains a blunder. Analysts who remember that managers may have their own agendas will not be persuaded that the executives are in reality making tough choices designed to yield long-run benefits not knowable at present by individuals outside the corporation.

Once armed with the attitude that the burden of proof lies with those making the disclosures, an analyst is prepared to tackle the basic financial statements. From that level right on up to the rendering of investment decisions, it will pay to keep the adversary's viewpoint in mind at all times.

Part Two

THE BASIC
FINANCIAL STATEMENTS

2

THE BALANCE SHEET

THE BALANCE SHEET is a remarkable invention, yet it has two fundamental shortcomings. First, while it is in theory quite useful to have a summary of the values of all the assets owned by an enterprise, these values frequently prove elusive in practice. Second, many kinds of things have value and could be construed, at least by the layperson, as assets. Not all of them can be assigned a specific value and recorded on a balance sheet, however. For example, proprietors of service businesses are fond of saying, "Our assets go down the elevator every night." Everybody acknowledges the value of a company's "human capital"—the skills and creativity of its employees—but no one has devised a means of valuing it precisely enough to reflect it on the balance sheet. Accountants do not go to the opposite extreme of banishing all intangible assets from the balance sheet, but the dividing line between the permitted and the prohibited is inevitably an arbitrary one.[1]

THE VALUE PROBLEM

The problems of value that accountants wrestle with have also historically plagued philosophers, economists, tax assessors, and the judiciary. Moral

---

[1]For the record, the accounting profession defines assets as "probable future economic benefits obtained or controlled by a particular entity as a result of past transactions or events" (Statement of Financial Accounting Concepts No. 6, Financial Accounting Standards Board, Stamford, Connecticut, December 1985, p. 10).

philosophers over the centuries grappled with the notion of a "fair" price for merchants to charge. Early economists attempted to derive a product's intrinsic value by calculating the units of labor embodied in it. Several distinct approaches have evolved for assessing real property. These include capitalization of rentals, inferring a value based on sales of comparable properties, and estimating the value a property would have if put to its "highest and best" use. Similar theories are involved when the courts seek to value the assets of bankrupt companies, although vigorous negotiations among the different classes of creditors play an essential role in the final determination.

With laudable clarity of vision, the accounting profession has cut through the thicket of valuation theories by establishing historical cost as the basis of its system. The cost of acquiring or constructing an asset has the great advantage of being an objective and verifiable figure. As a benchmark for value, it is, therefore, compatible with accountants' cardinal principle of conservatism.

Whatever its strengths, however, the historical cost system also has disadvantages that are apparent even to the beginning student of accounting. For example, basing valuation on transactions means that no asset can be reflected on the balance sheet unless it has been involved in a transaction. The most familiar difficulty that results from this convention involves goodwill. Company A has value above and beyond its tangible assets, in the form of well-regarded brand names and close relationships with merchants built up over many years. None of this intangible value appears on Company A's balance sheet, however, for it has never figured in a transaction. When Company A is acquired by Company B at a premium to book value, though, the intangibles are suddenly recognized. To the benefit of users of financial statements, Company A's assets are now more fully reflected. On the negative side, Company A's balance sheet now says it is more valuable than Company C, which has equivalent tangible and intangible assets but has never been acquired.

Liabilities, too, can become distorted under historical cost accounting. Long-term debt obligations floated at rates of 5% or lower during the 1950s and 1960s remained outstanding during the late 1970s and early 1980s, when rates on new corporate bonds soared to 15% and higher. The economic value of the low-coupon bonds, as evidenced by market quotations, plunged to as little as 40 cents on the dollar. At that point, corporations that had had the foresight (or simply the luck) to lock in low rates for 30 years or more enjoyed a significant cost advantage over their competitors. A company in this position could argue with some validity that its low-cost debt constituted an asset rather than a liability. On its books, however, the company continued to show a $1,000 liability for each $1,000 face amount of bonds. Consequently, its balance sheet did not reflect the value that an acquirer, for example, might capture by locking in a cheap cost of capital for an extended period.

While some would regard the prohibition of adjusting debt figures to the market as artificial, they might at least find it tolerable if it applied in every instance. Under Accounting Principles Board Opinion No. 16 ("Business Combinations"), however, it is mandatory, in acquisitions accounted for under the purchase method, to revalue the acquired company's debt to current market if its value differs significantly from face value as a consequence of a shift in interest rates since the debt was issued.

For example, following James River's 1987 acquisition of Crown Zellerbach, the long-term debt on Crown Zellerbach's balance sheet declined from $659 million to $482 million (Exhibit 2–1). The Notes to Financial Statements, however, reveal that this reduction in liability primarily reflected a change in the method of recording debt. As in the case of first-time recognition of goodwill, the historical cost principle in this

EXHIBIT 2–1   Balance Sheet

Crown Zellerbach Corporation
Liabilities and Capital
($000,000 omitted)

	January 25, 1987	April 27, 1986
Trade Accounts Payable	$ 70.3	$ 86.4
Accrued Income Taxes	10.2	3.8
Long-Term Debt, Current Portion	84.6	66.7
Other Current Liabilities	180.2	214.6
Total Current Liabilities	345.3	371.5
Long-Term Debt	482.4	659.3
Deferred Income Taxes	12.2	17.8
Other Liabilities	100.6	144.2
Common Stock	89.5	142.6
Additional Paid-In Capital	765.1	105.2
Retained Earnings	71.2	692.5
	$1,866.3	$2,133.1

Source: Crown Zellerbach Form 10-Q for the quarter ended January 25, 1987.

instance makes comparable companies appear quite dissimilar. A never-acquired company's "hidden asset value" in the form of low-cost debt will not be reflected on its balance sheet, even though it may be as great as Crown Zellerbach's.

The lack of comparability arising from the revaluation of the liability persists long after the acquisition is consummated, but the footnote detailing the adjustment eventually disappears from the acquired firm's annual report. In later years, readers receive no hint that the company's debts have been reduced—not in fact, but through one of accounting's convenient fictions.

Critics of accounting practices tend to deplore the quirks that give rise to such distortions, arguing that corporations should be made to report the true economic value of their assets. Such criticisms assume, however, that there *is* a true value. If so, determining it is a job better left to metaphysicians than to accountants. In the business world, it proves remarkably difficult to establish values with which all the interested parties concur.

The difficulties a person may encounter in the quest for true value are numerous. Consider, for example, a piece of specialized machinery, acquired for $50,000. On the day the equipment is put into service, even before any controversies surrounding depreciation rates arise, value is already a matter of opinion. The company that made the purchase would presumably not have paid $50,000 if it perceived the machine to be worth a lesser amount. A secured lender, however, is likely to take a more conservative view. For one thing, the lender will find it difficult in the future to monitor the value of the collateral through "comparables," since only a few similar machines (perhaps none, if the piece is customized) are produced each year. Furthermore, if the lender is ultimately forced to foreclose, there may be no ready purchaser of the machinery for $50,000, since its specialized nature makes it useful to only a small number of manufacturers. All of the potential purchasers, moreover, may be located hundreds of miles away, so that the machinery's value in a liquidation would be further reduced by the costs of transporting and reinstalling it.

The problems encountered in evaluating one-of-a-kind industrial equipment might appear to be eliminated when dealing with actively traded commodities such as crude oil reserves. Even this type of asset, however, resists precise, easily agreed on valuation. Since oil companies frequently buy and sell reserves "in the ground," current transaction prices are readily available. These transactions, however, are based on estimates of eventual production from unique geologic formations, for there is no means of directly measuring oil reserves. Even when petroleum engineers employ the most advanced technology, their estimates rely heavily on judgment and inference. It is not unheard of, moreover, for a well to begin to produce at the rate predicted by the best scientific methods, only to "peter out" a short time later, ultimately yielding just a fraction of its estimated reserves. With this degree of uncertainty, recording the "true" value of oil reserves is not a realistic objective for accountants. Users of financial statements can, at best, hope for informed guesses, and there is considerable room for honest people (not to mention rogues with vested interests) to disagree.

Because the value of many assets is so subjective, balance sheets are prone to sudden, arbitrary revisions. For example, on May 19, 1987, Citicorp announced a $3-billion addition to its loan loss reserves, acknowledging that—as everyone had long known—its Latin American loans were worth far less than their stated value. This dramatic decline in value did not occur in one day, or even in the period between Citicorp's last previously published financial statement and the reserve addition. That, however, is how the balance sheet told the story. Shortly after Citicorp's action, several other major bank holding companies also added to their reserves for Latin American loans. The aggregate "instantaneous" wipeout of balance sheet value exceeded $15 billion.

In view of the potential for stated asset values to vanish suddenly, users of financial statements should not assume that balance sheet figures correspond to the economic worth of the assets they represent. A more reasonable expectation is that the numbers have been calculated in accordance with GAAP. The trick is to understand the relationship between these accounting conventions and reality.

EXTERNAL INDICATORS OF VALUE

Often it becomes necessary to look outside the balance sheet to determine that the values shown on it are unrealistic, even though completely defensible under GAAP.

For example, the December 31, 1990 balance sheet of International Business Machines showed stockholders' equity of $36.7 billion. If accepted at face value, this figure would have been quite misleading. In the next two years, IBM recorded restructuring charges totaling $30.4 billion (after taxes). By the end of 1993, as shown in Exhibit 2–2, stockholders' equity was down to $19.7 billion. (Note that the 1991–1993 net losses were smaller than the special charges.)

EXHIBIT 2–2

International Business Machines Corporation
($000,000 omitted)
December 31, 1993

Assets
  Current Assets
    Cash $ 873
    Cash equivalents   4,988
    Marketable securities, at cost   1,272
    Notes and accounts receivable   11,676
    Sales-type leases available   6,428
    Other accounts receivable   1,308
    Inventories   7,565
    Prepaid expenses and other current assets   5,092
                                                                  39,202
Plant, Rental Machines and Other Property   47,504
Less accumulated depreciation   29,983
                                                                  17,521
Investments and Other Assets
    Software, less accumulated amortization   3,703
    Investments and sundry assets   20,687
                                                                  24,390
                                                                 $81,113

Liabilities and Stockholders' Equity
  Current Liabilities
    Taxes $ 1,589
    Short-term debt   12,097
    Accounts payable   3,400
    Compensation and benefits   2,053
    Deferred income   3,575
    Other accrued expenses and liabilities   10,436
                                                                  33,150
Long-term Debt   15,245
Other Liabilities   11,177
Deferred Income Taxes   1,803
Stockholders' Equity
    Preferred stock   1,091
    Common stock   6,980
    Retained earnings   10,009
    Translation adjustments   1,658
    Treasury stock
                                                                  19,738
                                                                 $81,113

Source: International Business Machines 1993 Annual Report.

As in the Citicorp example, the entire losses in value did not occur on the days that IBM recorded the write-offs. Frequently, in fact, companies make such wholesale reductions in shareholders' equity during the fourth quarter. These year-end "cleanups" reveal the arbitrariness of the timing.

An alert analyst might have suspected that IBM would decide to revalue its assets, even though the precise magnitude of the restructuring charges was not foreseeable. Beginning in 1986, the computer maker's annual ratio of net income to shareholders' equity had fallen from its customary level of more than 20% to the 14% range. Reflecting that decline, IBM had begun to receive a lower stock market valuation, relative to the stocks of other corporations. Regardless of what the financial statements indicated at the end of 1990, a dollar of IBM book value was worth less than formerly. The subsequent reductions in accounting values simply brought the balance sheet into line with economic realities.

Even at its reduced level of profitability, IBM continued to earn a respectable return, at least prior to the restructuring charges of 1991–1993. By way of comparison, the average return on the industrial corporations composing the Standard & Poor's 500 Index was 15.9% in the five years ending 1990. Many other companies, however, have chronically earned well-below-average returns on their book values. In such cases, analysts should consider the balance sheet assets overstated and expect write-offs, sooner or later.

It is not feasible to predict precisely the magnitude of future reductions in accounting values. Indeed, there is no guarantee that a company will fully come to grips with its overstated net worth, especially on the first round. To estimate the expected order of magnitude of future write-offs, however, an analyst can adjust the balance sheet's shareholders' value to the rate of return typically being earned by corporations.

To illustrate, suppose Company Z's average net income over the past five years has been $24 million. With most of the modest earnings being paid out in dividends, shareholders' equity has been stagnant at around $300 million. Assume further that during the same period, the average return of companies in the Standard & Poor's 400 index of industrial corporations has been 14%.

Does the figure $300 million accurately represent Company Z's equity value? If so, the implication is that investors are willing to accept a return of only 8% ($24 million divided by $300 million) to own the company's shares, even though a 14% return is available on other stocks. There is no obvious reason why investors would voluntarily make such a sacrifice, so Company Z's book value is almost certainly overstated.

A reasonable estimate of the low-profit company's true equity value would be the amount that produces a return on equity equivalent to the going rate:

$$\frac{\text{Company Z average earnings stream}}{x} = \frac{\text{Average return on equity}}{\text{for U.S. corporations}}$$

$$\frac{\$24 \text{ million}}{x} = 14\%$$

$$x = \$171 \text{ million}$$

Although useful as a general guideline, this method of adjusting the shareholders' equity of underperforming companies neglects a number of important subtleties. For one thing, Company Z may be considered riskier than the average company. In that case, shareholders would demand a return higher than 14% to hold its shares. Furthermore, cash flow may be a better indicator of economic performance than net income, implying that the adjustment should be made to the average ratio of market capitalization to cash flow, rather than average return on equity. Also, investors' rate-of-return requirements reflect expected future earnings, rather than past results. It might be reasonable to assume that Company Z will realize higher profits in the next five years than in the past five or, alternatively, that its profits will plunge further. By the same token, the peer group of stocks that represent alternative investments may be expected to produce a return higher or lower than 14% in coming years. The further the analyst travels in search of "true" value, it seems, the murkier the notion becomes.

The Illusion of Modest Debt

The IBM example shows that declining earnings may make a company's equity value lower than the balance sheet suggests. Analysts who accept the reported figure uncritically may have an unrealistically sanguine view of the company's financial strength. Similarly excessive confidence can arise in connection with debt. The value of a company's existing borrowings (and attendant financial risk) may be reflected accurately in its balance sheet, yet the potential for sharply increased indebtedness may be sizable.

The greatly expanded scope of merger and acquisition activity in recent years has been a source of vulnerability to a rise in debt levels. As shown in Exhibit 2–3, corporate combinations and recombinations grew dramatically during the 1980s, then began to climb again after a hiatus in the early 1990s.

The economic factors underlying mergers and acquisitions, as well as the manner in which they have been initiated, have varied over time. For the present discussion, the most important type of transaction was the "hostile" takeover, in which the target companies were characterized by depressed stock prices. That is, the acquirees did not solicit or welcome offers from their acquirers, who believed that the acquirees' shares were trading below their intrinsic value.

Transactions of this sort were more common in the mid-to-late 1980s than subsequently, but underperforming companies remained vulnerable to unsolicited bids. Moreover, hostile takeovers could again become a major component of mergers and acquisitions activity as a result of a general slump in the stock market.

The means by which hostile takeovers can cause financial leverage to rise involves the notion of "excess debt capacity." This term refers to the difference between the amount of debt a company can prudently incur and the amount (if lower) that it actually carries.

Before "merger mania" took hold in the 1980s, debt capacity was commonly regarded as a cushion that preserved financial flexibility. If a company's earnings unexpectedly turned down, a company with excess debt

EXHIBIT 2–3 Mergers and Acquisitions

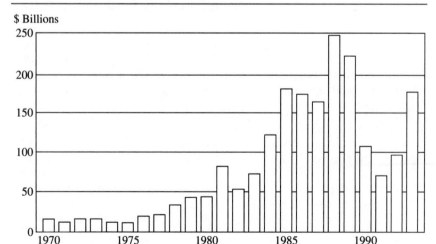

Source: Mergerstat Review—Division of Merrill Lynch Business Brokerage & Valuation.

capacity could borrow to finance any unplanned buildup in inventory. A company that was not already in debt up to the hilt when a recession hit could use its credit lines to maintain research and modernization programs while its competitors cut theirs back, at a cost to future market share.

By the early 1980s, a less constructive view of excess debt capacity had begun to gain favor. Companies that avoided borrowing, it was argued, were failing to use a cheap source of capital. Interest charges, after all, were deductible for income tax purposes, whereas dividends on common stock were not. Consequently, by relying on equity financing more than was necessary from the standpoint of prudence, corporate managers were delivering too little of their companies' pretax profits to shareholders.

Worse still, in an analysis pioneered by financial economist Michael Jensen,[2] corporations were reinvesting retained earnings in economically unrewarding ventures as a result of debt avoidance. As long as companies had sufficient earnings to cover their dividends (which were discretionary, in any case), they could continue plowing money back into low-return projects. Corporate managers benefited since they liked running bigger companies, but shareholders were denied the opportunity to recycle their profits into more remunerative investments. Greater reliance on debt financing, Jensen reasoned, would commit a larger portion of pretax earnings to nondiscretionary interest payments. (Failure to make a scheduled interest payment would constitute a default possibly forcing a change in control of the corporation.) More earnings would then be available for investors to put to the best use, while less would be trapped in projects of little merit.

Theorizing aside, excess debt capacity increasingly became a target that takeover specialists could use against target companies. Typically, the hostile bidders reckoned that by dislodging the incumbent management, they could reform the target's operating strategies, as well as its financial policies. Higher profits could help the acquirer to repay money borrowed in the process of eliminating excess debt capacity, but the transaction might succeed even without that benefit. A company's debt capacity can finance its own hostile takeover in the following manner:

Raider	**Target Company**
Long-term debt: $1.5 billion	Long-term debt: $ 50 million
Equity: $1.0 billion	Equity: $200 million

[2]Michael C. Jensen. "Agency Costs of Free Cash Flow, Corporate Finance, and Takeovers." *The American Economic Review* (May 1986), pp. 323–329.

The raider's capital structure, with $1.50 of debt for each dollar of equity, connotes a substantially higher tolerance of financial risk than at the target company, which has just 25 cents of debt for each dollar of equity.

Eyeing a takeover of the target company, the raider arranges temporary financing, through a syndicate of banks, to pay for the target company's shares.

Bank debt: $250 million	
Long-term debt: $1.5 billion	Long-term debt: $ 50 million
Equity: $1.0 billion	Equity: $200 million

The raider bids a 25% premium to book value and succeeds in acquiring the target company's stock for $250 million.

Long-term debt: $1.5 billion	Long-term debt: $300 million
Equity: $1.0 billion	Equity: $200 million

The acquired company is made to borrow $250 million, which it lends to its new parent. With the $250 million advance, the raider pays off its bank debt, leaving it with its original ratio of $1.50 of debt for each dollar of equity. The target company's ratio, meanwhile, has risen from 25 cents of debt for each dollar of equity to $1.50 of debt for each dollar of equity.

On a fully consolidated basis, the acquired company's equity drops out and the total entity has debt of $1.80 for each dollar of equity. This increase in total enterprise indebtedness will attract the notice of credit analysts but will not alter the raider's position relative to restrictive loan covenants. The raider's loan covenants limit only debt directly incurred by, or guaranteed by, the parent company or incurred by "restricted subsidiaries" designated by the parent; the newly acquired subsidiary is not so designated. Therefore, if the raider was in compliance with its debt covenants before taking over the target company, it remains in compliance afterward. In the end, then, the target company's previously unused capacity to borrow finances its takeover by a hostile entity that puts up no equity and remains free to incur debt for its next tender offer.

An early and chilling example of this process involved Diamond International, a forest products and packaging company that in 1982 caught the attention of Sir James Goldsmith, a renowned Anglo-French corporate raider. Diamond International's September 12, 1982, balance sheet (Exhibit 2–4) shows a conservative capital structure—just $170.7 million of total debt (short-term plus long-term, including current installments)

EXHIBIT 2–4   Balance Sheet

Diamond International and Its Wholly Owned Domestic and Foreign Subsidiaries
Balance Sheet
($000 omitted)

	December 31, 1982	September 12, 1982
Assets		
Current Assets		
Cash and short-term money market investments	$ 68,560	$ 18,220
Notes and accounts receivable—net	80,075	136,133
Inventories	122,787	134,896
Net assets of discontinued operations	32,823	92,195
	304,245	381,444
Property, Plant and Equipment—at Cost	605,298	678,505
Allowance for depreciation	319,508	340,573
	285,790	337,932
Standing Timber and Cutting Rights—Net	106,465	105,853
Investments and Other Assets	476,796	44,624
	$1,173,296	$ 869,853
Liabilities and Stockholders' Equity		
Current Liabilities		
Accounts payable and accrued liabilities	$ 116,878	$ 143,924
Short-term debt	727	64,612
Current installments of long-term debt	75,930	43,768
Dividends payable	323	287
	193,858	252,591
Long-Term Debt	426,626	62,456
Deferred Federal Income Taxes	27,600	28,000
Stockholders' Equity	525,212	526,806
	$1,173,296	$ 869,853

Source: Diamond International 1982 Annual Report and Form 10-Q for the quarter ended September 12, 1982.

against $526.8 million of equity, or a ratio of 32 cents of debt for each dollar of equity. Since many forest products companies at the time employed higher ratios of debt to equity, Diamond International could have been said to possess excess debt capacity. Goldsmith certainly held that view. Upon gaining control of the company, he sharply increased Diamond International's indebtedness—not merely to the industry norm, but well above it—to a ratio of 96 cents of debt for every dollar of equity as of December 31, 1982.

Contrary to the supposition of many who are not directly acquainted with the typical indentures of public bond issues, no restrictive covenants barred Goldsmith from radically increasing Diamond International's financial risk. To compound the injury, Goldsmith next utilized a Securities and Exchange Commission exemption from filing requirements for companies with fewer than 300 security holders. Bondholders were thereby deprived of further financial information.

At the time, Diamond International's radical financial restructuring was quite unusual in the world of large public companies. Over the next few years, however, similar—and even more drastic—recapitalizations became commonplace. Some companies, like Phillips Petroleum and Unocal, responded to hostile overtures by repurchasing substantial amounts of their stock with borrowed funds. Others, like Scott Paper and PPG, bought in large blocks of their shares to prevent them from falling into "unfriendly" hands. Stauffer Chemical purchased a company unrelated to its core business from Carl Icahn, a prominent raider, as part of the price of getting Icahn to drop his pursuit. Later, Stauffer was acquired by Chesebrough-Pond's, which sopped up excess debt capacity through the transaction.

One of the most sensational episodes occurred in 1982, when Bendix launched a hostile bid for Martin Marietta. Martin Marietta's response was immortalized in the media as the "Pac-Man Defense," in allusion to a popular video game of the time in which contestants vied to make their animated cartoon characters devour each other. Martin Marietta responded to the tender by making a bid of its own for Bendix. For a while, it appeared that Martin Marietta and Bendix might actually succeed in simultaneously acquiring each other. The fascinating legal questions that would have ensued were never answered, however. In the end, Martin Marietta remained independent but at a cost of buying in a substantial number of its shares, while Bendix was taken over by Allied Corporation. Credit quality deteriorated across the board as all three companies' capital structures became significantly more laden with debt.

As spectacular as the Martin Marietta-Bendix shootout was, however, the balance sheet effects had nowhere near the impact of the leveraged buyouts and recapitalizations that followed. In these transactions, equity often shrank from 60%–70% to 10%–15% of capital as companies repurchased large percentages of their outstanding shares, primarily with borrowed funds. FMC, Owens-Corning Fiberglas, and Burlington Industries were just a few of the prominent companies that embraced the idea.

The latter 1980s were characterized by intense competition to act as intermediaries in the transactions. Increasingly, the means of vying for the associated fees was to assume part of the risk of loss. Specifically, an investment bank might provide interim financing for a hostile takeover. If the acquirer failed to refinance the loan and was then unable to repay the borrowed funds through cash flow or asset sales, the intermediary was on the hook.

Through this device and others, acquirers shed a substantial portion of the risk, while retaining the potential profits of takeovers. Managers of leveraged buyout funds earned fee income by consummating transactions, whether or not the deals proved successful. In extreme cases, acquirers had little to lose and everything to gain by outbidding rival bidders, even if in the process they borrowed more than they could realistically hope to repay. Not surprisingly, many excessively indebted companies emerged from the takeover wars and a number went bankrupt. Among the prominent casualties were Federated Department Stores, R.H. Macy, Revco, and Southland. All had carried medium-to-high bond ratings, reflecting moderate use of debt, prior to the buyout wave.

The analytical lesson of the takeover movement, which could be reprised in the future, is that a modest level of debt is not guaranteed to last. Users of financial statements cannot ignore the context in which a company assumes a conservative posture. Circumstances could force management to boost corporate indebtedness substantially, even though nothing in the financial statements directly suggested the possibility.

The Importance of Management's Attitude toward Debt

Even in the absence of external pressures to step up the use of debt, a corporation may elect that means of enhancing shareholder value. Management's attitudes are nowhere to be found on the balance sheet, yet they can be pivotal in evaluating the continuity of present financial policies.

One case study that shows management attitudes as a positive force, curiously enough, involves Martin Marietta, the company mentioned previously in connection with its Pac-Man defense against a hostile tender offer from Bendix. Martin Marietta's defense consumed a substantial portion of its equity, but leveraging the balance sheet was a strategy adopted under duress. Historically, the company had followed a conservative financial course and undoubtedly would have continued to do so except that losing their independence was even more distasteful to Martin Marietta's senior managers than taking greater-than-customary risks.

Once the Bendix threat was eliminated, management moved swiftly to store the balance sheet strength to which it was committed by tradition and temperament. Exhibit 2–5 depicts the relative proportions of fixed obligations (debt and preferred stock) and common equity on Martin Marietta's balance sheet during 1979–1993. After depleting common equity severely through stock purchases in the 1982 defense against Bendix, management quickly began to replenish it. This was achieved partly by divesting operations that were tangential to the core aerospace business. In retrospect, Martin Marietta's 1982 surge in financial leverage was plainly an aberration.

A similar bar graph of the trend in debt leverage at Georgia-Pacific (Exhibit 2–6) tells a very different story. At the beginning of the period, the company was the subject of criticism for relying more heavily on borrowed funds than most of its peers in the forest products industry. Through 1986, Georgia-Pacific made steady progress in addressing those concerns. A simple analysis of financial ratios suggested that management had "gotten religion" and would henceforth adhere to a more conservative debt policy. Beginning in 1987, however, Georgia-Pacific reversed

EXHIBIT 2–5   Historical Financial Leverage: Martin Marietta Corporation

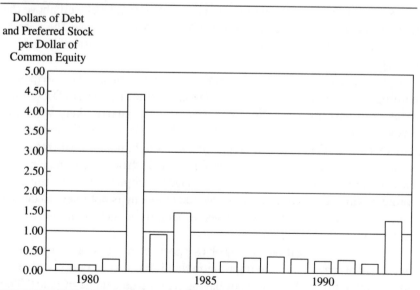

Dollars of Debt
and Preferred Stock
per Dollar of
Common Equity

Source: Martin Marietta 1979–1993 Annual Reports.

EXHIBIT 2–6   Historical Financial Leverage: Georgia-Pacific Corporation

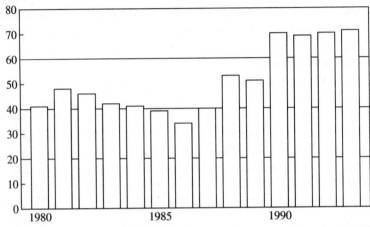

Debt and Other Long-Term
Liabilities as a Percentage
of Total Liabilities
and Equity

Source: Georgia-Pacific 1980–1993 Annual Reports.

course, eventually increasing its reliance on debt to a level well above the previous peak. In direct contrast to the Martin Marietta case, the aberration in Georgia-Pacific's record was the low point in use of financial leverage.

It sometimes happens that companies genuinely change their stripes. If nothing else, a new chief executive officer or chief financial officer may break with past practices. Such changes are particularly likely when the incumbent management is forced out, with its strategies discredited by the company's recent performance. Often, though, managerial transition is planned and orderly. The retiring CEO has a strong voice in selecting a successor from the ranks of senior managers steeped in the existing corporate culture. Under such conditions, the company is not likely to depart radically from past financial policies, especially if there is no perceived problem with the status quo.

The risk in such situations involves short-term corporate objectives. Management may create the impression that it has turned conservative, to curry favor with lenders, without having had a true change of heart. The company can reinforce the positive impression by temporarily reducing the proportion of debt in its capital structure. Then, after floating long-term bonds at an attractive rate, the corporation can return to its former, more aggressive policies. Bondholders wind up with a riskier investment than they bargained for, while the company retains the benefits of a highly leveraged balance sheet without incurring the penalty.

Not everybody is taken in by this ruse. Moody's and Standard & Poor's put heavy emphasis on management's attitude toward debt when assigning bond ratings. They strive to avoid upgrading companies in response to balance sheet improvements that are unlikely to last much beyond the completion of the next public debt offering. In reward for such vigilance, the agencies are accused of being backward-looking. The corporations complain that the bond raters are dwelling unduly on past, weaker financial ratios. In reality, the agencies are thinking ahead. Based on their experience with management, they are inferring that the recent reduction in financial leverage reflects expediency, rather than a longer-term shift in debt policy.

Users of financial statements are partly to blame for their victimization if they naively extrapolate a favorable trend in the proportion of debt in the capital structure. For starters, they should examine a longer term record, rather than the few recent years of history typically provided in a bond prospectus. If possible, analysts should also query management about its intentions and listen carefully for hedging statements. A common verbal escape clause is, "Continued debt reduction is a key objective for this company. Of course, if a once-in-a-lifetime acquisition opportunity came along, we might be forced to deviate for a bit. We would borrow, rather than dilute our shareholders by issuing new stock to finance the acquisition." Lenders who hear these words can generally assume that the once-in-a-lifetime opportunity will materialize sooner, rather than later.

THE COMMON FORM BALANCE SHEET

The Martin Marietta and Georgia-Pacific examples dramatize the value of studying a company's balance sheet in historical perspective. They serve so well as illustrations, however, precisely because the swings in their proportions of debt and equity are uncommonly wide. Most companies alter the mix of their assets, or their methods of financing them, in a more gradual fashion. To spot these subtle, yet frequently significant, changes, it is helpful to prepare a common form balance sheet.

Also known as the percentage balance sheet, the common form balance sheet converts each asset into a percentage of total assets and each liability or component of equity into a percentage of total liabilities and shareholders' equity. Exhibit 2–7 applies this technique to the 1993 balance sheet of International Flavors & Fragrances, Inc., which supplies ingredients to manufacturers of food and personal care products.

The analyst can view a company's common form balance sheets over several quarters to check, for example, whether inventory is increasing significantly as a percentage of total assets. An increase of that sort might signal involuntary inventory accumulation—a buildup resulting from an unanticipated slowdown in sales.

Pitfalls of Presentation

It would be a pity if a balance sheet reader who took a hard look at purported values and diligently studied the company's statements in historical perspective nevertheless came to erroneous conclusions because of the most mundane of problems—a confusing or misleading balance sheet format. Sadly, such errors can result from the range of choices that the accounting rules give companies in reporting their financial position. In striving to balance the principle of comparability (which implies standardization) against the flexibility required to report certain companies' unique circumstances fairly, accounting rulemakers have inadvertently created many opportunities for mistaken impressions to arise.

The variations in terminology applied to basic balance sheet accounts illustrate the variety of options available in the construction of financial statements. Each of the following two lists represents a variety of names currently being applied to corresponding accounts by different public companies.

Stockholders' equity	Cash
Shareowners' equity	Cash and temporary investments
Ownership	Cash and deposits
Shareholders' investment	Cash and marketable securities
Shareholders' equity	Cash and short-term investments
	Cash and temporary cash investments
	Cash and equivalents
	Cash and time deposits
	Cash and cash investments

For the most part, these semantic quirks cause no great consternation. The same freedom of choice that produces harmless variations in

EXHIBIT 2–7

International Flavors & Fragrances Inc.
Common Form Balance Sheet
($000 omitted)
December 31, 1993

Assets

Current Assets		
Cash and cash equivalents	$ 187,205	15.28%
Short-term investments	124,073	10.13
Receivables		
Trade	203,088	16.58
Allowance for doubtful accounts	(6,314)	(0.52)
Other	24,851	2.03
Inventories	302,926	24.72
Prepaid and deferred charges	43,194	3.53
	879,023	71.74
Property, Plant and Equipment	323,417	26.40
Other Assets	22,817	1.86
	$1,225,257	100.00%

Liabilities and Stockholders' Equity

Current Liabilities		
Bank loans	$ 30,937	2.52%
Accounts payable	43,771	3.57
Accrued payrolls and bonuses	11,749	0.96
Dividends payable	30,259	2.47
Income taxes	45,512	3.71
Other current liabilities	64,359	5.25
	226,587	18.49
Deferred income taxes	11,099	0.91
Retirement and other liabilities	95,702	7.81
Stockholders' Equity		
Common stock	14,470	1.18
Capital in excess of par	150,114	12.25
Retained earnings	860,640	70.24
Cumulative translation adjustment	448	0.04
Treasury stock	(133,803)	(10.92)
	891,869	72.79
	$1,225,257	100.00%

Source: International Flavors & Fragrances 1993 Annual Report.

nomenclature, however, can also lead to potentially serious misunderstandings, particularly with respect to optional approaches to aggregating accounts.

By way of illustration, the comparative capitalization figures for Arkla, Inc., (Exhibit 2–8) tell a positive story. Between December 31, 1986, and March 31, 1987, stockholders' equity rose from $616 million to $765 million. As a result of the large increase in equity, long-term debt (which fell slightly in absolute terms) declined from 52% to 46% of total capitalization. Lenders ordinarily regard reduced reliance on borrowed funds as a positive change. Even within the stockholders' equity category, Arkla apparently achieved a minor improvement by reducing its dependence on preferred and preference stock from $1.3 million to $260,000. (Because preferred and preference dividends, unlike common dividends, are contractually fixed and in many cases "cumulative," issuing preferred or preference stock creates somewhat greater financial risk than common stock, although not as much as debt does.)

On closer examination of Arkla's SEC Form 10-Q for March 31, 1987, a slightly less rosy picture emerges. As explained in the Notes to Consolidated Financial Statements, Arkla sold $130 million of convertible exchangeable preferred stock during March 1987, proceeds of which were subsequently applied to retire long-term debt. (The debt issue targeted for retirement appeared as a current liability on the March 31, 1987, balance sheet.) Why, then, did the March 31, 1987, statement show just

EXHIBIT 2–8   Capitalization Report

<table>
<tr><td colspan="3" align="center">Arkla, Inc.
Capitalization
($000 omitted)</td></tr>
<tr><td></td><td>March 31, 1987</td><td>December 31, 1986</td></tr>
<tr><td>Stockholders' Equity</td><td></td><td></td></tr>
<tr><td>Preference stock</td><td>$ —</td><td>$ 1,279</td></tr>
<tr><td>Preferred stock</td><td>260</td><td>—</td></tr>
<tr><td>Common stock</td><td>36,209</td><td>36,104</td></tr>
<tr><td>Capital surplus</td><td>266,264</td><td>137,206</td></tr>
<tr><td>Retained earnings</td><td>462,240</td><td>441,779</td></tr>
<tr><td>Total Stockholders' Equity</td><td>764,973</td><td>616,368</td></tr>
<tr><td>Long-Term Debt</td><td>653,272</td><td>677,709</td></tr>
<tr><td>Total Capitalization</td><td>$1,418,245</td><td>$1,294,077</td></tr>
</table>

Source: Arkla Form 10-Q for the quarter ended March 31, 1987.

$260,000 of preferred stock? The answer is that Arkla entered only the par amount of the preferred issue (10 cents for each $50 face amount share) in the preferred stock account, with the balance recorded as capital surplus. While this treatment is perfectly consistent with GAAP, it has the unfortunate effect of lumping the preferred proceeds in excess of par together with proceeds of previous common equity offerings. Accustomed to seeing preferred stock broken out separately, as in the presentation of Commonwealth Edison Company (Exhibit 2–9), most users would at least initially interpret Arkla's capital surplus account as consisting entirely of common equity. Only if they read the Notes would they arrive at the correct components of capitalization as of March 31, 1987:

($ 000 omitted)

Preferred stock	$ 130,000	=	9%
Common stock	634,973	=	45
Long-term debt	653,272	=	46
	$1,418,245	=	100%

These figures tell a less favorable story than did the initial interpretation. Long-term debt still falls from 52% to 46% of total capitalization, but that decline is more than offset by the creation of a 9% component of preferred stock. Besides being a contractually fixed obligation, this particular preferred is exchangeable, at the company's option, into debt. Admittedly, the holder also has an option—to convert to common equity, which would improve Arkla's capital structure—but holders will exercise

EXHIBIT 2–9 Capitalization Report

Commonwealth Edison Company Capitalization ($000 omitted)	
December 31, 1986	
Common Stock Equity	$ 6,406,973
Preferred and Preference Stocks without Mandatory Redemption Requirements	448,769
Preference Stock Subject to Mandatory Redemption Requirements	716,731
Long-Term Debt	6,425,777
	$13,998,250

Source: Commonwealth Edison 1986 Annual Report.

this option only if the common stock appreciates. In any case, the preferred stock creates greater risk than would exist if 54% of Arkla's capital consisted, rather than merely appeared to consist, of common equity.

As it turned out, Arkla's unconventional presentation proved short-lived. In its next quarterly statement, June 30, 1987, the company re-aggregated the equity accounts as shown in Exhibit 2–10. Instead of entering only the par value of its $130-million convertible preferred as preferred stock, the company now showed the full face amount in an account that combined preferred stock with preference stock, of which Arkla had a modest amount outstanding.

Arkla's March 31, 1987, presentation is a rare (although not unique) variant that may never cause the reader a problem. Nevertheless, it underscores the point that financial analysts cannot safely assume they will find a standard format in every balance sheet they examine. If they do, they will sooner or later apply an analytical technique in a mechanical fashion and come up with a "correct" answer that paints a completely false picture of economic reality. In light of such hazards, users of financial statements should adopt the following phrase as their motto: "When all else fails, think."

Actually, the Arkla example teaches two important lessons related to the freedom companies enjoy in choosing how they present information. As already discussed, analysts might be misled because the March 31, 1987, presentation differed from the format used by most companies.

EXHIBIT 2–10   Capitalization Report

	June 30, 1987	December 31, 1986
Arkla, Inc.		
Capitalization		
($000 omitted)		
Stockholders' Equity		
Preferred/Preference stock	$ 130,000	$ 1,279
Common stock	36,210	36,104
Capital surplus	136,097	137,206
Retained earnings	450,430	441,779
Total Stockholders' Equity	752,737	616,368
Long-Term Debt	717,500	677,709
Total Capitalization	$1,470,237	$1,294,077

Source: Arkla Form 10-Q for the quarter ended June 30, 1987.

The example also shows that a company can alter its presentation from one year to the next, sometimes with the effect of throwing financial analysts off the track.

Occidental Petroleum neatly illustrates this second point. Production payments, which are frequently found on oil companies' balance sheets, represent obligations to repay money advanced for oil reserves that will be extracted in the future. When these transactions first became popular, financial analysts had some difficulty in classifying them, since they appeared to have the character of asset sales. Gradually, though, analysts came to regard production payments as debt in another guise—perhaps even as a deliberate effort to hide debt from analysts and to circumvent loan covenants restricting indebtedness. Occidental's December 31, 1985, balance sheet (Exhibit 2–11) muddies the issue slightly by aggregating production payments ("Revenue from sale of future production") with other deferred income; a conservative analyst's tally of Occidental's debt would include the entire $122.0 million. In 1986, Occidental revised its presentation (Exhibit 2–12), reducing the three subheadings under "Deferred credits and other liabilities" to two. The production payments subheading was merged into 1985's "Other," resulting in a revised presentation of 1985's "Deferred credits and other liabilities" in the 1986 annual report (see Exhibit 2–12). Analysts viewing Occidental's balance sheet for the first time in 1986 would not have realized that a significant amount of debt had been buried in this fashion, unless they were conscientious and checked Note 1. There—in fairness to Occidental—it was disclosed that "Other" included revenue from the sale of future production and other deferred income of $122.0 million in 1985 and $81.9 million in 1986.

Occidental's format change demonstrates first of all the importance of carefully inspecting the Notes to Financial Statements. More germane to the present chapter is that a company can alter its presentation in an effort to stay a step ahead of analysts who are gradually gaining a better understanding of a new financing technique. The sort of reaggregation of accounts practiced by Occidental does not prevent an auditor from affirming that the financial statement presents the company's financial position "on a consistent basis." It is up to financial analysts to spot and investigate such changes in presentation. Admittedly, there are legitimate reasons for changing formats, but from time to time, valuable clues to a company's true financial state will reward the analyst with a sharp eye and a readiness to believe the worst.

EXHIBIT 2–11   Balance Sheet

**Occidental Petroleum Corporation and Consolidated Subsidiaries
Liabilities and Equity
($000 omitted)**

December 31, 1985

Current Liabilities

Current maturities of senior funded debt and capital lease liabilities	$ 228,308
Notes payable (Note 4)	112,486
Accounts payable	974,958
Accrued liabilities	730,516
Dividends payable	91,226
Domestic and foreign income and other taxes (Notes 1 and 9)	332,444
	2,469,938
Senior Funded Debt (Note 5)	1,954,877
Subordinated Debt (Note 5)	1,795,503
Capital Lease Liabilities (Note 6)	94,272
Deferred Credits and Other Liabilities	
Deferred and other domestic and foreign income taxes (Notes 1 and 9)	547,708
Revenue from sale of future production and other deferred income (Note 1)	121,980
Other	923,624
	1,593,312
Contingent Liabilities and Commitments (Notes 5, 6, 7, 8, 9, and 12)	—
Minority Equity in Subsidiaries and Partnerships (Note 1)	60,263
Redeemable Preferred Stocks	336,682

Shareholders' Equity (Notes 5 and 11)

Nonredeemable preferred stocks	329,366
Common shares	22,203
Additional paid-in capital	1,609,116
Retained earnings	1,342,648
Cumulative foreign currency translation adjustments (Note 1)	(22,312)
	3,281,021
	$11,585,868

Source: Occidental Petroleum 1985 Annual Report.

EXHIBIT 2–12   Balance Sheet

Occidental Petroleum Corporation and Consolidated Subsidiaries
Liabilities and Equity
($000 omitted)

	December 31, 1986	December 31, 1985
Current Liabilities		
Current maturities of senior funded debt and capital lease liabilities	$ 796,905	$ 222,308
Notes payable (Note 4)	32,174	112,486
Accounts payable	1,136,806	974,958
Accrued liabilities (Note 1)	1,052,102	730,516
Dividends payable	114,607	91,226
Domestic and foreign income and other taxes (Notes 1 and 9)	180,527	332,444
	3,313,121	2,469,938
Senior Funded Debt (Note 5)	5,612,769	1,954,877
Subordinated Debt (Note 5)	1,832,490	1,795,503
Capital Lease Liabilities (Note 6)	98,575	94,272
Deferred Credits and Other Liabilities		
Deferred and other domestic and foreign taxes (Notes 1 and 9)	566,062	547,708
Other (Note 1)	1,612,538	1,045,604
	2,178,600	1,593,312
Contingent Liabilities and Commitments (Notes 5, 6, 7, 8, 9, 10, and 12)	—	—
Minority Equity in Subsidiaries and Partnerships (Note 1)	109,531	60,263
Redeemable Preferred Stocks	13,350	336,682
Shareholders' Equity		
Nonredeemable preferred stocks	331,920	329,366
Common stock	32,942	22,203
Additional paid-in capital	2,914,213	1,609,116
Retained earnings	1,047,034	1,342,648
Cumulative foreign currency translation adjustments (Note 1)	(17,768)	(22,312)
	4,308,341	3,281,021
	$17,466,777	$11,585,868

Source: Occidental Petroleum 1986 Annual Report.

WHAT IS EQUITY?

Concentrating on substance rather than form has become more important than ever as a result of the radical financial restructuring undertaken by many corporations in recent years. In particular, it is dangerous to think conventionally about equity when corporations are treating it in an unconventional manner. Indeed, the accounting impact of leveraged buyouts and recapitalizations raises serious questions about the very meaningfulness of equity as a balance sheet account.

Consider the first recapitalization of Carter Hawley Hale Stores in 1987. As shown in Exhibit 2–13, the company's equity on May 2, 1987, was $633.2 million, including $300.0 million of preferred stock and $333.2 million of common equity. In its restructuring, Carter Hawley Hale first organized its specialty store divisions (Bergdorf Goodman,

EXHIBIT 2–13   Balance Sheet

Carter Hawley Hale Stores, Inc.
Balance Sheet
($000,000 omitted)

	May 2, 1987 (Actual)	(Pro Forma)
Current Assets	$1,264.8	$ 806.9
Property and Equipment, Net	797.6	534.0
Investment in Finance Subsidiaries	46.2	46.2
Other Assets	37.8	54.3
Total Assets	$2,146.4	$1,441.4
Current Liabilities	$ 659.2	$ 430.4
Long-Term Debt	576.9	979.6
Capital Lease Obligations	128.9	109.0
Other Liabilities	148.2	79.8
Redeemable Preferred Stock	300.0	—
Common Stockholders' Equity:		
Common stock	100.8	0.2*
Other paid-in capital	166.6	571.4
Accumulated earnings	65.8	(729.0)
	333.2	(157.4)
Total Liabilities and Equity	$2,146.4	$1,441.4

Source: Carter Hawley Hale Prospectus dated August 21, 1987.
*In connection with the restructuring, the par value of Carter Hawley Hale's common stock was reduced from $5.00 to $0.01 per share.

Contempo Casuals, and Neiman Marcus) into a new company and distributed the new company's shares to Carter Hawley Hale shareholders. The distribution reduced Carter Hawley Hale's total assets by $718.6 million. Offsetting that entry were a net $310.1-million reduction in liabilities and a $408.5-million reduction in common equity. Next, Carter Hawley Hale distributed $17 per share in cash to holders of its 20.2 million common shares, borrowing to fund the distribution. The $300-million preferred stock issue was eliminated by conversion into common and preferred stock of the newly created Specialty Stores Company. In all, this second round of distributions removed $382.1 million from Carter Hawley Hale's balance sheet. That figure, combined with the $408.5 million eliminated through distribution of the Specialty Stores shares, accounts for the $790.6 million difference between the actual preferred and common equity on May 2, 1987 ($633.2 million), and the pro forma account (negative $157.4 million).

Before pausing to reflect on the ramifications of a company's having stated equity of less than zero, consider the accounting treatment of a restructuring by another retailing firm at around the same time (Exhibit 2–14). Following a takeover struggle, a subsidiary of Campeau Corporation formed for the purpose of acquiring Allied Stores was merged into Allied. Allied's previous stockholders received $3.5 billion for their shares—mostly in cash borrowed by the acquiring entity, except for $150 million of new equity issued to Campeau Corporation. As in Carter Hawley Hale's case, the sum paid out to shareholders exceeded stockholders' equity ($1.3 billion plus Campeau Acquisition's $150 million as of November 1, 1986). Unlike Carter Hawley Hale, however, Allied Stores did not wind up with negative equity, but with positive equity of $273.1 million.

Why the difference in accounting? Under GAAP, the Carter Hawley Hale transaction was a case of a corporation buying back its own stock. In principle, a company cannot own part of itself, so reacquired shares are treated as unissued stock and recorded as a reduction in equity rather than as an acquisition of an asset. The Allied Stores transaction, on the other hand, involved the acquisition of one company by another (Campeau Acquisition Corp.). GAAP permitted the excess of the purchase price over Allied's book value to be reflected on the continuing company's balance sheet. This was accomplished through several entries, chief among them the creation of a $922.8-million account, "Excess of cost over net assets acquired," and a $1.1-billion writeup of "Property and equipment." When all the dust settled, Allied had positive equity and

EXHIBIT 2–14   Balance Sheet

Allied Stores Corporation
Balance Sheet
($000 omitted)

	November 1, 1986 Allied Stores Corporation	Campeau Acquisition Corp.	
	(Actual)	(Actual)	Pro Forma Combined
Current Assets	$1,829,171	$ 6,129	$2,394,674
Property and Equipment, Net	1,075,516		1,119,306
Investment in Allied		1,942,625	
Other Assets	20,629		12,671
Assets Held for Sale—Divisions			300,000
Excess of Cost over Net Assets Acquired	51,457		922,787
Total Assets	$2,976,773	$1,948,754	$4,749,438
Current Liabilities	$1,028,113	$ 23,754	$1,932,996
Long-Term Debt	523,705	1,775,000	2,543,342
Deferred Federal Income Taxes	104,641		—
Stockholders' Equity	1,320,314	150,000	273,100
Total Liabilities and Equity	$2,976,773	$1,948,754	$4,749,438

Source: Allied Stores Prospectus dated March 10, 1987.

Carter Hawley Hale had negative equity. In substance, both had borrowed to distribute cash greater than their book value to shareholders, but because the forms of the transactions differed, so did the accountants' handling of them.

This triumph of form over substance does not merely expose a technical problem in basing equity on historical cost, but casts doubt on the analytical validity of historical cost. The transaction-based method by which equity was calculated in both cases had the merit, extolled earlier in this chapter, of being objective and verifiable. Carter Hawley Hale paid a known amount for its shares, and Campeau Acquisition Corporation paid a known amount for the shares of Allied Stores. Both transactions, moreover, occurred in a free and competitive market, so the prices paid for the companies' shares should have reflected their true intrinsic value. No one would seriously argue, however, that Carter Hawley Hale's continuing shareholders left themselves with a company worth less than nothing, as the balance sheet seems to imply, while Allied Store's new owners shrewdly retained a positive equity. Furthermore, matters would still not be set entirely straight if, through a revision in GAAP, both companies ended up with negative equity. The notion of a company's having book value of less than zero dramatizes the distinction between what the financial analyst wants to know about a firm's value and what GAAP provides instead. This distinction is never sharper than when one is studying a firm with negative book value, yet it is a consideration in analyzing every company.

What financial analysts are actually seeking, but are unable to find in the financial statements, is equity as conceived by economists. In scholarly studies, the term *equity* generally refers not to accounting book value but to the present value of future cash flows accruing to the firm's owners. Consider a firm that is deriving huge earnings from a trademark that has no accounting value because it was developed internally rather than acquired. The present value of the profits derived from the trademark would be included in the economist's definition of equity, but not in the accountant's, potentially creating a gap of billions of dollars between the two. Negative equity, in the economist's terms, is synonymous with bankruptcy. The reasoning is that when a firm's liabilities exceed the present value of all future income, it is not rational for the owners to continue paying off the liabilities. At that point, either the creditors will attempt to recover their claims by forcing the firm into bankruptcy, or the firm will file voluntarily. In the latter case, the firm's hope is that the court will help it to reduce its liabilities to an amount less than the present value of its future cash flows, thereby making it rational to continue operating.

While logically sound, the economist's definition of equity is difficult to transfer to accounting, which favors items that can be objectively measured. Future earnings and cash flows, unfortunately, cannot. Moreover, calculating present value requires selecting a discount rate, or cost of capital. Determining the cost of capital is a controversial aspect of financial theory, complicated by tax considerations and risk adjustments that are extremely hard to make with any precision. Cost of capital is not, in short, the kind of number accountants like to deal with; their ideal value is a price on an invoice that can be independently verified by a canceled check.

In light of these difficulties, many financial analysts argue that it is pointless to make innumerable adjustments to book value to bend and squeeze it into conformity with equity in the economist's sense. Such struggles are senseless, they say, when there is available as an alternative an objectively verifiable number that reflects future, rather than past, cash flows and does not require the intermediate step of estimating a company's risk-adjusted cost of capital. This purportedly ideal measure of equity is market capitalization, defined as the market-determined value of all outstanding shares of a company's stock. With thousands of professional securities analysts and investors studying companies' future earnings prospects as the basis for their evaluations, say the advocates of market capitalization, no more accurate estimate of true equity value could be imagined. Moreover, up-to-the-minute market capitalization can be calculated on any day that the stock exchanges are open. This makes market capitalization immeasurably more useful than book value, which is available only once every three months. A company's market capitalization adjusts instantaneously to a new product announcement by a competitor, an explosion that halts production at a key plant, or a sudden hike in interest rates by the Federal Reserve Board. In contrast, these events may never be reflected in book value in a discrete, identifiable manner.

Against these advantages, however, the analyst must weigh several disadvantages of market capitalization as an approximation of "true" equity.

For one thing, while the objectivity of a price quotation established in a competitive market is indeed a benefit, it is obtainable only for publicly traded companies. A more subjective determination of equity value is required for private companies, which include a number of major industrial corporations that have withdrawn from the public realm in recent years through leveraged buyouts.

Leveraged buyouts and similar transactions likewise pose a problem with the use of market capitalization to monitor financial risk. Since a company's stock price discounts its future cash flows, a rise in the stock price logically implies either an increase in investors' expectations of future cash flows or a reduced discount rate.[3] The latter, in turn, suggests either a lower level of interest rates in the economy or a perception that operating risk has declined at the company in question. All these explanations bode well for a company's ability to meet its obligations: They suggest reduced financial risk. In an environment of hostile takeovers and leveraged buyouts, however, a rising stock price may signal just the opposite. The stock may begin to trade up for no reason related to the company's fundamentals or economic environment, but solely because a corporate raider has begun to accumulate shares. Often, the result of such activity is a successful takeover financed with the company's own unused debt capacity, as depicted earlier in this chapter. Alternatively,

---

[3]See Chapter 7 for a more detailed discussion of stock prices and their relationship to future cash flows.

the target company may fend off the raider by repurchasing a substantial portion of its own shares. This raises the value of the shares that remain outstanding and reduces the raider's incentive to go through with the takeover, since it will have already realized much of the initial potential for stock price appreciation. Reducing the equity base in this manner, however, increases financial risk by making the company proportionately more dependent on debt for its capital. The maximum increase in financial risk occurs when a company's defense against a hostile raid is a leveraged buyout or a recapitalization involving aggressive use of debt financing. With such outcomes increasingly common in recent years, it is no longer safe to view a rising stock price as a signal of declining financial risk; in many cases it heralds exactly the opposite trend.

Even when a change in market capitalization signals the correct direction of financial risk, analysts may be unwise to accept the signal at face value. Consider, for example, the September 30, 1987, market capitalization of Merck, a leading pharmaceutical maker. At $27.8 billion, market capitalization represented almost 10 times book value on the same date. Merck's balance sheet showed just two cents of debt for each dollar of market capitalization, implying an exceptionally low level of financial risk. Less than a month later, however, the picture changed dramatically. On Friday October 16, 1987, the Dow Jones Industrial Average fell by 109 points, its biggest-ever one-day drop. That record lasted only over the weekend, for October 19, 1987, was destined to be remembered as Meltdown Monday, the day the market index plummeted by 508 points. Merck, one of the stocks composing the Dow Jones Industrials, followed the harrowing pattern, falling from 190¼ to 184 on October 16 and then to 160 on October 19. In two trading sessions, then, Merck's market capitalization contracted by $3 billion.

Whatever theoretical arguments might be advanced for market capitalization, Meltdown Monday raised legitimate questions about the wisdom of relying uncritically on it as a measure of a company's financial well-being. Certainly, there was a strong suspicion that the stock market's plunge revealed more about investors' previously unbridled speculation than about short-run changes in companies' earnings prospects. The fact that the U.S. economy did not immediately plunge into a recession after October 19, 1987, reinforced the impression of many that the incident was purely a manifestation of the financial markets' structural flaws, rather than a reflection of changed earnings expectations. A financial analyst studying Merck is right to be skeptical about the magnitude and suddenness of the alteration in the company's earnings prospects implied by the 16% drop in its stock price in two sessions. Market capitalization, then, is a useful tool, but not one to be heeded blindly. In the end, "true" equity remains an elusive number and the analyst must use judgment to arrive at correct conclusions about a company's well-being.

ESCAPING THE GOODWILL TRAP

Whatever the potential pitfalls of market capitalization, the essential—and larger—point is that the financial analyst is free to look beyond book value. As discussed throughout this chapter, historical cost can produce an equity figure that leads to erroneous conclusions about a company's financial strength. Once the analyst makes the conceptual leap from book value to economic value (as approximated by market capitalization or any other means), many problems associated with historical cost suddenly become less vexing.

The difficulties attached to goodwill, for instance, are primarily accounting based, rather than elements of the reality that accounting attempts, with only limited success, to depict. Simply stated, in an acquisition accounted for under the purchase method, any premium paid over book value that cannot be attributed to the market value of tangible and identifiable intangible assets is assigned to an intangible account labeled "goodwill." Forever after, financial analysts who cling to book value will denigrate, debate, and adjust this item. The underlying problem is that goodwill is commonly regarded as a "soft" asset, in contrast to "hard" assets such as plants and inventories. Despite the arguments advanced earlier in this chapter about the elusiveness of "true" value—even in the case of solid and sturdy fixed assets—analysts perceive that in a company liquidation "hard" is better than "soft," from the creditor's standpoint. Reflecting this view, many analysts deduct goodwill from shareholders' equity, yet leave untouched the value of obsolete machinery that chronically fails to produce a competitive rate of return and would fetch only a tiny fraction of its book value on the auction block. Implicitly, the analyst who deducts goodwill is saying that any amount paid above the value of hard and semihard assets in an acquisition is a payment in exchange for nothing of value. In reality, this statement is true only if the acquiring company overpays.

By way of illustration, CPC International has been an active corporate acquirer over many years. It has ventured beyond its original corn products refining business into products as diverse as breadflats, mustard, and salad dressing. One result has been a large buildup of goodwill ("excess cost over net assets of businesses acquired"). In 1993, total intangibles of $774.7 million, with goodwill constituting the largest component, represented 44% of stockholders' equity (Exhibit 2–15).

Devotees of hard assets might dismiss that sizable chunk of net worth as so much fluff. CPC's rate of return, however, suggests that the company acquired something of genuine value for the premiums to book value that it paid in acquisitions. On an equity base of $1.769 billion, unadjusted for goodwill, CPC earned $454.5 million. That represented a return of 25.7%, a rate well above average for industrial corporations.

EXHIBIT 2–15

CPC International Inc.
($000,000 omitted)
December 31, 1993

Assets	
Current Assets	
Cash and cash equivalents	$ 166.3
Notes and accounts receivable	
Notes and drafts receivable	61.4
Accounts receivable-trade	782.6
—other	84.0
Allowances for doubtful accounts	(28.3)
Inventories	
Finished and in process	491.6
Raw materials	202.6
Manufacturing supplies and mechanical stores	136.0
Prepaid expenses	75.7
	1,971.9
Investment in unconsolidated affiliates	69.9
Property, Plant and Equipment	
Land	91.2
Buildings	736.7
Machinery and equipment	3,252.9
Less accumulated depreciation	(1,960.1)
	2,120.7
Intangibles	
Excess cost over net assets of business acquired	598.0
Other intangibles	309.0
Less accumulated amortization	(132.3)
	774.7
Other assets	123.6
	$5,060.8

(Continued)

EXHIBIT 2–15   *(Continued)*

CPC International Inc.
($000,000 omitted)
December 31, 1993

Liabilities and Stockholders' Equity

Current Liabilities	
Loans payable-banks	$ 200.4
Other notes and drafts payable	174.6
Accounts payable	352.9
Accrued expenses	
Accrued compensation	50.7
Accrued advertising and other	567.2
Taxes payable other than taxes on income	45.5
Income taxes	144.2
Dividends payable	47.9
	1,583.4
Employees' pension, indemnity, retirement, and related provisions	476.6
Other noncurrent liabilities	197.0
Minority stockholders' interest	94.9
	768.5
Long-term debt	897.7
Deferred taxes on equity	42.1
Stockholders' Equity	
Preferred stock	195.6
Common stock	48.8
Capital in excess of par	150.5
Retained earnings	2,774.5
Unearned ESOP compensation	(155.2)
Cumulative translation adjustment	(172.6)
Treasury stock	(1,072.5)
	1,769.1
	$5,060.8

Source: CPC International 1993 Annual Report.

Only if it were necessary to reduce CPC's equity base by the amount of its goodwill to derive a competitive rate of return on equity could it be said that the goodwill had no economic value. Instead, the evidence indicates that the intangible benefits represented by goodwill, such as the reputations of certain brand names, produced profits for CPC in 1993.

Similar results have been observed over a number of years. Reflecting the consistently high rate of profitability, CPC's year-end 1993 market capitalization stood at $7.1 billion. That figure confirmed that the company's economic value substantially exceeded its hard value (net assets less intangibles) of $994 million.

Soft assets, in short, can have demonstrable value. At the same time, it is possible for goodwill to lose its value more swiftly than it is amortized on the balance sheet. This danger has become especially pertinent during the 1990s as the value of brand names has increasingly come into question. Many manufacturers are finding it more difficult than in the past to obtain premium prices for products that offer consumers no special benefits, merely because their brand names are well known. As returns on equity decline at these companies, the goodwill components of their equity accounts may prove to be overstated.

UNDISCLOSED HAZARDS

Focusing on the economic value, rather than the accounting value of numbers reported in balance sheets, is a sound principle. It depends, however, on the numbers being available for the analyst's focus. In practice, companies' equity values can be significantly altered by items that are either undisclosed or disclosed only in a limited manner.

Early in 1994, for example, analysts were largely caught off guard by problems involving financial derivatives. (The collective term for these instruments reflects that their valuations derive from the values of other assets, e.g., commodities, indexes of securities.) For a number of years, corporations had used derivatives such as swaps and structured financings to hedge against swings in interest rates, currency exchange rates, and other cost factors.

As time went on, some corporate treasurers sought to capitalize further on expertise gained through hedging. Instead of merely trying to control risk, they hoped to profit by correctly predicting the direction of interest rates or the future relationship among various commodity prices. If their predictions proved wrong, trading losses would result.

As long as companies understood and limited the risks incurred in these transactions, they did not act irresponsibly. Often, the trading was profitable, providing a welcome supplement to earnings generated in more traditional activities.

As a comparatively new phenomenon, though, derivatives trading did not generate highly detailed mandatory disclosure. Typically, corporations divulged the scale, but not the terms or riskiness of the transactions. Some types of derivative were merely aggregated with the general cash accounts.

Just as accounting rulemakers were urging companies to expand their derivatives disclosure, while also considering new mandatory reporting on the subject, a sudden burst of interest rate volatility socked several major corporations with huge trading losses. Procter & Gamble took a one-time charge of $102 million on two interest rate swaps it had entered into in the United States and Germany. Air Products & Chemicals charged off $60 million on five swap contracts, acknowledging that with hindsight, its risk analysis had been faulty. Dell Computer sustained a $26.3 million loss on derivatives and other investments related to interest rates. (All figures are on an after-tax basis.)

The shock of these announcements probably moved companies toward greater conservatism in their use of derivatives. Additionally, the surprise losses strengthened the hand of those calling for fuller disclosure. At the same time, the incidents underscored the misfortunes that can befall even meticulous and thoughtful analysts. Users of financial statements can process only the information they have, and they do not always have the information they need.

Innovation in the financial markets is unlikely to abate, meaning that it will remain a challenge for accounting rulemakers to keep pace. To recognize possible undisclosed hazards, therefore, analysts must stay abreast of new types of transaction. Where feasible, users of financial statements should also solicit as much detail as management will disclose regarding risks not spelled out in the balance sheet or footnotes.

CONCLUSION

By closely examining the underlying values reflected in the balance sheet, this chapter emphasizes the need for a critical, rather than a passive, approach to financial statement analysis. The discussion of goodwill underscores the chapter's dominant theme, the elusiveness of "true" value. While the case studies in the chapter expose the weaknesses of historical cost accounting, the intricacies of goodwill accounting demonstrate that mere tinkering with historical cost does not necessarily improve the picture. Market capitalization may be a better approach in this instance, yet as shown in another case study, questions can be raised about the validity of a company's stock price as a standard of value. In the final analysis, users of financial statements cannot retreat behind the numbers derived by any one method, but must exercise judgment to draw sound conclusions.

3

THE INCOME STATEMENT

ANALYSIS OF THE income statement consists of two distinct tasks. The first is to determine how truly the statement does what it purports to do, that is, to report accurately the issuer's revenues, expenses and, most important, earnings. A thorough analyst must be conscious of imperfections in the accounting system that frequently can distort the reflection of economic reality. Accordingly, case studies dealing with the integrity of income statements make up the first section in this chapter. A special category of analytical pitfalls ("Extraordinary and Nonrecurring Items") is addressed separately. The second task in income statement analysis, discussed in the section entitled "Making the Numbers Talk," is to determine whether the story that the income statement tells is good, bad, or indifferent. Accomplishing this objective requires that the income statement be put into context (compared with prior statements and with statements of other companies).

HOW REAL ARE THE NUMBERS?

Many individuals are attracted to business careers not only by monetary rewards but by the opportunity, lacking in many other professions, to be measured against an objective standard. The personal desire to improve the bottom line, that is, a company's net profit, challenges a businessperson in much the same way that an athlete is motivated by the quantifiable goal of breaking a world record. The income statement is the stopwatch against which a company runs; net profit is the corporation's record of wins and losses for the season.

The analogy between business and athletics extends to the fact— apparent to any close observer—that championships are not won solely by superior skills and teamwork. A baseball manager can intimidate the umpire by heatedly protesting a call on the basepaths, hoping thereby to have the next close ruling go in his team's favor. A corporation has the power to fire its auditor, and may use that power to influence accounting decisions that are matters of judgment, rather than clear-cut reporting standards. A baseball team's front office can shorten the right-field fence in its home stadium to favor a lineup stocked with left-handed power hitters; a corporation's management can select the accounting method that shows its results in the most favorable light. Collectively, the team owners can urge the Rules Committee to lower the pitching mound if they believe that a consequent increase in base hits and runs will boost attendance. Similarly, a group of corporations can try to block the introduction of new accounting standards that might reduce their reported earnings.

Attempts to transform the yardstick become most vigorous when the measure of achievement becomes more important to participants than the accuracy of the measure itself. Regrettably, this is often the case when corporations seek to motivate managers by linking their compensation to the attainment of specific financial goals. Executives whose bonuses rise in tandem with earnings-per-share have a strong incentive not only to generate bona fide earnings, but also to use every lawful means of inflating the figures through accounting sleight of hand.

It would take many more pages than are allotted to this chapter to detail all the ways that companies can manipulate the accounting rules to inflate their earnings. Instead, the following examples should convey to the reader the thought process involved in this rule bending. Equipped with an understanding of how the rule benders think, users of financial statements will be able to detect other ruses they are sure to encounter.

Revenue Acceleration at Pan Am

One of the simplest ways to boost the bottom line is to beef up the top line. Selling more goods or services is the best means of doing this, from an economic standpoint, but from the standpoint of reported earnings, a bookkeeping gimmick serves just as well.

Pan Am Corporation's 1986 third-quarter income statement (Exhibit 3–1) exemplifies the latter approach. By way of background, Pan Am had

EXHIBIT 3–1   Statement of Operations

Pan Am Corporation
Consolidated Statements of Operations
($000 omitted)

	Quarter Ended September 30	
	1986	1985
Operating Revenues		
Airline		
Passenger	$ 693,162	$ 817,956
Freight and mail	53,229	63,240
Charter and other	38,048	41,323
Total Airline	784,439	922,519
World Services	104,350	99,674
Total operating revenues	888,789	1,022,193
Operating Expenses		
Airline		
Salaries and benefits	260,667	270,153
Fuel and oil	122,469	223,157
Advertising and commissions	90,553	102,686
Depreciation and amortization	40,636	50,949
Other operating expenses	235,124	236,621
Total Airline	749,429	883,566
World Services		
Salaries and benefits	51,297	54,201
Other operating expenses	47,286	41,503
Total World Services	98,583	95,704
Total operating expenses	848,012	979,270
Operating Income	40,777	42,923
Other Income (Expense)		
Interest expense	(29,032)	(32,148)
Interest income	9,325	8,577
Capital gains (losses)	(1,977)	2,155
Foreign exchange gain (losses)	(12,425)	739
Miscellaneous	(1,788)	(399)
Total other income (expense)	(35,897)	(21,076)
Income before Income Taxes	4,880	21,847
Provision (credit) for income taxes	628	(751)
Net Income	$ 5,508	$ 21,096

Source: Pan Am September 30, 1986, Form 10-Q.

lost money in each year from 1981 through 1985 and was in the red for 1986 at the halfway mark. Management was under considerable pressure from shareholders to demonstrate that the company could pull out of its tailspin.

Responding to a securities analyst's question, Chairman C. Edward Acker vowed in May 1986 that Pan Am would turn a profit in the third quarter. Acker made good on his prediction, for although earnings declined sharply from $21.1 million in 1985's third quarter, Pan Am stayed in the black with a bare $5.5 million profit. At last, it seemed, there was cause for investors to be hopeful.

In reality, Pan Am's profit was the product of a special effort in booking—rather than in generating—revenues. The third-quarter Management's Discussion and Analysis section disclosed the following: "The results of operations for the third quarter reflect a $30 million favorable adjustment to passenger revenue based on the annual review of tickets and refunds processed in 1986, but sold in 1985. A favorable adjustment of $10 million was booked in the fourth quarter a year ago based on the 1985 review."

The nature of the "annual review of tickets and refunds" was explained in the Notes to Consolidated Financial Statements:

> Passenger ticket sales are initially recorded in the air traffic liability account. When the transportation is provided by Pan Am, passenger revenue is recorded and the liability is reduced. The liability is also reduced by refunds to customers and by billings from other airlines that provided the transportation. The balance of the air traffic liability account at year-end is adjusted in the fourth quarter of the subsequent year, if necessary, on completion of a detailed review of the tickets and refunds processed during such subsequent year. In 1986, based on the early completion of the review of tickets and refunds, the adjustment was booked in the third quarter.

Pan Am's 1986 third quarter, in other words, was not comparable to its 1985 third quarter. By speeding up its annual review of tickets and refunds, the company managed to recognize in the third quarter some $30 million of revenue that under normal circumstances would not have hit the books until the fourth quarter. With the extra revenue, Pan Am squeezed out a profit for the period, thereby fulfilling its chairman's pledge. Analysts can only speculate whether management would have pressed as hard for early completion of the review of tickets and refunds had it expected a negative adjustment, rather than a $30 million addition to revenues.

Other Methods of Exaggerating Revenues

Unfortunately for analysts, companies do not always spell out in the Notes to Financial Statements the means by which they have artificially inflated their revenues. Many techniques subtler than those Pan Am employed do not necessitate special disclosure. For example, a company might lower the credit standards it applies to prospective customers without simultaneously raising the percentage of reserves it establishes for losses on receivables. The result would be a rise in both revenues and earnings, in the current period, with the corresponding increase in credit losses not becoming apparent until a later period. Alternatively, a manufacturer may institute short-term discounts that encourage its dealers or wholesalers to place orders earlier than they otherwise would. In this case, sales and earnings will be higher in the current quarter than they would be in the absence of the incentives, but the difference will represent merely a shifting of revenues from a later to an earlier period. Analysts will face disappointment if they regard such inflated quarterly sales as indicative of the future.

Although the current-period income statement may offer no clues that these gambits have been used, several techniques can help the analyst detect artificial expansion of revenues. On a retrospective basis, a surge in credit losses or an unexpected shortfall in revenues may indicate that revenues were inflated in an earlier period with the techniques described in the preceding paragraph. (Hindsight of this kind is not without value; an analyst who finds a historical pattern of hyperbolized sales will be appropriately skeptical about future income statements that look surprisingly strong.) On a current basis, analysts should take notice if a company registers a sales increase significantly above the gains posted by its competitors. If discussions with the company and other industry sources fail to elicit a satisfactory explanation (such as the introduction of a successful new product), artificial methods may be the cause. Industry sources can also provide direct testimony about tactics being used to shift revenues from future periods to the present.

NOT ALL SALES ARE FINAL

"Take care of the top line and the bottom line will take care of itself." So goes a business bromide, which underscores the importance of revenues (the "top line") to net income ("the bottom line"). The point is that if a company wants to cure an earnings problem, it should concentrate on bringing in more sales.

Generally, this is sound advice, as long as the needed sales are brought in by the salesforce. A company can compound its problems, however, if the financial staff makes up the shortfall in revenues through accounting gimmicks.

Some revenue-inflating tricks are achievable within GAAP boundaries, while others clearly fall outside the law. They all produce similar ill effects, however. Enhancements to reported sales boost reported earnings without increasing cash flow commensurately.

Often, a company's earnings and cash flow diverge to an extent that becomes unsustainable. The eventual result is an abrupt adjustment to the financial statements of previous periods. In the process, earnings and cash flow come back into alignment, but management's credibility plummets.

Even when no such shock occurs, the practice of pumping up revenues through discretionary accounting decisions represents a hazard for analysts. At a minimum, it reduces the comparability of a company's financial statements from one period to the next.

By way of illustration, the revenue recognition practices of International Business Machines came in for criticism when competition heated up in the computer business during the late 1980s. Management responded by becoming more accommodating in its marketing practices. The company stretched out payment periods, offered to make partial refunds if prices were subsequently reduced, and allowed customers to try out equipment without making any initial payments.

These innovations called for conservatism in recognizing revenues, lest the top line lose comparability with the past. In fact, though, a 1988 memorandum from IBM's chief outside auditor to its controller suggested that the company's accounting was fairly aggressive.

Price Waterhouse's Donald Chandler criticized the booking of revenues on shipment to dealers, who had the right to return the computers. IBM even recognized revenue in some instances when it merely shipped equipment to its owned warehouses, a practice that to Chandler seemed "clearly inappropriate." Additionally, Chandler was troubled by IBM's recognition of the full sales price on orders that entailed price protection, notwithstanding "ample evidence" that subsequent price cuts were likely.

Both IBM and Chandler's successor as lead partner on the audit defended the recognition of revenue on shipment. They noted that allowances were made for returns and argued that the terms of shipments to dealers were less lenient than Chandler believed. According to a company accounting official, shipments to an IBM warehouse resulted in booking of revenues only when the product was temporarily in storage, en route to a customer, and installation was expected within 30 days. Finally, IBM contended that its broad allowance for revenue adjustments provided adequately for the risk of "price-protected" orders.

Some companies in IBM's high-technology peer group, however, claimed that they followed far more conservative revenue recognition practices. For example, Amdahl, a competitor in the computer mainframe business, said that it refrained from booking a sale until a machine was installed and a field engineering unit verified that it was up and running.

IBM's aggressiveness in recognizing revenue helped to delay analysts' awareness of its decline in real profitability. Between 1984 and 1989, the company's return on equity fell from 26.5% to 9.6%, as data-processing technology moved away from reliance on mainframe computers. Over that same period, IBM's stock price fell from 123⅛ to 94⅛ a share. An early indication of the slowdown in true revenue growth could have been extremely valuable to investors.

The financial statements of another computer manufacturer provided just such a hint of future problems in the area of revenue recognition. Shortly before Kendall Square Research's October 1993 revision of its previously reported earnings, a research service known as *Financial Statement Alert* warned that the company was recognizing revenues too early.

Kendall Square reported $45.4 million in revenue in the first six quarters after it went public in March 1992. Loren Kellogg, copublisher of *Financial Statement Alert,* compared this income statement information with a figure from the company's statement of cash flows. Over the same 18-month period, Kendall Square's "cash received from customers" was just $25.7 million. Kellogg viewed the $19.7 million disparity between the two numbers as evidence that a large proportion of sales being booked by Kendall were dubious.

The warning proved prescient. Less than a month after Kellogg's analysis was reported in *The Wall Street Journal,* Kendall Square disclosed that its third quarter 1993 revenues would be "substantially below" securities analysts' expectations. In lieu of earnings per share of 11 cents (the consensus forecast according to the forecast-tracking firm of Zacks Investment Research), the company said that it would report a loss. Additionally, Kendall Square delayed the release of its third-quarter earnings and announced the resignation of its senior vice president/treasurer, who had joined the company only a month earlier. All these developments, by the way, were classic indications of serious corporate problems.

Revenue recognition controversies were central to Kendall Square's difficulties. The company indicated that while third-quarter shipments were "generally in line with expectations," there was some question about the proper amount of revenue to recognize from the shipments. Jeffry Canin, an analyst at Salomon Brothers, speculated about a possible area of disagreement within the company. Some officials, he suggested, may have objected to counting as revenue rebates that might have been given to customers who agreed to upgrade to Kendall's next generation of computers. Smith Barney Shearson analyst Barry Bosak proposed the possibility that Kendall Square had been hurt by its reliance on sales to universities. A number of these institutions, which were in turn dependent on diminishing government funding, proved unable to pay. Indeed, some critics insinuated that Kendall Square had made research grants to educational institutions as quid pro quos for orders, a charge that management denied.

At any rate, Kendall Square's troubles continued as auditor Price Waterhouse withdrew its clean opinion from the company's 1992 financial statements. Management revealed that the year's sales figure, originally reported as $20.5 million, included $4.2 million of "improperly recognized" revenue. Unaudited numbers for the first half of 1993 would also require restatement, the company added.

In the wake of these announcements, Kendall Square demoted and then fired its president, its chief financial officer, and the head of its technical products group. The company's acting chief executive officer announced that henceforth, Kendall Square would concentrate on building computers to order, instead of creating inventories in anticipation of orders. That reform was likely to reduce problems associated with revenue recognition, but by the time it was introduced, the damage to users of financial statements was substantial. At $7\frac{1}{2}$, the company's stock price was down by about 70% from its peak three months earlier.

Will it be possible to foresee future revenue problems by comparing revenues and cash received from customers, as analyst Kellogg did in the case of Kendall Square Research? Unfortunately, cash received is not an item broken out in the statements of cash flows of most companies. It is not even a widespread disclosure among companies in Kendall Square's business.

One exception to the rule is Cray Research, a supercomputer manufacturer substantially larger and longer established than Kendall Square. The statement of cash flows in Cray's annual report includes the item, "Receipts from customers" (Exhibit 3–2).

EXHIBIT 3–2

Cray Research, Inc., and Subsidiaries
Ratio of Cash Received to Revenue
($000 omitted)

	1992	1991	1990	Total
Receipts from customers	$904,266	$765,836	$838,715	$2,508,817
Total revenue	797,578	862,457	804,380	$2,464,415
Ratio (times)	1.13	0.89	1.04	1.02

Source: Cray Research 1992 Annual Report.

Cray does not break out the number in its quarterly statements, so we cannot directly compare its ratio of cash received to sales to Kendall Square's through June 30, 1993. For the three years ended December 31, 1992, though, Cray's ratio was 1.02:1. Against that backdrop, Kendall Square's 0.57:1 ratio ($25.7 million divided by $45.4 million) certainly deserved to be viewed as a red flag.

Even without the helpful disclosure of cash received from customers, analysts still may be able to detect warning signs of revenue problems ahead. Suppose, for example, that accounts receivable begin to rise more rapidly than sales. The cause may be that a growing number of customers are unable to pay, due to deteriorating economic conditions. Alternatively, they may not be truly committed to pay, by terms of their purchase agreements. Sooner or later, the company will have to reconcile the widening gap between sales and collections by canceling a portion of its previously recognized revenues.

Restatements of revenues and earnings arise in a wide range of circumstances. Many well-publicized cases involve young companies in comparatively new industries. Until the potential abuses have been demonstrated, managements may be able to take greater liberties than the auditors will countenance at a later point. On the other hand, major, long-established corporations are sometimes overzealous in booking sales. Mature companies may pump up revenues out of a desire to meet high expectations created by earlier, rapid growth.

After the fact, companies variously attribute excesses in reporting to misjudgment, bookkeeping errors, deliberate misrepresentation by "rogue managers," or some combination of the three. Seasoned analysts, having been burned on many occasions by revenue revisions, tend to doubt that overstatements are ever innocent mistakes. To gain some of the veterans' perspective, if not necessarily their jaundiced view of human nature, it is worthwhile to review a few case histories of adjustments to previously recorded revenues.

In November 1991, Citicorp restated $23 million in revenues associated with its credit card processing division. The bank holding company dismissed the unit's head and several other officials, saying they had been misreporting data for nearly two years. Financial executives were among those involved in the scam, which helped to explain why it had gone undetected for so long. Deadpanned *The Wall Street Journal*, "[Citicorp] officials didn't specify why the employees had been inflating revenue, although their bonuses were tied directly to the unit's performance."

Cincinnati Milacron credited an anonymous tip for its uncovering of a $2.3 million overstatement of sales in the first half of 1993. The "isolated" incident, said the company, involved a failure by the Sano plastic machinery unit to observe the "sales cutoff" rule. Contrary to Cincinnati Milacron's policy, Sano had counted in sales units that had not been shipped. The obligatory firing centered on a senior manager, while others escaped with reprimands.

First Financial Management blamed accounting errors, rather than policy violations, for its restatement of revenues for the first nine months of 1991. (Some of the employees at fault were fired, all the same.) The problem arose in the Basis Information Technologies subsidiary, a unit that First Financial had formed by consolidating 19 separate companies. Basis Information Technologies reportedly lost track of certain accruals of revenue, which should have been reduced as contracts expired. While uncovering the mess, First Financial also found that certain acquisition-related expenses had been amortized improperly.

In July 1993, T2 Medical placed in *Fortune*'s list of the 25 fastest-growing companies. The following month, the manager of home infusion therapy centers acknowledged that accounting irregularities had contributed to its remarkable sales growth. T2 (pronounced "T squared") had evidently recognized revenues on billings that neither patients nor insurers would cover. On the same day that T2's financial reporting came under a cloud, the Department of Health and Human Services announced it was investigating possible Medicare fraud at the company.

T2's president resigned in the wake of the disclosures and the company's stock price promptly fell 35% to $8.875. Only three months earlier, rumors of a management-led buyout of T2 had been rife, with one securities analyst speculating that the stock might run to $20 in such a scenario.

Equity Funding's Fabulous Fiction

As the foregoing examples show, revenues are not always as concrete and quantifiable as the dimes and quarters that trickle into the cash register at the local candy store. Thanks to accrual accounting, revenues can often be recorded in a manner intended to shift reported earnings from one period to another, as management desires. In most instances, the combined constraint of auditors and accounting rules suffices to prevent such distortions from getting completely out of hand. On occasion, however, unscrupulous executives successfully evade these controls and create grossly false impressions of their revenues and profits.

Unfortunately, the user of financial statements has little chance of prevailing over outright fraud. It is generally an implicit assumption in analyzing an audited income statement that the audit it underwent was honest and reasonably thorough. Such confidence is not always warranted.

Study of the following description of one of history's most spectacular financial reporting frauds is not guaranteed to improve the reader's ability to spot phony numbers. The narrative should nevertheless serve as a cautionary tale, reminding financial statement analysts that it is normally best to err on the side of skepticism. If one company's management was dishonest and cunning enough to conceive and successfully execute the deceptions practiced by Equity Funding, how many more are willing to bend the rules as far as possible without actually breaking the law? The answer, regrettably, is that many of the information statements an analyst will review are compromised to a considerable extent by managers' willingness to substitute artificial earnings for bona fide profits— particularly when the value of their stock holdings stands to benefit.

Inflating the share price, in fact, appears to have been a primary motive of the perpetrators of the Equity Funding fraud.[1] For an astonishingly long period, the scam succeeded. A $1,000 investment in the company's stock in 1961 rose to a value of over $200,000 in eight years. The ostensible foundation of this phenomenal appreciation was the company's success with an innovative approach to life insurance. Instead of buying a conventional whole life policy—in essence a combination of insurance coverage and a savings plan that provides a modest return—an Equity Funding customer purchased mutual fund shares. The buyer then borrowed against the shares to pay the premium on an insurance policy.

---

[1]A fascinating account of Equity Funding's rise and fall can be found in Raymond L. Dirks and Leonard Gross, *The Great Wall Street Scandal* (New York: McGraw-Hill Book Company, 1974).

For the cost of the interest on the loan, the customer received insurance protection plus appreciation on the mutual fund shares, which was likely to exceed returns provided by whole life's savings component. Not only did Equity Funding's sales skyrocket with the aid of this innovative marketing technique, but the company earned two commissions from each customer—one on the mutual fund shares and one on the policy.

As it turned out, this legitimate business strategy accounted for only part of the meteoric rise of Equity Funding's stock. In 1964, the company began to supplement its reported revenues through fictitious insurance policies. As the scheme evolved, Equity Funding generated additional revenues by selling the fake policies to reinsurers. (Reinsurers take over the risk on insurance policies from the original underwriters in exchange for future premiums.) From time to time, Equity Funding would kill off one of its imaginary policyholders by filing a forged death claim to the reinsurer. Since there was no beneficiary to pay, Equity Funding simply pocketed the death benefit when it arrived.

As the years went on, legitimate revenues represented a declining portion of the total reported by the company. A 1973 indictment estimated that at least 30% of Equity Funding's 1971 income from insurance premiums and commissions, plus at least 46% of its income from securities, represented nothing more than bookkeeping entries. Pretax earnings, reported as $26.6 million, were in truth no better than a $400,000 loss, according to the federal grand jury empaneled in the case.

When the colossal fraud was discovered in 1973, the disturbing question for financial analysts—who were accustomed to relying on auditors' opinions—was "How could the scheme have gone undetected for so long?" Surely the auditors must have attempted to verify the existence of the policies that the company claimed to have sold. Furthermore, if sales that never occurred were recorded, then the cash those sales should have produced (or other assets into which that cash was supposedly converted) would have been missing when the auditors came around. Finally, even if the auditors failed to uncover the discrepancies, the state insurance regulators' examinations certainly would have. With all these safeguards in the system, it seemed inconceivable that the deception could have continued for nearly a decade.

As it turned out, all the safeguards were systematically and effectively circumvented. When a nonexistent customer file was requested to verify a policy listed on a computer tape, company executives worked into the night filling out bogus applications and fabricating medical examination records. Coming up with cash was no problem, despite the missing sales; on the strength of its spectacular (albeit phony) earnings,

Equity Funding easily raised new capital. If the company's financial records indicated that the proceeds of fictitious policy sales had been invested in corporate bonds, a company printer could be put to work after hours producing counterfeit bond certificates. Auditors were also hoodwinked by falsified documents; a letter confirming that $20 million of bonds were on deposit at the American National Bank turned out to be a forgery. The additional surveillance provided by understaffed state insurance commissions proved ineffective.

To top off the whole sad story, the audit process was not merely outwitted, it was totally subverted. Two of the twenty-two individuals indicted by the federal grand jury were members of the accounting firm Equity Funding had used since its founding. In 1970, when Equity Funding applied to have its shares listed on the New York Stock Exchange, the exchange demanded that the company replace its auditors, Wolfson, Weiner, with a nationally recognized accounting firm. Wolfson, Weiner then parlayed its client relationship with Equity Funding into a merger with Seidman & Seidman, a larger firm acceptable to the exchange. After the lid blew off the Equity Funding scandal, exchange officials were shocked to discover that the Seidman & Seidman professionals policing Equity Funding were the very same individuals who had been auditing the books ever since the phony insurance began to be written in 1964.

With any luck, the reader will never be victimized by larceny on the grand scale with which it was executed through Equity Funding's financial statements. Still, the tale is worth remembering when something does not look quite right about a company's revenues. Giving management the benefit of the doubt in such instances can prove costly. A worst-case scenario, as demonstrated by Equity Funding's financial horror story, may be many times worse than anyone dreams.

Is Fraud Detectable?

Outright misrepresentation falls into a category entirely separate from the mere exploitation of financial reporting loopholes. Moreover, the gravity of such misconduct is not solely a matter of temporal law. In 1992, the Roman Catholic Church officially classified fraudulent accounting as a sin. A catechism unveiled in that year listed book-cooking in a series of "new" transgressions, that is, offenses not known in 1566—the time of the last previous overhaul of church teachings.

Neither fear of prosecution nor concern for spiritual well-being, however, entirely deters dishonest presenters of financial information. Audits, even when conducted in good faith, sometimes fail to uncover dangerous fictions. Financial analysts must therefore strive to protect themselves from the consequences of fraud.

No method is guaranteed to uncover malfeasance in financial reporting, but neither are analysts obliged to accept a clean auditor's opinion as final. Even without the resources that are available to a major accounting firm, it is feasible to find valuable clues about the integrity of financial statements.

In the case of Equity Funding, analysts overlooked a discrepancy that potentially could have exposed the fraud six years before it became public. The company claimed, in a 1967 prospectus, that during the preceding year it had sold $226.3 million face amount of life insurance and placed the "greater part" with the Pennsylvania Life Insurance Company. In its own prospectus, however, Pennsylvania Life indicated that it had underwritten only $58.6 million of Equity Funding policies in 1966.

More typically, hints of trouble emerge without the necessity of comparing one company's statements with another's. Classic red flags include an unexplained lurch in earnings, replacement of the auditor, and a delay in the release of quarterly or annual financials. A sudden buildup in inventories or receivables, if not proportionate to the growth in sales, can likewise be a reason for concern.

Messod Daniel Beneish, Associate Professor at the Fuqua School of Business at Duke University, has developed a model for identifying companies that are likely to manipulate their earnings, based on numbers reported in their financial statements. (Beneish defines manipulation to include both earnings or disclosure management within GAAP and actual fraud. In either case, his definition specifies that the company subsequently must have been required to restate results; write off assets; or change its accounting estimates or policies at the behest of its auditors, an internal investigation, or a Securities and Exchange Commission probe.) Beneish finds, by statistical analysis, that the presence of any of the following factors increases the probability of earnings manipulation:

1. Increasing days sales in receivables.
2. Deteriorating gross margins.
3. Decreasing rates of depreciation.
4. Decreasing asset quality (defined as the ratio of noncurrent assets other than property, plant, and equipment to total assets).
5. Growing sales.

Note that Beneish does not characterize these indicators as irrefutable evidence of accounting malfeasance. Indeed, it would be disheartening if every company registering high sales growth were shown to be achieving its results artificially. Nevertheless, Beneish's data suggest a strong association between the five phenomena he lists and earnings manipulation.

Capitalizing on Accounting Discretion: Orion Pictures

In the arithmetic of the income statement, the main method of increasing reported income—besides artificially increasing revenues, as shown in the preceding examples—is to reduce expenses by similar sleight of hand.

One of the richest opportunities for manipulating expenses is the capitalization of selected expenditures. The practice has a legitimate basis in the accounting objective of matching revenues and expenses by period. Current-year outlays that will generate revenues in future years should not be completely expensed right away, but rather deducted year by year as the value created by the outlay diminishes. As with so many accounting practices, the concept is sound, but problems arise in the execution. Usually, the victim of inappropriate capitalization practices is not the company that mistakenly (or deliberately) recognized its expenses too slowly, but the financial statement user who made decisions based on the originally reported figures.

To be sure, the rulemakers have tried to prevent obvious abuses. They have even barred altogether the capitalization of certain outlays—including advertising and research and development—that have undoubted future-year benefits. Despite such pronouncements, however, a fair amount of discretion remains for the issuers of financial statements. Even the most respectable companies use this discretion to their advantage at times, and more marginal firms exploit it to inflate their earnings artificially for as long as possible.

The history of Orion Pictures, an entertainment company, vividly illustrates the imperfections in current rules for capitalizing expenditures.

Following a "quasi-reorganization" that became effective on February 28, 1982, Orion earned a steady $7 million annually—give or take a few hundred thousand dollars—for the next three years. Granted, revenues were rising sharply during this period, hence profit margins were declining, but in the volatile world of show business, Orion's stable bottom line was impressive.

In fiscal 1986, however, Orion's consistency suddenly (or so it appeared) flew out the window as the company suffered a $31.9 million loss (Exhibit 3–3).

EXHIBIT 3–3 Income Statement

Orion Pictures Corporation
Consolidated Income Statement
($000 omitted)

	Fiscal Years Ended February 28 (29)		
	1986	1985	1984
Revenues	$198,122	$223,025	$154,728
Costs and Expenses			
Cost of rentals	192,280	181,740	120,998
Selling, general, and administrative	28,201	25,004	20,793
Interest expense, net	15,108	7,582	3,275
	235,589	214,326	145,066
Income (Loss) before Income Taxes	(37,467)	8,699	9,662
Provision (benefit) for income taxes	(5,605)	2,080	2,330
Net Income (Loss)	$(31,862)	$ 6,619	$ 7,332

Source: Orion Pictures 1985 and 1986 Annual Reports.

On closer examination, Orion's loss was not a sudden development confined to fiscal 1985. Rather, it was a reflection of expenses that were previously unrecognized, resulting in artificially inflated earnings—courtesy of special accounting practices permitted for film companies. Under Statement of Financial Accounting Standards (SFAS) 53, a company can capitalize most of the cost of producing a film. It can then write off the capitalized amount over the film's economic life, which may extend several years. The amounts to be charged off in each year are determined in advance by forecasting annual revenues from the film. Theater rentals will flow in during the early years, to be followed later in the film's economic life by the sale of videocassettes and television broadcast rights. If sales follow the predicted pattern, expenses will match revenues over the film's life. On the other hand, if a film flops at the box office, making it clear that future revenues will fall far short of expectations, the diminution in the film's value will not be recognized immediately. Instead, the capitalized costs will remain on the books as an asset. The economic loss signified by the film's box office failure, in other words, will be stretched out over several years for reporting purposes.

This was the situation that developed during fiscal 1982–1984 at Orion Pictures. Instead of recognizing losses as they became apparent through lower-than-expected box office receipts, Orion postponed the inevitable decline in its reported earnings by amortizing production costs according to the originally projected revenues of its films. In fiscal 1986, however, Orion finally faced up to the reduced value of its inventory, writing down more than 30 films to their net realizable value. In addition, the company wrote down one film that was nearly two years behind schedule for its release date and stepped up the amortization of certain fiscal 1986 releases that had drawn poorly at the theaters.

The benefit of this particular case history is that analysts can learn from it not merely a specific variety of earnings management but also a method of detecting it in advance of the inevitable write-off.

John Tinker, who was at the time a securities analyst employed at Balis & Zorn, Inc., published an analysis of Orion in December 1985. In his report, he calculated for each of nine leading film studios the ratio of revenue on the income statement to the amount of film inventories on the business. Orion, at 1.0 times, had a lower ratio than any of its peers, which averaged 2.5 times. This strongly suggested that Orion's inventories—and hence equity—were significantly overstated. Tinker also pointed out that Disney would have had a 1.1 times revenue-to-film-inventory ratio had that company not recently written off 50% of its film inventory, bringing its ratio up to a more normal 2.4 times. Just as Tinker predicted, Orion followed Disney's pattern, taking a write-off that was foreshadowed by a financial ratio well out of line with the industry norm.

A Rubber Ruler for Detroit's Expenses

In 1990, General Motors demonstrated an effective technique for creating earnings through an accounting change in a time of need. Analysts had to be on their toes to notice the alteration, which was overshadowed by larger developments.

An analysis of GM's income statements (Exhibit 3–4) indicates that sales fell by more than $2 billion between 1989 and 1990. At the same time, the three largest categories of costs and expenses showed increases. Clearly, 1990 was fated to be a down year for the company, regardless of revisions in accounting assumptions.

Equally clear was the impact of factors beyond management's control, notably Iraq's invasion of Kuwait and the resulting threat of war. As chairman Robert C. Stempel noted in his letter to shareholders, "world events began to have a negative impact on automotive markets" within hours of his assuming the helm on August 1, 1990.

EXHIBIT 3–4

General Motors Corporation and Consolidated Subsidiaries
Income Statement
($000,000 omitted)

	1990	1989	1988
Net Sales and Revenues (Note 1)			
Manufactured products	$107,477.0	$109,610.3	$107,815.0
Financial services	11,756.3	11,216.9	10,664.0
Computer systems service	2,787.5	2,384.6	1,907.0
Other income (Note 2)	2,684.3	3,720.1	3,253.0
Total net sales and revenues	124,705.1	126,931.9	123,639.0
Costs and Expenses			
Cost of sale and other operating expenses exclusive of items listed below	96,155.7	93,817.9	92,506.0
Selling, general, and administrative expenses	10,030.9	9,447.9	8,735.0
Interest expense (Note 15)	8,771.7	8,757.2	7,232.0
Depreciation of real estate, plants, and equipment (Note 1)	5,104.1	5,157.8	5,047.0
Amortization of special tools (Note 1)	1,805.8	1,441.8	1,432.0
Amortization of intangible assets (Note 1)	451.7	568.6	601.9
Other deductions (Note 2)	1,288.3	1,342.4	1,351.0
Special provision for scheduled plant closings and other restructurings (Note 7)	3,314.0	—	—
Total costs and expenses	126,922.2	120,533.6	116,904.9
Income (loss) before income taxes	(2,217.1)	6,398.3	6,734.1
United States, foreign, and other income taxes (credit) (Note 9)	(231.4)	2,174.0	2,102.8
Income (loss) before cumulative effect of accounting change	(1,985.7)	4,224.3	4,631.3
Cumulative effect of accounting change (Note 1)			224.2
Net income (loss)	$ (1,985.7)	$ 4,224.3	$ 4,855.5

Source: General Motors 1990 Annual Report.

Stempel did not seek to absolve GM's leadership altogether, though. "We cannot blame the financial results totally on the conflict in the Middle East, the plunge in consumer confidence, or the emerging U.S. recession," he declared. There was a need, said the new chief executive officer, "to position the company for stronger performance in the future."

Accordingly, General Motors took a special $2.1 billion restructuring charge in the very quarter that Stempel became chairman. For the full year, the automaker booked $3.3 billion of such special charges, transforming a sharp decline in earnings into an outright loss.

On the face of it, unqualified praise should have greeted GM's willingness to overhaul its operations, even at a sacrifice of reported earnings. Experience has bred a certain amount of cynicism, however, because the timing of restructuring charges can be somewhat arbitrary, in relation to the actual deterioration of economic value that they represent.

From a corporation's standpoint, it may be advantageous to bite the bullet when profits are down, anyway. By "taking a big bath," the company can ensure that pending charges will not drag down earnings during the next upturn, when the stock price (and executive compensation) stand to benefit in a big way. The implication, though, is that management was overstating earnings in previous periods, while it waited for an opportune time to restructure.

A new chief executive officer may be especially eager to undertake a major restructuring soon after coming into office. For one thing, scuttling moribund operations creates the impression of bold reforms. Perhaps even more important, the losses associated with a restructuring are likely to be blamed on the previous CEO if they come early in the newcomer's tenure. Within a year's time, the new chief may be able to take credit for a turnaround, based on an improvement in earnings from a large loss attributable to his predecessor.

Outsiders cannot know what went on in the minds of management in a specific case such as General Motors in 1990. Still, analysts should consider that at any given time, a corporation may be sweeping problems under the rug. Accumulated losses in value may subsequently be uncovered through a restructuring charge when senior management turns over.

In any event, GM's $3.3 billion of special charges in 1990 were partially offset by an accounting change. Unlike several other items, the change was not flagged in the income statement by a reference to the Notes to Consolidated Statements. Neither did the chairman's letter to shareholders mention it. Analysts noticed the change only if they checked the Notes on their own, which is always a good practice. There, in a discussion of the company's pension program, was a one-sentence mention of a not-inconsequential earnings booster:

> Certain changes in actuarial assumptions had the effect of reducing 1990 consolidated net loss by $289.8 million or $0.48 per share of $1 2/3 par value common stock.

The annual report did not elaborate further, but in general, the actuarial assumptions referred to deal with such factors as employees' projected length of service and life expectancy following retirement. Over time, it may be appropriate to alter these assumptions. For example, more employees than expected may leave the company before becoming entitled to receive pension benefits. By their nature, though, changes in the variables influencing future pension costs tend to be gradual. Therefore, the timing of revisions in actuarial assumptions can be even more arbitrary than the timing of restructuring charges.

A recession year, when earnings are depressed, may be a convenient moment to conclude that a retirement plan will be less of a burden than previously supposed. General Motors' archrival, Ford Motor Company, made that determination in 1980, when its earnings turned negative. Instead of revising its assumptions about vesting or employee lifespans, however, Ford boosted the assumed rate of return on the investments made by its pension fund.

Perhaps the adjustment in projected returns was warranted, considering that interest rates were then much higher than in previous years. Still, it is striking that in 1981, when Ford continued to suffer losses, the company again raised its assumed rate of return. One additional year of investment experience seems an inherently short period on which to base a change in assumed returns over the next several decades. On the other hand, the gap between the rate of return assumed in the 1970s and the rate that could be justified by the 1980s represented a sort of hidden reserve. Ford was able to tap the reserve when needed to boost its earnings and was not obliged to exhaust this source of incremental income in a single year.

Note that GAAP does not require the retirement expense reflected on the income statement to equate to the cash actually contributed to the pension fund during the period. On that basis, one might imagine that managements would not worry inordinately about the accounting values assigned to provisions for postretirement benefits. Companies could assume that analysts would not care very much, given the separation of the earnings impact from cash flow.

In fact, though, the reporting of postretirement benefits has long been a major bone of contention between the accounting rulemakers and providers of financial statements. By their actions, corporations have shown that they attribute considerable importance to the effects on reported income.

After FASB mandated a change from "pay-as-you-go" to accrual accounting for nonpension benefits (SFAS 106), corporations began to take a harder line in negotiating these benefits. Some companies announced curtailments of medical benefits to workers who had already retired, a policy change that predictably met stiff resistance from labor. In a strictly economic sense, the cutbacks must have been no less justifiable prior to, than after, the promulgation of SFAS 106. Nevertheless, corporations appeared to become much more strongly motivated once provisions for postretirement health care began to affect their reported earnings, as well as the economic reality.

MAKING THE MOST OF DEPRECIATION AND AMORTIZATION

Along with employee retirement costs, another major expense category that can be controlled through assumptions is depreciation. As a check against possible abuses, analysts should compare a company's ratio of depreciation to property, plant, and equipment with the ratios of its industry peers. An unusually low ratio may indicate that management is being unrealistic in acknowledging the pace of wear and tear on fixed assets. Understatement of expenses and overstatement of earnings would result.

Knowing that astute analysts will compare their depreciation policies with competitors' practices, companies commonly represent accounting changes in this area as efforts to get into line with industry norms. They do not ordinarily stress another plausible motive, namely, a desire to pump up earnings. Verbs such as "extend" and "liberalize" are considered expendable in the press releases disclosing revisions in depreciable lives.

Depreciation Assumptions—Fort Howard and Weirton Steel

Fort Howard produced a typical announcement of a change in depreciation assumptions in April 1992:

> During the first quarter of 1992, the company prospectively changed its estimates of the depreciable lives of certain machinery and equipment. These changes were made to better reflect the estimated periods during which such assets will remain in service. As a result, the lives over which the company depreciates the cost of its operating equipment and other capital assets will more closely approximate

industry norms. For the three months ended March 31, 1992, the change had the effect of reducing depreciation expense by $9.9 million and reducing net loss by $6.1 million.

In the same month, Weirton Steel was even more terse in describing a change in accounting for depreciation. The company did not alter the depreciable lives of the assets, but instead switched its accounting method:

> Weirton reported a change in depreciation method (accounting principle) effective January 1, 1992, for its steelmaking facilities from the straight-line method to a production-variable method, which adjusts straight-line depreciation to reflect production levels.

In explaining the change, the company did not emphasize a yearning for conformity with its fellow steelmakers. Nevertheless, Weirton was not the first in its group to abandon straight-line depreciation (already a less conservative technique than the various accelerated methods), for the still more liberal production-variable approach. During the first quarter of 1992, Weirton's switch in depreciation accounting had the convenient effect of reducing its net loss by nearly half.

A method that "adjusts straight-line depreciation to reflect production levels" may sound innocuous. Analysts should keep in mind, however, that the adjustment is far more likely to be downward than upward. As demand falls, the plant will incur more idle time and the company will record less depreciation expense. The same will be true if the facility turns unprofitable and temporarily shuts down, while lower-cost, more technologically advanced facilities owned by competitors continue to operate. Under these conditions, the book value of the plant will decline more slowly, even as approaching obsolescence causes its economic value to decline more rapidly.

Knogo Puts a New Spin on Depreciable Lives

As noted in the preceding section, stretching out the depreciable lives of assets is a common gambit for pumping up reported earnings. Consequently, users of financial statements can easily remember to be on the lookout for it. Like many other subtleties of financial reporting, however, depreciation schedules can trip up analysts who approach their job too mechanically.

Consider a change undertaken by Knogo Corporation in its fiscal 1989 statements. As suggested by its name (pronounced "no go"), Knogo manufactures systems that help retailers protect their merchandise against shoplifters. Effective December 1, 1988, the company revised its estimate of the economic lives of its security devices from ten to six years. The stated rationale was to reflect more accurately certain changes in Knogo's business and marketplace.

On its face, a shortening of depreciable lives is a commendably conservative action. The result, ordinarily, is to increase annual depreciation charges, leading to lower stated income.

In this case, though, the change had the opposite effect on earnings. Under the accounting rules, the company was obliged to depreciate security devices on lease over their remaining estimated economic lives, not to exceed six years. Revising the estimates forced certain five-year leases to be reclassified from sales-type leases to operating leases, in accordance with Statement of Financial Accounting Standards 13. The net result was to *increase* fiscal 1989 net income by approximately $750,000.

Such convenient boosts to reported earnings are not invariably signals that problems lie ahead. Still, a brief survey of Knogo's subsequent history underscores the wisdom of being on guard when companies generate profits from accounting changes.

Knogo's president began his fiscal 1990 letter to shareholders with a literary allusion:

> Robert Burns, the 18th-century Scottish poet, must have had our Fiscal 1990 in mind when he penned "The best laid schemes o' mice an' men gang aft a-gley." Interestingly, when you assess our Company's results, and look beyond the bottom line, we come in pretty well according to our operating plan and strategy, but we had a number of substantial unanticipated one-time expenses which adversely impacted upon our bottom line.

In support of his thesis that Knogo's 86% drop in net income from the previous year was a function of "a variety of unforeseen factors," the president cited four items. They included a settlement with the Internal Revenue Service, a reserve for extended warranty costs, settlement of patent litigation, and a special tax provision associated with upstreaming funds from Puerto Rican operations.

Notwithstanding such uncontrollable events, the letter to shareholders suggested that the company was on the right track, operationally speaking. "Even a casual assessment" would show that to be the case, the president wrote. Perhaps so, but more intense scrutiny might have yielded a hint of the coming restructuring charge and other provisions that largely caused a $14.7 million loss in Knogo's fiscal 1992 third quarter.

Responding to the disappointing performance, the board of directors suspended the company's dividend. In retrospect, the shareholders who were thereby deprived of income would have been prudent to begin taking a skeptical view of Knogo's reported profits when the depreciation schedule changed.

EXTRAORDINARY AND NONRECURRING ITEMS

To most individuals who examine a company's income statement, the document is less important for what it tells about the past than for what it implies about future years.[2] Last year's earnings, for example, have no direct impact on a company's stock price, which represents a discounting of a future stream of earnings (see Chapter 7). An equity investor is therefore interested in a company's income statement from the preceding year primarily as a basis for forecasting future earnings. Similarly, a company's creditors already know whether they were paid the interest that came due in the previous year before the income statement arrives. Their motivation for studying the document is to form an opinion about the likelihood of payment in the current year and in years to come.

In addition to recognizing that readers of its income statement will view the document primarily as an indicator of the future, a company knows that creating more favorable expectations about the future can raise its stock price and lower its borrowing cost. It is therefore in the company's interest to persuade readers that a major development that hurt earnings last year will not adversely affect earnings in future years. One way of achieving this is to suggest that any large loss suffered by the company was somehow outside the normal course of business, anomalous and, by implication, unlikely to recur.

To create the desired impression that a loss was alien to the company's normal pattern of behavior, the loss can be shown on a separate line on

---

[2]This generalization is not without exceptions. Tax collectors, for example, examine a company's income statement to determine its tax liability. For them, *next* year is irrelevant because they can assess a tax only on what has already been earned.

the income statement and labeled an "extraordinary item." Note that an extraordinary item is reported on an after-tax basis, below the line of income (or loss) from continuing operations. This presentation creates the strongest possible impression that the loss was outside the normal course of business. It maximizes the probability that analysts of the income statement will give it little weight in forecasting future performance.

Because the effect created by a "below-the-line" treatment is so strong, the accounting rules carefully limit its use. To qualify as extraordinary under the relevant APB opinion, events must be "distinguished by their unusual nature and by the infrequency of their occurrence."[3] These criteria are not easily satisfied, for as the opinion goes on to say, "unusual nature" means that "the underlying event or transaction should possess a high degree of abnormality and be of a type clearly unrelated to, or only incidentally related to, the ordinary and typical activities of the entity, taking into account the environment in which the entity operates." Furthermore, to ensure that the "extraordinary" label will not be employed indiscriminately, the opinion prohibits its use for several types of events considered "usual in nature" under the strict standard being applied. Among these are write-offs of receivables and inventories; gains or losses on foreign currency translation (even when they result from major devaluations and revaluations); and gains or losses on disposal of a segment of a business or the sale or abandonment of property, plant, or equipment.

Considering the exacting tests that an item must meet to be considered extraordinary, analysts may think themselves on solid ground if they largely disregard any such item in forecasting future earnings. The APB opinion, after all, adds that "infrequency of occurrence" means that the event or transaction in question must be "of a type not reasonably expected to recur in the foreseeable future."[4]

Unfortunately, it is not always possible to foresee the recurrence of an event deemed extraordinary. One of the most dramatic examples of this analytical difficulty involved Westinghouse Electric. In 1977, the company posted a $20.55 million extraordinary loss on settlements of uranium contract litigation. The following year, Westinghouse reported a $67.9 million loss attributable to the same cause. Finally, in 1979, came a $405.0 million extraordinary loss. Once again, the loss resulted from

---

[3]Financial Accounting Standards: Original Pronouncements, as of June 1, 1980, Financial Account Standards Board, Stamford, Connecticut, pp. 371–73.
[4]The APB opinion described here became effective on October 1, 1973.

settlements of uranium contract litigation, an item that the 1977 financial statements implied was likely to be infrequent.

The label "extraordinary"—which can be conferred only on items that meet a rigorous test—can be quite fallible as a guide to what will ultimately prove to be infrequent in occurrence. How much more suspect, then, are items that fail the test but are nevertheless reported in a manner implying they are one-time aberrations?

The reporting method frequently employed for a loss or gain not deemed extraordinary by the accounting profession, yet somehow exceptional in nature, is to break out the item separately "above the line," that is, on a pretax basis. Use of a term such as "nonrecurring" creates the desired impression, but has no official standing under GAAP. Sometimes the label is the more neutral "special charges," but even this terminology leaves the impression that the company has put the problem behind itself.

In recent years, "restructuring" has become a catchall for charges that companies wish analysts to consider outside the normal course of business, but which do not qualify for below-the-line treatment. The term has a positive connotation, typically implying that the corporation has cast off its money-losing operations and positioned itself for significantly improved profitability.

Users of financial statements should not necessarily infer finality from the appearance of the phrase "restructuring," however. Some corporations have a habit of remaking themselves year after year. In these cases, the baseline for forecasting future profitability should be pretax earnings after, rather than before, restructuring charges.

Times Mirror's income statements (Exhibit 3–5) reveal the publisher to be a serial restructurer. In 1991, the charges arose from voluntary early retirement and separation programs at the *Los Angeles Times* and *The Baltimore Sun.* The following year, Times Mirror recorded charges involving severance and pay-related actions, leased facilities, and the restructuring of its Matthew Bender unit. Further charges associated with severance, pay-related actions, and leased facilities came in 1993.

There is no suggestion that Times Mirror's management tried to mislead analysts about the possibility of future restructuring charges. By the same token, it would have been a mistake in 1991 to assume that a flat year in 1992 would result in operating earnings of $325 million (the 1991 figure before restructuring charges). Instead, a second round of restructuring caused operating profit to plunge by nearly 50% in 1992, even though revenues and costs were within 2% of their 1991 levels.

EXHIBIT 3–5

The Times Mirror Company and Subsidiaries
Statements of Consolidated Income
($000 omitted)

	Year Ended December 31		
	1993	**1992**	**1991**
Revenues	$3,714,158	$3,594,044	$3,519,975
Costs and Expenses			
Cost of sales	2,039,034	1,977,862	1,943,204
Selling, general and administrative	1,299,431	1,266,753	1,251,656
Restructuring charges	80,164	202,700	42,300
	3,418,629	3,447,315	3,237,160
Operating Profit	295,529	146,729	282,815
Interest expense	(85,237)	(74,501)	(77,403)
Nonrecurring gains (charges)	86,799	8,673	(71,503)
Other, net	4,626	4,896	9,977
Income from continuing operations			
become income taxes	301,717	85,797	143,886
Income taxes	137,604	50,480	75,932
Income from continuing operations	164,113	35,317	67,954
Discontinued operations			
Income from discontinued operations, net of income taxes	21,344	21,458	14,000
Gain on sale of discontinued operations, net of income taxes	131,702	0	0
Income before cumulative effect of changes in accounting principles	317,159	56,775	81,954
Cumulative effect of changes			
Postretirement benefits, net of income tax benefit of $84,931	0	(133,376)	0
Income taxes	0	10,000	0
Net Income (Loss)	$ 317,159	($66,601)	$ 81,954

Source: 1993 Times Mirror Company Annual Report.

Expunging Losses

Restructuring, if abused, can be a means of creating too rosy a picture of past performance. It can entrap the unwary analyst by downplaying the significance of blots on a company's earnings record.

The award for ingenuity in dressing up history, however, should probably go to Brooke Group. In 1990, the diversified company booked a special gain of $433 million. The gain arose from a reversal of a previously recognized loss generated by Brooke's 50.1% interest in New Valley

Corporation (formerly Western Union). By reducing its voting interest in New Valley to less than a majority, Brooke contrived to deconsolidate the company and erase the red ink retroactively.

MAKING THE NUMBERS TALK

The discussion of the income statement up to this point has been designed to help the reader assess the integrity of the numbers that purport to represent revenues, expenses, and earnings. After doing all that is possible in that vein, the analyst must focus on deriving meaning from the numbers.

By observing an income statement in its raw form (Exhibit 3–6), the reader can perform useful, but only very rudimentary, analysis. Pfizer's 1993 income statement shows, for example, that the company was profitable rather than unprofitable. The statement also gives some sense of the firm's cost structure; selling, informational, and administrative expenses

EXHIBIT 3–6

Pfizer, Inc., and Subsidiary Companies
Consolidated Statement of Income
($000,000 omitted)

	1993
Net Sales	$7,477.7
Operating Costs and Expenses	
Cost of sales	1,772.0
Selling, informational, and administrative expenses	3,066.0
Research and development expenses	974.4
Divestitures, restructuring, and unusual items-net	752.0
Income from Operations	913.3
Interest income	163.5
Interest expense	(106.5)
Other income	34.6
Other deductions	(153.5)
Nonoperating income (deductions)-net	(61.9)
Income before Provision for Taxes on Income, Minority Interests, and cumulative effect of Accounting Changes	851.4
Provision for taxes on income	191.3
Minority interests	2.6
Net Income	$ 657.5

Source: Pfizer 1993 Annual Report.

were the largest component of total costs, while interest expense was a comparatively small factor. An analyst would infer from this distribution of costs that Pfizer's earnings are not especially sensitive to fluctuations in interest rates. In contrast, changes in borrowing costs can have a far greater impact on banks and finance companies, which have a much larger component of interest expense in their cost structures.

One of the most powerful tools for advancing beyond such simple conclusions is the percentage income statement. In this mode of presentation, each income statement item is expressed as a percentage of the "top line" (sales or revenues), which is represented as 100%. Recasting the figures in this way permits the analyst to compare an income statement with any other income statement. The percentage income statement's facilitation of comparisons gives rise to its other name, the "common form income statement." Much can be learned by comparing an income statement with previous years' statements of the same company, as well as with statements of other companies in the same industry.

Exhibit 3–7 converts Pfizer's 1993 income statement to percentages and compares the year's results with the company's 1992 figures. The potential for enriched analytical insight is readily apparent.

To begin with, Pfizer's cost of sales declined from 28.7% of sales in 1992 to 23.7% in 1993. Several possible explanations for this improvement come to mind. The company might have raised prices while holding costs steady or it may have realized economies of scale through increased production levels. As it happens, though, the Financial Review section of the 1993 annual report attributes the gross margin improvement to divestitures of low-margin businesses, cost reductions, and a shift of the product mix toward more pharmaceuticals. (Pfizer also makes hospital products, consumer health care items, food ingredients, and animal health products.)

Less favorably, the tilt toward the higher-margin pharmaceuticals sector also contributed to a rise in selling, informational, and administrative expenses from 40.1% to 41.0% of sales. As the Financial Review notes, marketing new drugs entails substantial outlays for communicating clinical information to doctors. Another special cost in the pharmaceuticals business arises from its research-intensive nature. Research and development expenses increased from 11.9% to 13.0% of Pfizer's sales in 1993.

On balance, the year-to-year comparison of percentage income statements suggests that Pfizer's underlying profitability improved in 1993. Before taking into account the net impact of divestitures, restructuring, and unusual items, operating income rose from 20.0% in 1992 to 22.3%

EXHIBIT 3-7

Pfizer, Inc., and Subsidiary Companies
Historical Percentage Income Statements
($000,000 omitted)

	1993		1992	
	Amount	Percentage	Amount	Percentage
Net Sales	$7,477.7	100.0%	$7,230.2	100.0%
Operating Costs and Expenses				
Cost of sales	1,772.0	23.7	2,024.3	28.0
Selling, informational, and administrative expenses	3,066.0	41.0	2,899.3	40.1
Research and development expenses	974.4	13.0	863.2	11.9
Divestitures, restructuring, and unusual items-net	752.0	10.1	(110.5)	(1.5)
Income from Operations	913.3	12.2	1,553.9	21.5
Interest income	163.5	2.2	184.6	2.6
Interest expense	(106.5)	(1.4)	(103.4)	(1.4)
Other income	34.6	0.5	34.6	0.5
Other deductions	(153.5)	(2.1)	(134.9)	(1.9)
Nonoperating income (deductions)-net	(61.9)	(0.8)	(19.1)	(0.3)
Income before Provision for Taxes on Income, Minority Interests, and cumulative effect of Accounting Changes	851.4	11.4	1,534.8	21.2
Provision for taxes on income	191.3	2.6	438.6	6.1
Minority interests	2.6	N.M	2.7	N.M
Income before Cumulative Effect of Accounting Changes	657.5	8.8	1093.5	15.1
Cumulative effect of change in accounting for:				
Postretirement benefits, net of income taxes	0.0	0.0	(312.6)	(4.3)
Income taxes	0.0	0.0	30.0	0.4
Net Income	$ 657.5	8.8%	$ 810.9	11.2%

Source: Pfizer 1993 Annual Report.

in 1993. Without translating the raw figures into percentages, this trend would be more difficult to discern.

At the same time, the shedding of low-margin operations had a cost. Divestitures and restructuring charges contributed to a 10.1% penalty to income from operations. Any additional discarding of underperformers would likely clip earnings in a similar fashion. The percentage income statement, though, helps to identify the ongoing benefits of such short-run sacrifices.

Besides facilitating comparisons between a company's present and past results, the percentage income statement can highlight important facts about a company's competitive standing. Exhibit 3–8 displays the 1993 performance of Pfizer alongside that of an industry peer, Schering-Plough.

The two companies' percentage income statements were generally similar in 1993. For example, both spent about 13% of sales on research and development. Still, certain contrasts emerge from the matchup. Cost of sales consumed 23.7 cents of Pfizer's sales dollar in 1993, but only 20.9 cents in Schering-Plough's case. Pfizer likewise showed a cost disadvantage (41.0 cents vs. 40.3 cents) in the selling, general, and administrative expenses category. Consequently, Pfizer earned less from operations

EXHIBIT 3–8

Pfizer Inc., and Schering-Plough Corporation
Comparative Percentage Income Statements
1993

	Pfizer	Schering-Plough
Net sales	100.0%	100.0%
Operating Cost and Expenses		
Cost of sales	23.7	20.9
Selling, general, and administrative expenses	41.0	40.3
Research and development expenses	13.0	13.3
Unusual items	10.1	0.0
Income from operations	12.2	25.5
Interest income	2.2	0.5
Interest expense	(1.4)	(1.1)
Other	(1.6)	(0.1)
Nonoperating income (expense)	(0.8)	(0.7)
Income before Provision for Taxes on		
Income and Minority Interests	11.4	24.8
Provision for taxes on income	2.6	5.8
Cumulative effect of accounting changes	0.0	2.2
Net Income	8.8%	16.8%

Source: Pfizer and Schering-Plough 1993 Annual Reports.

(22.3% vs. 25.5% of sales), even before taking into account its unusual items.

In this case, analysis of comparative percentage income statements is an effective technique. Since Pfizer and Schering-Plough operate within the same industry cost structure, it is meaningful to compare the efficiency of the two operations by identifying modest differences in the breakdown of their respective sales dollars.

Not every comparison within an industry proves as fruitful, however. Frequently, the analysis is complicated by corporate diversification. Some pharmaceutical manufacturers, for example, are also involved in other sectors of the health care industry, which have very different cost structures.

Bristol-Myers Squibb derived only 57% of its 1993 sales from pharmaceuticals, with the balance coming from medical devices, nonprescription health products, toiletries, and beauty aids. The company's 22.5% ratio of operating income to sales was close to Pfizer's 22.3%, but it was derived in a rather different manner. Bristol-Myers Squibb's cost of sales accounted for 26.5% of sales versus 23.7% for Pfizer. Its research and development outlays were considerably lower, in percentage terms, than Pfizer's (9.9% vs. 13.0%).

These relationships are not surprising, given the typically low product costs and high degree of research-intensity of the pharmaceuticals business. With a greater concentration in that area, Pfizer ought to have a cost structure somewhat different from Bristol-Myers Squibb's. Unfortunately, Bristol-Myers Squibb's standard segment reporting does not provide sufficient detail for a full comparison, along the lines of Exhibit 3–8, of the pharmaceuticals businesses only. (To complicate matters further, Pfizer reports its pharmaceuticals and hospital products businesses as a single health care segment.)

Differences in lines of business, even among companies ostensibly within the same industry, make it imperative to exercise caution in interpreting a comparative percentage income statement analysis. A company tagged as an inefficient competitor may be doing a good job, in reality, of utilizing assets and controlling costs in light of its unique business mix.

CONCLUSION

At several points in this chapter, analysis of the income statement has posed questions that could be answered only by looking outside the statement. Indeed, mere study of reported financial figures can never lead to a fully informed judgment about the issuer. Financial statements cannot capture certain nonquantitative factors (e.g., industry conditions, corporate culture, management's ability to anticipate and respond to change) that may be essential to an evaluation.

In a few situations, the limitations of income statement analysis pose no difficulty. For example, an investment organization may be permitted to buy the bonds only of companies that meet a specific financial ratio test. If the analyst's task is narrowly defined as calculating the ratio to see whether it meets the guideline, then there is no need to go beyond the financial statements themselves. If, on the other hand, the objective is to assess the likelihood that the company's future financial performance will be satisfactory, analyzing the statements is merely a jumping-off point. Armed with an understanding of what happened in past periods, the analyst can approach the issuer and other sources to find out why.

4

THE STATEMENT OF CASH FLOWS

THE PRESENT VERSION of the statement that traces the flow of funds in and out of the firm, the statement of cash flows (see Exhibit 4–1 for an example) became mandatory, under SFAS 95, for issuers with fiscal years ending after July 15, 1988. Its predecessor, the statement of changes in financial position (which is used in several of this chapter's historical examples), was first required, under APB 19, in 1971.

Prior to that time, going as far back as the introduction of double-entry accounting in Italy during the fifteenth century, financial analysts had muddled through with only the balance sheet and the income statement. Anyone with a sense of history will surely conclude that the introduction of the cash flow statement must have been premised by expectations of great new analytical insights. Such an inference is in fact well founded. The advantages of a cash flow statement correspond to the shortcomings of the income statement, and more specifically, of the concept of profit. Over time, profit has proven so malleable a quantity, so easily enlarged or reduced to suit management's needs, as to make it useless, in many instances, as the basis of a fair comparison among companies.

One example of the erroneous comparisons that can arise involves the contrasting objectives that public and private companies have in preparing their income statements.

For financial-reporting (as opposed to tax-accounting) purposes, a publicly owned company generally seeks to maximize its reported net

EXHIBIT 4–1

Consolidated Statement of Cash Flows
Rubbermaid Incorporated
($000 omitted)

1993 Cash Flows from Operating Activities

Net earnings	$211,413
Adjustments to reconcile net earnings to net cash from operating activities	
Depreciation	80,860
Employee benefits	14,204
Provision for losses on accounts receivable	4,687
Other	9,077
Changes in:	
Receivables	(31,949)
Inventories	(31,520)
Prepaid expenses and other assets	(12,546)
Payables	16,783
Accrued liabilities	28,426
Deferred income taxes and credits	(2,039)
Net cash from operating activities	287,396
Cash Flows from Investing Activities	
Additions to property, plant, and equipment	(141,697)
Additions to marketable securities	(66,260)
Other, net	87
Net cash from investing activities	(207,870)
Cash Flows from Financing Activities	
Net change in notes payable	(5,630)
Repayment of long-term debt, net	(3,650)
Cash dividends paid	(64,938)
Other, net	0
Net cash from financing activities	(74,218)
Net change in cash and cash equivalents	5,308
Cash and cash equivalents at beginning of year	122,494
Cash and cash equivalents at the end of the year	$127,802

Source: Rubbermaid 1993 Annual Report.

income, which investors use as a basis for valuing its shares. Therefore, its incentive in any situation where the accounting rules permit discretion is to minimize expenses. The firm will capitalize whatever expenditures it can and depreciate its fixed assets over as long a period as possible. All that restrains the public company in this respect (other than conscience) is the wish to avoid being perceived as employing liberal accounting practices, which may lead to a lower market valuation of its reported earnings. Using depreciation schedules much longer than those of other companies in the same industry could give rise to such a perception.

In contrast, a privately held company has no public shareholders to impress. Unlike a public company, which shows one set of statements to the public and another to the Internal Revenue Service, a private company typically prepares one set of statements, with the tax authorities foremost in its thinking. Its incentive is not to maximize, but to minimize, the income it reports, thereby minimizing its tax bill as well. If an analyst examines its income statement and tries to compare it with those of public companies in the same industry, the result will be an undeservedly poor showing by the private company.

THE CASH FLOW STATEMENT AND THE LBO

Net income becomes even less relevant when one analyzes the statements of a company that has been acquired in a leveraged buyout, or LBO (Exhibit 4–2). In a classic LBO, a group of investors acquires a business by putting up a small amount of equity and borrowing the balance (90% in this example) of the purchase price. As a result of this highly leveraged capital structure, interest expense is so large that the formerly quite profitable company reports a loss in its first year as an LBO (1995). Hardly an attractive investment, on the face of it, and one might also question the wisdom of lenders who provide funds to an enterprise that is assured of losing money.

A closer study, however, shows that the equity investors are no fools. In 1995 the company's sales are expected to bring in $1,500 million in cash. Cash outlays include cost of sales ($840 million), selling, general, and administrative expense ($300 million), and interest expense ($265 million), for a total of $1,405 million. Adding in depreciation of $105 million produces total expenses of $1,510 million, which when subtracted from sales results in a $10-million pretax loss. The amount attributable to depreciation, however, does not represent an outlay of cash in the current year. Rather, it is a bookkeeping entry intended to represent the gradual reduction in value, through use, of physical assets. Therefore, the funds generated by the leveraged buyout firm equal sales less the cash expenses only. (Note that the credit for income taxes is a reduction of cash outlays.)

EXHIBIT 4–2   Leveraged Buyout Forecast—Base Case ($000,000 omitted)

Leveraged Buyout Forecast—Base Case ($000,000 omitted)

Capitalization

December 31, 1994

Senior Debt	$1,375	55 %
Subordinated Debt	875	35 %
Total debt	2,250	90 %
Common Equity	250	10 %
Total capital	$2,500	100 %

Projected Income Statement

	1994 (Actual)	1995	1996	1997	1998	1999
Sales	$1,429	$1,500	$1,575	$1,654	$1,737	$1,824
Cost of sales	800	840	882	926	973	1,021
Depreciation	100	105	110	116	122	128
Selling, general, and administrative expense	286	300	315	331	347	365
Operating Income	243	255	268	281	295	310
Interest Expense	70	265	265	263	251	257
Income before Income Taxes	173	(10)	3	18	44	53
Provision (Credit) for Income Taxes	61	(3)	1	6	12	18
Net Income	$ 112	$ (7)	$ 2	$ 12	$ 22	$ 35

Projected Cash Flow

	1995	1996	1997	1998	1999
Net Income	$ (7)	$ 2	$ 12	$ 22	$ 35
Depreciation	105	110	116	122	128
Cash from operations	98	112	128	144	163
Less: Property and equipment additions	95	100	105	110	116
Cash Available for Debt Reduction	$ 3	$ 12	$ 23	$ 34	$ 47

(Continued)

EXHIBIT 4–2   *(Continued)*

	1994 (Actual)	1995	1996	1997	1998	1999
Projected Capitalization						
Senior Debt	$1,375	$1,372	$1,360	$1,337	$1,303	$1,256
Subordinated Debt	875	875	875	875	875	875
Total debt	2,250	2,247	2,235	2,212	2,178	2,131
Common Equity	250	243	245	257	279	314
Total capital	$2,500	$2,490	$2,480	$2,469	$2,457	$2,445

	Sales	$1,500 million
Less:	Cash expenses	
	Cost of sales	840
	Selling, general and administrative expense	300
	Interest expense	265
	Provision (credit) for income taxes	(3)
Equals:	Cash generated	$ 98 million

The same figure can be derived by simply adding back depreciation to net income.[1]

	Net income	$ (7) million
Plus:	Depreciation	105
Equals:	Cash generated	$ 98 million

Viewed in terms of cash inflows and outflows, rather than earnings, the leveraged buyout begins to look like a sound venture. Projected net income remains negative, but as shown under "Projected Cash Flow," cash generation should slightly exceed cash use in 1995. (Note that the equity investors take no dividends but instead dedicate any surplus cash generated to reduction of debt.)

---

[1]Exhibit 4–2 and the accompanying narrative simplify the concept of cash flow in order to introduce it to the reader. Only the two major sources of cash—net income and depreciation—appear here, leaving to subsequent exhibits refinements such as deferred taxes, which arise from timing differences between the recognition and payment of taxes. Similarly, the uses of cash exclude a working capital factor, which is discussed in connection with Exhibit 4–10.

The story improves even more during subsequent years. As sales grow at a 5% annual rate, the Projected Income Statement shows a steady increase in operating income. In addition, a gradual paydown of debt causes interest expense to decline a bit, so net income increases over time. With depreciation rising as well, funds from operations in this example keep modestly ahead of the growing capital expenditure requirements.

If the projections prove accurate, the equity investors will, by the end of 1999, own a company with $1.8 billion in sales and $310 million of operating income, up from $1.4 billion and $243 million, respectively, in 1994. They will have captured that growth without having injected any additional cash beyond their original $250-million investment.

Suppose the investors then decide to monetize the increase in firm value represented by the growth in earnings. Assuming they can sell the company for the same multiple of EBITDA (earnings before interest, taxes, depreciation and amortization)[2] that they paid for it, they will realize net proceeds of $685 million, derived as follows ($000 omitted):

1. Calculate the multiple of EBITDA paid in 1994

$$= \frac{\text{Purchase price (Equity plus borrowed funds)}}{\text{Net income + Income taxes + Interest expense} \atop \text{+ Depreciation + Amortization}}$$

$$= \frac{\$2,500}{\$112,000 + \$61,000 + \$70,000 + \$100,000}$$

$$= 7.3$$

2. Multiply this factor by 1999 EBITDA to determine sale price in that year.

$(7.3) \times (\$18,000 + \$53,000 + \$257,000 + \$128,000) = \$3,328,800$

3. From this figure subtract remaining debt to determine pretax proceeds.

$$\begin{array}{r} \$3,328,800 \\ -2,131,000 \\ \hline \$1,197,800 \end{array}$$

---

[2]For a detailed rationale for use of the EBITDA multiple to evaluate a firm, see Chapter 7, under the heading "Valuation via Restructuring Potential."

4. Subtract taxes on the gain over original equity investment to determine net proceeds.

$1,197,800	Pretax proceeds
− 250,000	Original equity investment
947,800	Capital gain
× .34	Capital gains tax rate
$ 322,252	Tax on capital gain

$1,197,800	Pretax proceeds
− 322,252	Tax on capital gain
$ 875,548	Net proceeds

The increase in the equity holders' investment from $250 million to $876 million over five years represents a compounded annual return of 28.5% after tax. Interestingly, the annual return on equity (based on reported net income and the book value of equity) averages only 4% during the period of the projection. Analysts evaluating the investment merits of the LBO proposal would miss the point if they focused on earnings rather than cash flow.

The same emphasis on cash flow, rather than reported earnings, is equally important in analyzing the downside in a leveraged buyout.

As one might expect, the equity investors do not reap such spectacular gains without incurring significant risk. There is a danger that everything will not go according to plan and that they will lose their entire investment. Specifically, there is a risk that sales and operating earnings will fall short of expectations, perhaps as a result of a recession or because the investors' expectations were unrealistically high at the outset. With a less debt-heavy capital structure, a shortfall in operating earnings might not be worrisome. In a leveraged buyout, however, the high interest expense can quickly turn disappointing operating income into a sizable net loss (Exhibit 4–3). The loss may be so large that even after depreciation is added back, the company's funds generated from operations may decline to zero or to a negative figure. (Note that the shortfall shown here resulted from deviations of just 8% each in the projections for sales, cost of sales, and selling, general and administrative expense, shown in Exhibit 4–3.)

Now the future does not look so rosy for the equity investors. If they cannot reduce operating expenses sufficiently to halt the cash drain, they will lack the cash required for the heavy interest expenses they have incurred, much less the scheduled principal payments. Unfortunately, most

EXHIBIT 4–3 Leveraged Buyout Forecast—Pessimistic Case
($000,000 omitted)

Projected Income Statement	
	1995
Sales	$1,380
Cost of sales	907
Depreciation	105
Selling, general, and administrative expense	324
Operating Income	44
Interest Expense	265
Income before Income Taxes	(221)
Provision (Credit) for income taxes	(75)
Net Income	$ (146)

	Net income	$(146) million
Plus:	Depreciation	105
Equals:	Cash generated	$ (41) million

of the choices available in the event they cannot cut costs sufficiently are unappealing. One option is for the investors to inject more equity into the company. This will cause any profits they ultimately realize to represent a smaller percentage return on the equity invested, besides possibly straining the investors' finances. Alternatively, the existing equity holders can sell equity to a new group of investors. The disadvantage of this strategy is that anyone putting in new capital at a time when the venture is perceived to be in trouble is likely to exact terms that will severely dilute the original investors' interest and, possibly, control. Comparably harsh terms may be expected from lenders who are willing (if any are) to let the company try to borrow its way out of its problems. A distressed exchange offer, in which bondholders accept reduced interest or a postponement of principal repayment, may be more attractive for the equity holders but is likely to meet stiff resistance.

If all these options prove unpalatable or unfeasible, the leveraged company will default on its debt. At that point, the lenders may force the firm into bankruptcy, which could result in a total loss for the equity investors. Alternatively, the lenders may agree to reduce the interest rates on their loans and postpone mandatory principal repayments, but they will ordinarily agree to such concessions only in exchange for a larger influence on the company's management. In short, once cash flow turns negative, the potential outcomes generally look bleak to the equity investors.

The key point here is that the cash flow statement—not the income statement—provides the best information about a highly leveraged firm's financial health. Given the overriding importance of generating (and retaining) cash to retire debt, and because the equity investors have no desire for dividends, there is no advantage in showing an accounting profit, the main consequence of which is incurrence of taxes, resulting in turn in reduced cash flow. Neither are there public shareholders clamoring for increases in earnings per share. The cash flow statement is the most useful tool for analyzing highly leveraged companies, because it reflects the true motivation of the firm's owners—to generate cash, rather than to maximize reported income.

ANALYTICAL APPLICATIONS

While privately held and highly leveraged companies illustrate most vividly the advantages of the cash flow statement, the statement also has considerable utility in analyzing publicly owned and more conventionally capitalized firms. One important application lies in determining where a company is in its life cycle—whether it is starting up, "taking off," growing rapidly, maturing, or declining. Different types of risk characterize these various stages of the life cycle, so knowing which stage a company is in can focus the analyst's efforts on the key analytical factors. A second use of the cash flow statement is to assess a company's financial flexibility. This term refers to a company's capacity, in the event of a business downturn, to continue making expenditures that, over the long term, minimize its cost of capital and enhance its competitive position. Finally, the cash flow statement is the key statement to examine when analyzing a troubled company. When a company is verging on bankruptcy, its balance sheet may overstate its asset value (by virtue of write-offs having lagged the deterioration in its business) or fail to reflect the full value of certain assets recorded at historical cost, which the company might sell to raise cash. The income statement is not especially relevant, since the company's key objective for the moment is to survive, not to maintain an impeccable earnings record. The cash flow statement forms the basis for answering the most pertinent question: Will the company succeed in keeping its creditors at bay?

CASH FLOW AND THE COMPANY LIFE CYCLE

Business enterprises typically go through phases of development that are in many respects analogous to a human being's stages of life. Just as children are susceptible to illnesses different from those of the elderly, the risks incurred when investing in start-up companies are different from the risks inherent in mature companies. Accordingly, it is useful when analyzing a company to understand which portion of the life cycle it is in and which financial pitfalls it is therefore most likely to face.

Exhibit 4–4 depicts the business life cycle in terms of sales and earnings growth over time. Revenues build gradually during the start-up phase, during which time the company is just organizing itself and launching its products. Growth and profits accelerate rapidly during the emerging growth phase, as the company's products begin to penetrate the market and the firm achieves an economic scale of production. During the established growth period, sales and earnings growth decelerates as the market nears saturation. In the mature industry phase, sales opportunities are limited to the replacement of products previously sold, plus new sales derived from growth in the population. Price competition often intensifies at this stage, as companies seek growth through increased market share (a larger piece of a more slowly growing pie). The declining

EXHIBIT 4–4   The Business Life Cycle

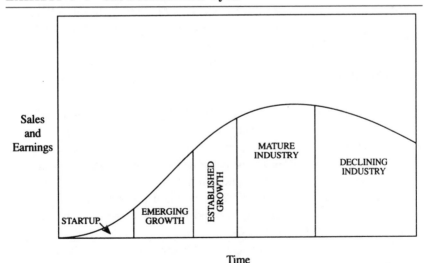

industry stage does not automatically follow maturity, but over long periods some industries do get swept away by technological change. Sharply declining sales and earnings, ultimately resulting in corporate bankruptcies, characterize industries in decline.

The characteristic growth patterns of firms at various stages in the company life cycle correspond to typical patterns of cash generation and usage. Exhibits 4–5 and 4–8 are cash flow statements of actual examples of the types described immediately below.

Start-up companies are voracious cash users. They require funds to acquire facilities and pay the salaries of employees who plan the initial attempts to produce goods and make sales. With no revenues yet coming in, the risk is high that the organization will fail to gel. If its backers are not well capitalized, they may be forced to abandon the venture by unexpected delays in bringing the product to market or by unanticipated expenses.

Grand Casinos illustrates the cash flow pattern observed in a start-up company (Exhibit 4–5). The company commenced business in 1990 as a manager of gaming facilities owned by Native American tribes. In 1993, Grand Casinos began to generate revenue from properties that it both owned and operated. Along with a number of other start-ups, Grand Casinos was investing heavily in ventures made possible by the legalization of casino gambling in states that had not permitted it previously.

The key cash flow sources of net earnings, depreciation and amortization (including amortization of debt-related items) totaled $28.0 million in 1993. Grand Casinos boosted its overall cash flow from operating activities to $38.5 million, mainly by building up accrued expenses and income taxes. That left the company about $100 million shy of its capital spending requirements for the year ($142.8 million). Issuance of long-term debt filled the gap and Grand Casinos stockpiled an additional $164.1 million by selling common equity.

A large need for external financing is a common characteristic of start-up companies. Grand Casinos enjoyed good access to capital markets at a time when investors were eager to participate in the rapid expansion of casino gambling into new jurisdictions. Not all start-ups are so fortunate. With internal cash generation falling considerably short of cash needs, a cutoff of outside financing could prove fatal for a young company. It is therefore prudent to build up a cash cushion when funds are available, as Grand Casinos did in 1993.

Emerging growth companies' cash requirements outstrip their ability to generate cash. They must aggressively expand their productive facilities to capitalize on demand, but this requires more cash than they can

EXHIBIT 4–5

Consolidated Statement of Cash Flows
Grand Casinos, Inc., and Subsidiaries
($000 omitted)

1993 Cash Flows from Operating Activities	
Net earnings	$ 18,750
Adjustments to reconcile net earnings to net cash	
from operating activities	
Depreciation and amortization	7,592
Amortization of original issue discount	1,668
Gain on sale of investment	(4,600)
Equity in loss of unconsolidated affiliate	214
Increase in deferred income taxes	1,925
Changes in:	
Other current assets	(7,212)
Accounts payables-trade	1,701
Accrued expenses and income taxes	18,453
Net cash from operating activities	38,491
Cash Flows from Investing Activities	
Payments for notes payables	(24,363)
Investment in and notes receivables from affiliates	(8,057)
Proceeds from repayment of notes receivables	3,825
Payments for property and equipment	(142,805)
Proceeds from sale of investment	500
Payments for other long-term assets	(13,752)
Net cash from investing activities	(184,652)
Cash Flows from Financing Activities	
Increase in accounts payable-construction	25,671
Proceeds from issuance of common stock, net	164,135
Proceeds from original issue discount	9,823
Debt issuance costs-First Mortgage Notes	(6,490)
Proceeds from issuance of long-term debt	107,177
Payments on long-term debt and capital lease obligation	(3,301)
Net cash from financing activities	297,015
Net change in cash and cash equivalents	150,854
Cash and cash equivalents at beginning of year	7,209
Cash and cash equivalents at the end of the year	$158,063

Source: Grand Casinos and Subsidiaries 1993 Annual Report.

generate from earnings and depreciation. Although they are beyond the start-up phase, these companies remain financially fragile. A growth industry typically attracts more start-up firms than the industry can ultimately support. Unless a firm can grow rapidly enough to achieve an economic scale of production, it will be one of the firms "shaken out" in the inevitable consolidation achieved through both the absorption (in mergers) of some firms and the failure of others. An emerging growth company, then, has no choice but to grow rapidly if it is to survive, yet its management may lack the know-how to maintain control of operations as the organization inevitably becomes more complex. Furthermore, a slump in demand for new stock of growth companies could prove fatal for a company so dependent on external funding.

United States Cellular (Exhibit 4–6) illustrates the cash flow pattern of an emerging growth company. Competing in the fast-growing cellular telecommunications field, the company increased its revenues steadily from $10.3 million in 1987 to $247.3 million in 1993. Operations continued to generate losses, however, making U.S. Cellular dependent primarily on depreciation and amortization for cash flow. Even with a $29.0 million boost from accrued interest, total cash flow from operations fell about $50 million short of the $84.9 million capital budget. The company made up the difference by issuing common shares and borrowing on its revolving credit line. As demonstrated by U.S. Cellular's statement of cash flows, access to outside capital remains a vital concern for companies that progress from the start-up to the emerging growth stage.

Established growth companies are more nearly able to fund their growth internally. Depreciation is now substantial, and with a large portion of the potential market penetrated, the rate of required capacity additions slows down. Some of the problems of rapid growth remain, but in a less severe form. Having survived the industry shakeout, the firm must now meet the challenges of intensifying competition for a more slowly growing market. Pitfalls include product obsolescence and failure to satisfy increasingly sophisticated customers' demands for improved service support or a wider range of product options.

McDonald's (Exhibit 4–7) displays the typical business characteristics of an established growth company. In 1993, earnings increased by a quite respectable 12.9% over 1992, which in turn was up 11.5% over 1991. The restaurant chain continued to expand more rapidly than the overall economy, but it was past the hypergrowth phase that can make a company impervious to fluctuations in general business conditions. Earnings growth had slackened to 7.1% in 1991 as McDonald's failed to escape the impact of consumers tightening their purse strings in the face of an uncertain economic outlook. A major challenge for the company was finding attractive new sites, which meant in part looking outside its established geographic markets. Additionally, McDonald's had to answer competitors' initiatives in pricing and new products. Increasingly, the company's key tasks were beginning to resemble those of a mature business.

EXHIBIT 4–6

Consolidated Statement of Cash Flows
U.S. Cellular
($000 omitted)

1993 Cash Flows from Operating Activities

Net earnings	($25,441)
Adjustments to reconcile net earnings to net cash from operating activities	
Depreciation	45,944
Investment income	(16,922)
Gain on sale of cellular interests	(4,851)
Minority share of operating income	3,496
Other noncash expense	499
Changes in:	
Accounts receivable	(7,343)
Accounts payable	5,836
Accrued interest	29,009
Accrued taxes	177
Other assets and liabilities	4,899
Net cash from operating activities	35,303

Cash Flows from Financing Activities

Long-term debt borrowings	64
Repayment of long-term debt	(15,851)
Change in revolving credit agreement	45,446
Common shares issued	36,813
Minority partner capital	(1,075)
Net cash from financing activities	65,397

Cash Flows from Investing Activities

Additions to property, plant and equipment	(84,889)
Investments in and advances to minority partnerships	(16,279)
Distributions from partnerships	11,265
Proceeds from sale of investments	6,750
Acquisitions, excluding cash acquired	(9,964)
Other investments	(5,439)
Net cash from investing activities	(98,556)
Net change in cash and cash equivalents	2,144
Cash and cash equivalents at beginning of year	4,130
Cash and cash equivalents at the end of the year	$ 6,274

Source: U.S. Cellular 1993 Annual Report.

EXHIBIT 4-7

Consolidated Statement of Cash Flows
McDonald's Corporation
($000 omitted)

1993 Cash Flows from Operating Activities

Net earnings	$1,083
Adjustments to reconcile net earnings to net cash from operating activities	
Depreciation and amortization	568
Deferred income taxes	52
Changes in:	
Accounts receivable	(48)
Inventories and prepaid expenses	(10)
Accounts payable	45
Accrued interest	(5)
Taxes and other liabilities	27
Other-net	(32)
Net cash from operating activities	1,680

Cash Flows from Investing Activities

Property and equipment expenditures	(1,317)
Sales of restaurant businesses	114
Purchases of restaurant businesses	(64)
Notes receivables additions	(33)
Property sales	62
Notes receivables reductions	76
Other	(55)
Net cash from investing activities	(1,218)

Cash Flows from Financing Activities

Notes payable and commercial paper net borrowings	(9)
Other long-term financing issuances	1,241
Other long-term financing repayments	(1,186)
Treasury stock purchases	(620)
Common and preferred stock dividends	(201)
Other	63
Net cash from financing activities	(713)
Net change in cash and cash equivalents	(251)
Cash and cash equivalents at beginning of year	437
Cash and cash equivalents at the end of the year	$ 186

Source: McDonald's 1993 Annual Report.

Reaping the benefits of past investments, McDonald's earned more than a billion dollars in 1993. That sum, combined with over a half billion dollars of depreciation and amortization, more than covered capital expenditures of $1.3 billion. Changes in operating working capital items had little net impact.

McDonald's positive net cash flow enabled it to pay out substantial dividends to shareholders, an option not generally available to companies at much earlier stages of growth. Far from requiring external financing, McDonald's was able to repurchase $620.1 million of its stock, a further benefit to shareholders. (The long-term financing undertaken in 1993 essentially replaced outstanding borrowings.) As an established growth company, McDonald's was far less vulnerable to disruptions in the capital markets than its start-up and emerging growth counterparts.

Mature industry companies have modest capital requirements. Demand for their products grows slowly, necessitating only a moderate pace of additions to manufacturing capacity. Monsanto (Exhibit 4–8), like many other companies in mature industries, has diversified into businesses that promise higher growth and wider profit margins. In addition to its long-established chemical, plastic, and synthetic fibers, it produces more technologically dynamic items, including pharmaceuticals, food sweeteners, and agricultural products enhanced by biotechnology. On the whole, though, its revenues have expanded slowly in recent years. Between 1988 and 1993, net sales grew at only about 1% annually. During that period, earnings were repeatedly penalized by restructuring charges.

Depreciation and amortization alone covered Monsanto's 1993 capital expenditures of $437 million, continuing the pattern observed in preceding years. Put another way, the company was in a position of net negative reinvestment in its business. This was true even before considering that as a result of inflation, the replacement cost of capital equipment typically exceeds the historical cost basis of its reported depreciation. (Note, however, that an excess of depreciation over capital expenditures can also represent a shift to less capital-intensive businesses.)

As a further sign of maturity, Monsanto paid out 56% of its earnings in dividends in 1993. Faster-growing, more cash-hungry companies tend to retain a larger portion of earnings for reinvestment in their businesses. Unquestionably, a single year's dividend payout ratio may be misleading. Earnings can fluctuate substantially from year to year, while boards of directors generally gear dividends to normalized earnings expectations over periods of several years. In Monsanto's case, though, the company raised its dividend each year from 1989 to 1993, for a cumulative increase

EXHIBIT 4–8

Consolidated Statement of Cash Flows
Monsanto
($000,000 omitted)

1993 Cash Flows from Operating Activities

Income from continuing operations	$ 494
Add incomes taxes - continuing operations	235
Income from continuing operations before taxes	729
Adjustments to reconcile to cash provided by continuing operations	
Income tax payments	(166)
Depreciation and amortization	572
Restructuring expenses - net	5
Incremental SFAS 106 expenses	48
Other	(19)
Changes in:	
Accounts receivable	62
Inventories	(31)
Accounts payable and accrued liabilities	(202)
Other	34
Other items	(10)
Cash from continuing operations	1,022
Cash from discontinued operations	(291)
Net cash from operating activities	731

Cash Flows from Investing Activities

Property and equipment purchases	(437)
Acquisition and investment payments	(510)
Investment and property disposal proceeds	298
Net cash from investing activities	(649)

Cash Flows from Financing Activities

Net change in short-term financing	(31)
Long-term debt proceeds	379
Long-term debt reductions	(299)
Treasury stock purchases	(380)
Dividend payments	(275)
Other financing activities	68
Net cash from financing activities	(538)
Net change in cash and cash equivalents	(456)
Cash and cash equivalents at beginning of year	729
Cash and cash equivalents at the end of the year	$ 273

Source: Monsanto 1993 Annual Report.

of 56%. Over the five years ending in 1993, operating earnings per share fluctuated substantially, finishing just 4% above the 1988 level. The clear effect, whatever the intent may have been, was to return more cash to shareholders and to reinvest less in the business. This overall tendency was reinforced by repeated stock repurchases, including $380 million in 1993.

Declining industry companies encounter the kinds of problems reflected in Asarco's 1993 cash flow statement (Exhibit 4–9). The nonferrous metal producer could not generate the funds required for reinvestment in its business from the combination of its slim profits and its depreciation flows. To alleviate its cash flow shortfall, the company incurred a net increase in debt and liquidated securities and property. In addition, Asarco's dividend payments ($20.8 million) were down substantially from earlier years.

Like an emerging growth company, a company in a declining industry is typically a net cash user, but for different reasons. Instead of having an excess of attractive investment opportunities, the declining industry company has difficulty maintaining its present businesses, as a consequence of their low profitability. Instead of returning substantial amounts of cash to investors for deployment in higher-return ventures, like a company in a mature industry, a company in a declining industry commonly struggles to preserve its dividend and borrows to remain viable.

Studying the cash flow statement will not fully equip the analyst to predict whether a firm—whatever the stage of its development—will meet the challenges it faces. Thinking about the types of problems a company is likely to encounter at a particular point in its life cycle can, however, steer the analyst into the most pertinent areas of further investigation. By helping the analyst to characterize the firm's relative maturity, the cash flow statement can be an objective counterbalance to overly upbeat comments disseminated by management outside the financial statements proper. A company has strong incentives to dampen investors' awareness that it is undergoing a normal and inevitable transition from rapid to moderate growth or from moderate growth to contraction. Analysts who remain conscious of how the cash is flowing are unlikely to have their perceptions altered by such mind-bending techniques.

THE CONCEPT OF FINANCIAL FLEXIBILITY

Besides reflecting a firm's stage of development, and therefore the categories of risk it is most likely to face, the cash flow statement provides

EXHIBIT 4–9

Consolidated Statement of Cash Flows
Asarco Inc.
($000 omitted)

1993 Cash Flows from Operating Activities

Net earnings	$ 15,619
Adjustments to reconcile net earnings to net cash from operating activities	
Depreciation and depletion	80,641
Provision for deferred taxes	(19,639)
Treasury stock used for employee benefits	4,743
Undistributed equity earnings	(26,114)
Net gain on sale of investments and property	(18,823)
Cumulative effect of change in accounting principle	(86,295)
Provision for plant closures and disposals	13,156
Reserves for closed plant and environmental matters	(38,012)
Changes in:	
Accounts receivable	21,765
Inventories	37,462
Accounts payable and accrued liabilities	42,231
Other operating liabilities and reserves	12,149
Other operating assets	(709)
Foreign currency transaction losses	687
Net cash from operating activities	38,861

Cash Flows from Investing Activities

Capital expenditures	(112,315)
Proceeds from sale of securities and property	176,024
Purchase of investments	(139,592)
Net cash from investing activities	(75,883)

Cash Flows from Financing Activities

Debt incurred	387,788
Debt retired	(349,371)
Net treasury stock transactions	321
Dividends paid	(20,792)
Net cash from financing activities	17,946
Effect of exchange rate changes in cash	(1,672)
Net change in cash and cash equivalents	(20,748)
Cash and cash equivalents at beginning of year	33,248
Cash and cash equivalents at the end of the year	$ 12,500

Source: Asarco 1993 Annual Report.

essential information about a firm's financial flexibility. By studying the statement, an analyst can make informed judgments on such questions as

- How "safe" is the company's dividend?
- Could the company fund its needs internally if external sources of capital suddenly become scarce or prohibitively expensive?
- Would the company be able to continue meeting its obligations if its business turned down sharply?

Exhibit 4–10 provides a condensed format that can help answer these questions. At the top is basic cash flow, defined as net income (excluding noncash components), depreciation, and deferred income taxes. The various uses of cash are deducted in order, from least to most discretionary. In difficult times, when a company must cut back on various expenditures to conserve cash, management faces many difficult choices. A key objective is to avoid damage to the company's long-term health. Financial flexibility, as elucidated by the presentation in Exhibit 4–10, is critical to meeting this objective.

EXHIBIT 4–10

Analysis of Financial Flexibility Kellogg Company and Subsidiaries ($000,000 omitted)	
	1993
Basic Cash Flow[1]	$869.6
Less: Increase in adjusted working capital[2]	69.4
Operating Cash Flow	800.2
Less: Capital expenditures	449.7
Discretionary Cash Flow	350.5
Less: Dividends	305.2
Less: Asset sales and other investing activities	(89.5)
Cash Flow before Financing	134.8
Less: Net (increase) in long-term debt	(206.6)
Less: Net (increase) in notes payable	(176.7)
Less: Net purchase of company's common stock	545.2
Less: Miscellaneous	1.1
(Decrease) in Cash and Temporary Investments	($28.2)

Source: Kellogg 1993 Annual Report.

[1]Includes net earnings, depreciation, and deferred income taxes, less items in net earnings not providing cash.

[2]Excludes cash and notes payable.

Kellogg Company, a producer of breakfast cereals and other foods, exhibited considerable financial flexibility in 1993. After satisfying all its capital and dividend requirements, the company had additional cash available, even before considering $89.5 million (net) provided by asset sales and other investing activities. Kellogg chose to allocate the $134.8 million generated before financing partly to repurchasing common stock. (The stock buyback was also financed by increases in long-term debt and notes payable.) A key analytical point is that the stock repurchase was a discretionary expenditure that could have been eliminated without long-term harm to the company.

While Kellogg's performance was excellent, the analyst must recognize that it was achieved in the context of a strong economy. If business conditions tightened to the point where Kellogg could no longer build cash, repurchase stock, or (if it chose) pay down debt, the company would have to consider various austerity measures. Given a sufficiently depressed economy, those measures could become quite painful.

Cutting or completely omitting the dividend is a step companies avoid except under extremely difficult circumstances, even though the format in Exhibit 4–10 makes the dividend decision look like a residual of other operating and capital expenditure choices. In some cases, maintaining the dividend by, for example, cutting back on capital expenditures sacrifices long-range competitiveness. On the other hand, a slowdown in demand may postpone the need for new capacity and make a cut in the capital budget not merely responsible but advisable (to avoid construction of costly idle facilities).

In a real pinch, the company can cut back to its maintenance level of capital spending, the bare amount required to keep the equipment operating and in good repair. Asking a company to estimate its maintenance level of capital spending (and verifying through other industry sources that the figure is realistic) can greatly aid the analyst's assessment of financial flexibility.

For example, in 1993 Kellogg's discretionary cash flow, at $350.5 million, covered its dividend of $305.2 million by 1.15 times. Suppose earnings were to fall by $100 million from their 1993 level of $680.7 million, while all other elements of discretionary cash flow remained constant. Discretionary cash flow would then fall to approximately $55 million below the indicated dividend level. If the company did not happen to have sizable asset sales in the works, it might be forced to borrow to pay its dividend.

To avoid that step, which is not a prudent practice over a prolonged period, Kellogg could instead reduce its capital expenditures. A cut of only

12%, or $55 million, would restore discretionary cash flow to the dividend level. Provided a reduction of that magnitude would not impair Kellogg's long-term competitiveness, an analyst could conclude that the company had considerable flexibility to maintain its dividend in difficult times.

Note, too, that flexibility is partly a function of the likelihood of an earnings decline large enough to cause discretionary cash flow to fall below the indicated dividend level. As a strong competitor in a comparatively noncyclical industry, Kellogg is less susceptible to wide swings in earnings than producers of commodities such as cement and steel. At many companies, a ratio of discretionary cash flow to dividends as low as Kellogg's 1.15 times would be too small a cushion to suggest dividend continuity.

A final item in the analysis of financial flexibility is the change in adjusted working capital. In general, rising sales necessitate increased inventories and generate higher levels of accounts receivable. To the extent that this funds requirement cannot be met by expansion of accounts payable or other liabilities, a net use of funds occurred. In 1993, this use amounted to $69.4 million for Kellogg—a modest deduction from the company's $869.6 million of basic cash flow.

Note that, unlike conventional working capital, the adjusted figure of $69.4 million excludes notes payable, as well as cash and short-term investments. The former item shows up as part of Kellogg's financing for the year. Changes in cash and short-term investments are treated as a residual in the analysis of financial flexibility.

During 1993, Kellogg's cash and short-term investments declined from $126.3 million to $98.1 million. This reduction was not driven by sales, which rose from $6,190.6 million to $6,295.4 million. Rather, having generated more cash in previous years than it could invest internally at attractive returns, Kellogg decided to retain the surplus in a liquid form. Doing so further enhanced the company's financial flexibility. When stock repurchases appeared attractive in 1993, drawing down cash was one means (along with increasing debt) of financing the opportunistic transactions.

Kellogg's 1993 increase in adjusted working capital represented a modest cash requirement brought about by a healthy rise in sales. Some companies are able to fund needs of this type entirely by increasing accounts payable and other current liabilities. Their balance sheets perennially show negative working capital, which does not indicate lack of liquidity, but rather high confidence on the part of their creditors.

Unfortunately, not every company enjoys relative independence from the credit markets year in and year out. Sometimes a company experiences a sudden surge in sales, resulting in so large an increase in inventories and receivables that its operating cash flow turns negative, even though net income is rising. As long as its profits are healthy, a company will generally not have difficulty in obtaining credit to fund the shortfall. More problematic is the case in which a sudden drop-off in sales causes involuntary inventory accumulation. Until the company realizes that its goods are moving more slowly and it cuts back on production, inventory levels rise, creating a funds need. When this cash drain is combined with an earnings decline resulting from the sales drop-off, the financial squeeze can be acute. Often, too, the sales decline results from tight money conditions—exactly the circumstances that make it most difficult for a company to fund itself.

Conditions are tough enough when credit is scarce or prohibitively expensive, but sometimes a company finds itself actually prohibited from borrowing. Bank credit agreements typically impose restrictive covenants, which may include limitations on total indebtedness. Beyond a certain point, a firm bound by such covenants cannot continue borrowing to meet its obligations.

When a company's squeeze becomes this severe, management must cut back on discretionary expenditures to avoid losing control—one consequence of violating debt covenants or filing bankruptcy. Unfortunately, many of the items that a company can cut without disrupting operations in the short run are outlays that are essential to its long-term health. Advertising and research are obvious targets, since they tend to have future-period benefits; the cash savings are immediately apparent, while the cost to future revenues is not. Over many years, a company that habitually scrimps on such expenditures can impair its competitiveness, thereby transforming a short-term problem into a long-term one.

Avoiding this pattern of decline is the primary benefit of financial flexibility. If during good times a company can generate positive cash flow before financing, it will not have to cut deeply into capital expenditures and other outlays that represent investments in its future. Nor, in all likelihood, will a company that maintains some slack be forced to cut its dividend under duress, tarnishing its image in the capital markets and raising the cost of future financings.

Despite the blessings that financial flexibility confers, however, maintaining a funds cushion is not universally regarded as a wise corporate policy. The opposing view is based on a definition of free cash flow as "cash flow in excess of that required to fund all of a firm's projects that have positive net present values when discounted at the relevant cost of capital."[3] A firm's management should, according to the argument, dividend all excess cash flow to shareholders. The only alternative is to invest it in low-return projects (or possibly even lower-return marketable securities), thereby preventing shareholders from earning their required returns on a portion of their capital. Left to their own devices, argue the proponents of this view, managers will trap cash in low-return investments because their compensation tends to be positively related to the growth of assets under their control. Therefore, pressure—including the threat of hostile takeover—should be exerted to force management to remit all excess cash.

This argument certainly sounds logical and is, moreover, supported by numerous studies[4] indicating the tendency of companies to continue investing even after they have exhausted their good opportunities. Growing as it does out of economic theory, though, the argument must be applied judiciously in practice. Overinvestment has unquestionably led, in many industries, to prolonged periods of excess capacity, producing in turn chronically poor profitability. In retrospect, the firms involved would have done better by their shareholders if they had increased their dividend payouts or repurchased stock, instead of constructing new plants. That judgment, however, benefits from hindsight. Managers may have overinvested because they believed forecasts of economic growth that ultimately proved too optimistic. Had demand grown at the expected rate, a firm that had declined to expand capacity might have been unable to maintain its market share. In the long run, failing to keep up with the scale economies achieved by more expansion-minded competitors could have harmed shareholders more than a few years of excess capacity. The financial analyst's job includes making judgments about a firm's reinvestment policies—without the benefit of hindsight—and does not consist of passively accepting the prevailing wisdom that low returns in the near term are proof that an industry has no future opportunities worth exploiting.

A subtler point not easily captured by theorists is that financial flexibility can translate directly into operating flexibility. Keeping cash "trapped" in marketable securities can enable a firm to gain an edge over

---

[3]Michael C. Jensen, "The Free Cash Flow Theory of Takeovers: A Financial Perspective on Mergers and Acquisitions and the Economy," in *The Merger Boom,* Proceedings of a Conference Held in October 1978, edited by Lynn E. Browne and Eric S. Rosengren, Federal Reserve Bank of Boston, pp. 102–37. This article provides the basis for the synopsis of the free cash flow argument described here, as well as the definition quoted.

[4]Ibid.

"lean-and-mean" competitors when tight credit conditions make it difficult to finance working capital needs. Another less obvious cost of eschewing financial flexibility involves the danger of permanently losing experienced skilled workers through temporary layoffs occasioned by recessions. Productivity subsequently suffers when laid-off skilled employees find permanent jobs elsewhere. It may therefore be economical to keep plants running, thereby deliberately building up inventory, in order to keep valued workers on the payroll. This strategy is difficult to implement without some capability of adjusting to a sudden increase in working capital financing requirements.

CONCLUSION

Thanks to the wide diversity of companies available for investment today, the cash flow statement has become a valuable complement to the other statements, aiding in situations where the balance sheet and income statement provide only limited insight. For example, the income statement is a dubious measure of the success of a highly leveraged company that is being managed to minimize, rather than maximize, reported profits. Similarly, it is largely irrelevant whether a company with an already substantially depleted net worth reports 10% lower equity in the current quarter than in the previous one. The primary concern of the investor or creditor at such times is whether the firm can continue meeting its obligations long enough to solve its operating problems.

The cash flow statement not only facilitates the analysis of a number of different types of companies facing different types of risks, it also helps to identify the categories into which companies fit. At all stages of development, and whatever the nature of the challenges a company faces, financial flexibility—which is best measured by studying the flow of funds—is essential to meeting those challenges. Financial flexibility is not merely a security blanket for squeamish investors, as it is sometimes portrayed. In the hands of an aggressive but prudent management, it can be a weapon for gaining an advantage over competitors by maintaining long-term investment spending at times when other firms are forced to cut back.

Part Three

FORECASTS, ANALYSIS, AND SPECIAL CASES

5

FORECASTING FINANCIAL STATEMENTS

ANALYSIS OF A company's current financial statements—as discussed in the three preceding chapters—is enlightening, but not as enlightening as the analysis of its *future* financial statements. After all, it is future earnings and dividends that determine the value of a company's stock (see Chapter 7) and the relative likelihood of future timely payments of debt service that determines credit quality (see Chapter 6). To be sure, investors rely to some extent on the past as an indication of the future. Because already-reported financials are available to everyone, however, studying them is unlikely to provide any significant advantage over competing investors. To capture fundamental value that is not already reflected in securities prices, the analyst must act on the earnings and credit quality measures that will appear on future statements.

Naturally, the analyst cannot know with certainty what a company's future financial statements will look like, but neither are financial projections mere guesswork. Rather, the process is an extension of historical patterns and relationships, based on assumptions about future economic conditions, market behavior, and managerial actions.

Financial projections will correspond to actual future results only to the extent that the assumptions prove accurate. Analysts should therefore energetically gather information beyond the statements themselves, seeking constantly to improve the quality of their assumptions.

A TYPICAL ONE-YEAR PROJECTION

The following one-year projection works through the effects of the analyst's assumptions on all three basic financial statements. There is probably no better way than following the numbers in this way to appreciate the interrelatedness of the income statement, the cash flow statement, and the balance sheet.

Exhibit 5–1 displays the current financial statements of a fictitious company, Colossal Chemical Corporation. The historical statements

EXHIBIT 5–1   Financial Statements

Financial Statements of Colossal Chemical Corporation
Year Ended December 31, 1994
($000,000 omitted)

Income Statement		Statement of Cash Flows	
Sales	$1,991	Sources:	
Cost of goods sold	1,334	Net income	$ 85
Selling, general and			
administrative expense	299	Depreciation	119
Depreciation	119	Deferred income taxes	20
Research and development	80	Working capital changes, excluding	
		cash and borrowings	(8)
Total costs and expenses	1,832	Funds provided by operations	216
		Uses:	
Operating Income	159	Additions to property, plant, and	
Interest expense	36	equipment	125
Interest (income)	(6)	Dividends	28
Earnings before income taxes	129	Reduction of long-term debt	60
Provision for income taxes	44	Funds used by operations	213
Net Income	$ 85	Net Increase in Funds	$ 3

Balance Sheet			
Cash and marketable securities	$ 69	Notes payable	$ 21
Accounts receivable	439	Accounts payable	263
		Current portion of long-term debt	
Inventories	351		32
Total Current Assets	859	Total Current Liabilities	316
Property, Plant, and Equipment	895	Long-Term Debt	379
	$1,754	Deferred Income Taxes	70
		Shareholders' Equity	989
			$1,754

constitute a starting point for the projection by affirming the reasonableness of assumptions about future financial performance. Indeed, it will be assumed throughout the commentary on the Colossal Chemical projection that the analyst has studied the company's results over not only the preceding year but also over the past several years.

Projected Income Statement

The financial projection begins with an earnings forecast (Exhibit 5–2). Two key figures from the projected income statement—net income and depreciation—will later be incorporated into a projected statement of cash flows, which will in turn supply data for constructing a projected balance sheet. The analyst will have to make additional assumptions at each subsequent stage, but the logical flow begins with a forecast of earnings, which will significantly shape the appearance of all three statements.

Immediately below is a discussion of the assumptions underlying each line in the income statement, presented in order from top (sales) to bottom (net income).

Sales. The projected $2.110 billion for 1995 represents an assumed rise of 6% over the actual figure for 1994 shown in Exhibit 5–1. Of this

EXHIBIT 5–2   Earnings Forecast

Colossal Chemical Corporation Projected Income Statement ($000,000 omitted)

	1995
Sales	$2,110
Cost of goods sold	1,393
Selling, general and administrative expense	317
Depreciation and amortization	121
Research and development	84
Total costs and expenses	1,915
Operating Income	195
Interest expense	34
Interest (income)	(5)
Earnings before Income Taxes	166
Provision for Income Taxes	56
Net Income	$ 110

increase, 2% will be accounted for by higher shipments and 4% by higher prices.

To arrive at these figures, the analyst builds a forecast "from the ground up," using the historical segment data shown in Exhibit 5–3. Sales projections for the company's business—basic chemicals, plastics, and industrial chemicals—can be developed with the help of such sources as trade publications, trade associations, and firms that sell econometric forecasting models. Certain assumptions about economic growth (increase in Gross Domestic Product) in the coming year underlie all such forecasts. The analyst must be careful to ascertain the forecaster's assumptions and judge whether they seem realistic.

If the analyst is expected to produce an earnings projection that is consistent with an in-house economic forecast, then it will be critical to establish a historical relationship between key indicators and the shipments of the company's various business segments. For example, a particular

EXHIBIT 5–3 Sales Forecast

Colossal Chemical Corporation Results by Industry Segment
($000,000 omitted)

	1994	1993	1992	1991	1990
Sales					
Basic chemicals	975	$ 921	$ 878	$ 807	$ 786
Plastics	433	422	399	370	373
Industrial chemicals	583	546	531	475	461
Total	$1,991	$1,889	$1,808	$1,652	$1,620
Operating Income					
Basic chemicals	$ 94	$ 82	$ 65	$ 52	$ 59
Plastics	24	16	25	41	26
Industrial chemicals	41	35	28	31	28
Total	$159	$133	$118	$124	$113
Depreciation					
Basic chemicals	$ 55	$ 51	$ 50	$ 46	$ 46
Plastics	27	25	22	20	19
Industrial chemicals	37	36	35	31	31
Total	$119	$112	$107	$ 97	$ 96
Identifiable Assets					
Basic chemicals	$ 813	$ 772	$ 741	$ 676	$ 674
Plastics	390	369	352	314	309
Industrial chemicals	551	530	510	457	456
Total	$1,754	$1,671	$1,603	$1,447	$1,439

segment's shipments may have historically grown at 1.5 times the rate of industrial production or have fluctuated in essentially direct proportion to housing starts. Similarly, price increases should be linked to the expected inflation level—represented by either the Consumer Price Index or the Producer Price Index, depending on the product.

Note that basic industries such as chemicals, paper, and capital goods tend to lend themselves best to the macroeconomic-based approach described here. In technology-driven industries and "hits" business such as motion pictures and toys, the connection between sales and the general economic trend will tend to be looser. Forecasting in such circumstances depends largely on developing contacts within the industry being studied in order to make intelligent guesses about the probable success of a company's new products.

A history of sales by geographic area (Exhibit 5–4) provides another input into the sales projection. An analyst can modify the figures derived from industry segment forecasts to reflect expectations of unusually strong or unusually weak economic performance in a particular region of the globe. Likewise, a company may be experiencing an unusual problem, such as a dispute with a foreign government. The geographic sales breakdown can furnish some insight into the magnitude of the expected impact of such occurrences.

EXHIBIT 5–4 Colossal Chemical Corporation Results by Geographic Area ($000,000 omitted)

Colossal Chemical Corporation Results by Geographic Area ($000,000 omitted)					
	1994	1993	1992	1991	1990
Sales					
North America	$1,077	$1,019	$ 968	$ 896	$ 873
Europe	649	622	601	551	526
Latin America	102	87	90	99	103
Far East	163	161	149	106	118
	$1,991	$1,889	$1,808	$1,652	$1,620
Operating Income					
North America	$ 43	$ 36	$ 29	$ 32	$ 25
Europe	77	62	61	47	52
Latin America	26	16	17	24	17
Far East	13	19	11	21	19
	$159	$133	$118	$124	$113

Cost of Goods Sold.   The $1.393-billion cost-of-goods-sold figure in Exhibit 5–2 represents 66% of projected sales, or a gross margin of 34%—a slight improvement over the preceding year's 33%.

The projected gross margin for a company in turn reflects expectations about changes in costs of labor and material, as well as the intensity of industry competition, which affects a company's ability to pass cost increases on to customers or to retain cost decreases. In a capital-intensive business such as basic chemicals, the projected capacity utilization percentage (for both the company and the industry) is a key variable. At full capacity, fixed costs are spread out over the largest possible volume, so unit costs are minimized. Furthermore, if demand exceeds capacity so that all producers are running flat out, none will have an incentive to increase volume by cutting prices. When such conditions prevail, cost increases will be fully (or more than fully) passed on and gross margins will widen—at least until new industry capacity is built, bringing supply and demand back into balance. Conversely, if demand were expected to fall rather than rise in 1995, leading to a decline in capacity utilization, Exhibit 5–2's projected gross margin would probably be lower than in 1994, rather than higher.

As with sales, the analyst can project cost of goods sold from the bottom up, segment by segment. Since the segment information in Exhibit 5–3 shows only operating income, and not gross margin, the analyst must add segment depreciation to operating income, then make assumptions about the allocation of selling, general, and administrative expense, and research and development expense by segment. For example, operating income by segment for 1994 works out as shown in Exhibit 5–5, if SG&A and R&D expenses are allocated in proportion to segment sales.

By compiling this data for a period of several years, the analyst can devise models for forecasting gross margin percentage on a segment-by-segment basis.

Selling, General, and Administrative Expense.   The forecast in Exhibit 5–2 assumes continuation of a stable relationship in which SG&A expense has historically approximated 15% of sales. The analyst would vary this percentage for forecasting purposes if, for example, recent quarterly income statements or comments by management suggested a trend to a higher or lower level.

Depreciation.   Depreciation expense is essentially a function of the amount of a company's fixed assets and the average number of years over

EXHIBIT 5–5   Colossal Chemical Corporation Operating Income by Segment

	Basic Chemicals	Plastics	Industrial Chemicals	Total
Operating income	$ 94	$ 24	$ 41	$159
Plus: Depreciation	55	27	37	119
Plus: SG&A	146	65	88	299
Plus: R&D	39	17	24	80
Equals: Gross Margin	$334	$133	$190	$657
Sales	$975	$433	$583	$1,991
Gross Margin Percentage	34.3%	30.7%	32.6%	33.0%
Memo: Segment Sales as Percentage of Total:	49.0%	21.7%	29.3%	100.0%

which it writes them off. If on average, all classes of the company's property, plant, and equipment are depreciated (PP&E) over eight years, then on a straight-line basis the company will write off one-eighth (12.5%) each year. From year to year, the base of depreciable assets will grow to the extent that additions to PP&E exceed depreciation charges.

Exhibit 5–2 forecasts depreciation expenses equivalent to 13.5% of PP&E as of the preceding year end, based on a stable ratio between the two items over an extended period. Naturally, a projection should incorporate any foreseeable variances from historical patterns. For example, a company may lengthen or shorten its average write-off period, either because it becomes more liberal or more conservative in its accounting practices, or because such adjustments are warranted by changes in the rate of obsolescence of equipment. Also, a company's mix of assets may change. The average write-off period should gradually decline, for instance, as comparatively short-lived assets, such as data-processing equipment, increase as a percentage of capital expenditures and long-lived assets, such as "bricks and mortar," decline.

Research and Development.   R&D, along with advertising, is an expense that is typically budgeted on a percentage-of-sales basis. The R&D percentage may change if, for example, the company makes a sizable acquisition in an industry that is either significantly more, or significantly less, research-intensive than its existing operations. In addition, changing incentives for research, such as extended or reduced patent protection periods, may alter the percentage of sales a company believes it must spend on research to remain competitive. Barring developments of this sort, however, the analyst can feel fairly confident in expecting that the coming year's R&D expense will represent about the same percentage of sales as it did last year. That is the assumption (at 4% of sales) built into Exhibit 5–2.

Interest Expense.　After summing the four projected expense lines to derive total costs and expense—which is subtracted from projected sales to calculate projected operating income of $195 million—the forecasting process moves on to interest expense.

Exhibit 5–6 displays information found in the Notes to Financial Statements that can be used to estimate the coming year's interest expense. (Note that not all annual reports provide the amount of detail

EXHIBIT 5–6　Details of Long-Term Debt, Short-Term Debt, and Interest Expense*

Colossal Chemical Corporation ($000,000 omitted)		
Long-Term Debt	**1994**	**1993**
(Excluding current maturities)		
10.0% notes payable 1992	52	78
8.1% notes payable 1996	77	111
9.5% debentures due 1999	75	75
8.875% debentures due 2003	125	125
6.5% industrial development bonds due 2006	50	50
	$379	$439
Short-Term Debt	**1994**	
Average interest rate for year	8.5%	
Average annual amount outstanding	$29	
Annual maturities of long-term debt for the next five years are as follows:		
1995	$27 million	
1996	$13 million	
1997	$22 million	
1998	$18 million	
1999	$31 million	
Interest Expense	**1994**	
Interest Incurred	41	
Capitalized Interest	5	
Interest Expense	36	

*From Notes to Consolidated Financial Statements.

shown here. Greater reliance on assumptions is required when the information is sketchier.)

The key to the forecasting method employed here is to estimate Colossal Chemical's embedded cost of debt, that is, the weighted average interest rate on the company's existing long-term debt. Using the details of individual long-term issues shown in Exhibit 5–5, the calculation goes as follows:

($000,000 omitted)

(1993 Amount + 1994 Amount)	÷ 2	=	Average Amount Outstanding	@ Rate	=	Estimated Interest Charges on Long-Term Debt
(78 + 52)	÷ 2	=	65	@ 10.0%	=	$ 6.500
	÷ 2	=	94	@ 8.1%	=	7.614
(75 + 75)	÷ 2	=	75	@ 9.5%	=	7.125
(125 + 125)	÷ 2	=	125	@ 8.875%	=	11.094
(50 + 50)	÷ 2	=	50	@ 6.5%	=	3.250
						$35.583

Interest Charges on Long-Term Debt		Average Amount of Total Long-Term Debt Outstanding		Embedded Cost of Long-Term Debt
$35.583	÷	([$439 + $379] ÷ 2)	=	8.7%

Applying the embedded cost of 8.7% to Colossal's 1994 year-end long-term debt (*including* current maturities, which are assumed to carry the same average interest rate) produces projected interest charges of $35.8 million. (As shown in Exhibit 5–6, the 1995 cash flow projection suggests no substantial reduction in debt outstanding during 1995, so the method employed here, while merely an approximation, should not prove far off the mark.)

To the $35.8-million figure, the forecaster must add interest charges related to short-term debt. These projections assume an average outstanding balance of $32 million, 10% higher than in 1994, and an average rate of 9%, based on an expectation of slightly higher rates in 1995.

($000,000 omitted)

Interest charges on long-term debt	$35.8
Interest charges on short-term debt ($32 @ 9%)	2.9
Total interest charges	$38.7

The $38.7-million figure represents total interest that Colossal is expected to incur in 1995. From this amount the forecaster must subtract an assumed level of capitalized interest to obtain projected interest expense. Exhibit 5–2 simply projects capitalized interest at the same level in 1995 as in 1994.

($000,000 omitted)	
Interest incurred	$39
Capitalized interest	$ 5
Interest expense	$34

Readers should remember when employing the method described here that it involves a certain amount of simplification. Applied retroactively, it will not necessarily produce the precise interest expense shown in the historical financial statements. (For one thing, paydowns of long-term debt will not come uniformly at mid-year, as implicitly assumed by the estimation procedure for average amounts of long-term debt outstanding.) Certainly, analysts should recognize and adjust for major, foreseeable changes in interest costs, such as refinancing of high-coupon bonds with cheaper borrowings. By the same token, forecasters should not go overboard in seeking precision on this particular item. For conservatively capitalized industrial corporations, interest expense typically runs in the range of 1% to 2% of sales, so a 10% error in estimating the item will have little impact on the net earnings forecast. Analysts should reserve their energy in projecting interest expense for more highly leveraged companies, the financial viability of which may depend on the size of the interest expense "nut" they must cover each quarter.

Interest Income.   Consistent with assumptions discussed in *Increase in Notes Payable* (page 179), Exhibit 5–2 incorporates a forecast of an unchanged cash balance for 1995. Based on expectations of an average money market rate of return of 7.0% on corporate cash, the average balance of $69 million will generate (in round figures) $5 million of interest income.

Provision for Income Taxes.   Following the deduction of interest expense and the addition of interest income, earnings before income taxes stand at $166 million. The forecast reduces this figure by the statutory tax rate of 34%, based on Colossal's effective rate having historically approximated the statutory rate. For other companies, effective rates could vary widely as a result of tax loss carryforwards and investment tax credits, among other items. Management will ordinarily be able to provide some guidance regarding major changes in the effective rate, while changes in the statutory rate are widely publicized by media coverage of federal tax legislation.

Projected Statement of Cash Flows

The completed income statement projection supplies the first two lines of the projected statement of cash flows (Exhibit 5–7). Net income of $110 million and depreciation of $121 million come directly from Exhibit 5–2 and largely determine the total sources (funds provided by operations) figure. The other two items have only a small impact on the projections.

Deferred Income Taxes.   This figure can vary somewhat unpredictably from year to year, based on changes in the gap between tax and book

EXHIBIT 5–7   Projected Statement of Cash Flows, 1995

Colossal Chemical Corporation ($000,000 omitted)		
Sources:		
Net income	$ 110	
Depreciation	121	
Deferred income taxes	25	
Working capital changes, excluding cash and borrowings	(43)	
Cash provided by operations	213	
Uses:		
Additions to property, plant, and equipment	165	
Dividends	37	
Repayment of current maturities of long-term debt	32	
Cash used by operations	234	
Net cash provided (used) by operations	$ (21)	
Increase in notes payable	$ 21	
Changes in Working Capital		
Decrease (increase) in accounts receivable		$(25)
Decrease (increase) in inventories		(29)
Increase (decrease) in accounts payable		11
		$(43)

depreciation and miscellaneous factors such as leases, installment receivables, and unremitted earnings of foreign subsidiaries. Input from company management may help in the forecasting of this figure. The $25-million figure shown in Exhibit 5–6 is a trend-line projection.

Working Capital Changes (Excluding Cash and Borrowings). Details of the derivation of the $43-million projection appear at the bottom of Exhibit 5–7. The forecast assumes that each working capital item remains at the same percentage of sales shown in the historical statements in Exhibit 5–1. Accounts receivable, for example, at 22% of sales, rises from $439 million to $464 million (an increase of $25 million) as sales grow from $1,991 million in 1994 to a projected $2,110 million in 1995. Before assuming a constant-percentage relationship, the analyst must verify that the most recent year's ratios are representative of experience over several years. Potential deviations from historical experience must likewise be considered. For example, a sharp drop in sales may produce involuntary inventory accumulation or a rise in accounts receivable as the company attempts to stimulate its sales by offering easier credit terms.

Additions to Property, Plant, and Equipment. The first and largest of the uses on this cash flow projection is capital expenditures. A company may provide a specific capital spending projection in its annual report, then, as the year progresses, update its estimate in its quarterly statements or 10-Q reports and in press releases. Even if the company does not publish a specific number, its investor-relations officer will ordinarily respond to questions about the range, or at least the direction (up, down, or flat) for the coming year.

Dividends. The $37-million figure shown assumes that Colossal will continue its stated policy of paying out in dividends approximately one-third of its sustainable earnings (excluding extraordinary gains and losses). Typically, this sort of guideline is interpreted as an average payout over time, so that the dividend rate does not fluctuate over a normal business cycle to the same extent that earnings do. A company may even avoid cutting its dividend through a year or more of losses, borrowing to maintain the payout if necessary. This practice often invites criticism and may stir debate within the board of directors, where the authority to declare dividends resides.

Until the board officially announces its decision, an analyst attempting to project future dividends can make only an educated guess. Moreover, in a difficult earnings environment a decision to maintain the dividend in one quarter is no assurance that the board will decide the same way three months later.

Repayment of Current Maturities of Long-Term Debt. The $32-million figure shown comes directly from the current liabilities section of the balance sheet in Exhibit 5–1.

Increase in Notes Payable. Subtracting $234 million of cash used in operations from the $213 million provided by operations produces a net use of $21 million. This projection assumes, based on the company's stated objectives—and some knowledge of how faithfully management has stuck to its plans in the past—that any net cash generated will be applied to debt retirement. A net cash use, on the other hand, will be made up through drawing down short-term bank lines. Other assumptions might be more appropriate in other circumstances. For example, a net provision or use of cash might be offset by a reduction or increase in cash and marketable securities. A sizable net cash provision might be presumed to be directed toward share repurchase, reducing shareholders' equity, if management has indicated a desire to buy in stock and is authorized to do so by its board of directors. Instead of making up a large cash shortfall with short-term debt, a company might instead fund the borrowings as quickly as possible (add to its long-term debt). Alternatively, a company may have a practice of financing any large cash need with a combination of long-term debt and equity, using the proportions of each that are required to keep its ratio of debt to equity at some constant level.

Projected Balance Sheet

Constructing the projected balance sheet (Exhibit 5–8) requires no additional assumptions beyond those made in projecting the income statement and statement of cash flows. The analyst simply updates the historical balance sheet in Exhibit 5–1 on the basis of information drawn from the other statements.

Most of the required information appears in the projected statement of cash flows (Exhibit 5–7). Accounts receivable, inventories, and accounts

EXHIBIT 5–8   Projected Balance Sheet

Colossal Chemical Corporation
Projected Balance Sheet
December 31, 1995
($000,000 omitted)

Cash and marketable securities	$ 69	Notes payable	$ 42
Accounts receivable	464	Accounts payable	274
Inventories	380	Current portion of long-term debt	27
Total Current Assets	913	Total Current Liabilities	343
		Long-Term Debt	352
		Deferred Income Taxes	95
Property, Plant, and Equipment	939	Shareholders' Equity	1,062
	$1,852		$1,852

payable, for example, reflect the projected changes in working capital. The cash flow projection would likewise show any increase or decrease in cash and marketable securities, an item that in this case remains flat. Property, plant, and equipment rises from the prior year's level of $895 million by $165 million of additions, less $121 million of depreciation. The projected cash flow statement also furnishes the increases in notes payable and deferred income taxes, as well as the change in shareholders' equity (net income less dividends).

The details of long-term debt in the historical balance sheet (Exhibit 5–6) provides the figures needed to complete the projection of long-term debt. With the 1994 current maturities of long-term debt ($32 million) having been paid off, the 1995 current maturities ($27 million) take their place on the balance sheet. The $27-million figure is also deducted from 1994's (noncurrent) long-term debt of $379 million to produce the new figure of $352 million. (Any further adjustments to long-term debt—of which there are none in these projections—would appear in the projected statement of cash flows.)

SENSITIVITY ANALYSIS WITH PROJECTED FINANCIAL STATEMENTS

Preparing a set of projected financial statements provides a glimpse at a company's future financial condition, given certain assumptions. The analyst can study the projected statements with the same techniques that Chapters 2 through 4 discussed in conjunction with the historical statements and also use them to calculate the ratios employed in credit analysis (Chapter 6) and equity analysis (Chapter 7). Based on the projections in Exhibits 5–1 through 5–8, for example, Colossal Chemical's credit quality measures will improve in 1995 (Exhibit 5–9). Total debt will decline, not only in absolute terms, but also as a percentage of total capital—from 29.0% to 26.7%. Cash provided by operations, meanwhile, will rise from 51.9% to 60.8% of total debt. As explained in Chapter 6, both of these trends indicate reduced financial risk. Unfortunately, these projected ratios are only as reliable as the assumptions underlying the projected statements that generated them. Logical though they may seem, the assumptions rest heavily on macroeconomic forecasting, which is— to put it charitably—far from an exact science. Frequently, the analyst must modify the assumptions—and therefore the projections—several times during the year as economic indicators point to GDP growth coming in above or below expectations.

Knowing that conditions can, and in all likelihood will, change, wise investors and lenders will not base their decisions entirely on a single set

EXHIBIT 5–9   Trend of Credit Quality Measures—Base Case

Colossal Chemical Corporation
($000,000 omitted)

	1995 (Projected)*	1994 (Actual)**
Total Debt		
Notes payable	$ 42	$ 21
Current portion of long-term debt	27	32
Long-term debt	352	379
	421	432
Deferred Income Taxes	95	70
Shareholders' Equity	1,062	989
Total Capital	$1,578	$1,491
Total Debt as a Percentage of Total Capital	26.7%	29.0%
Cash Provided by Operations (Before working capital changes)	256	224
Total Debt	421	432
Cash Provided as a Percentage of Total Debt	60.8%	51.9%

*From Exhibit 5–8.
**From Exhibit 5–1.

of projections, or "point forecast." Instead, they will assess the risks and potential rewards in light of a range of possible outcomes.

Exhibit 5–10 provides one example of how the analyst can modify the underlying assumptions and then observe the extent to which projected ratios will be altered—a process known as sensitivity analysis. In this instance, the analyst projects a sales increase over the preceding year of just 3%—half the growth rate assumed in the base case (the most probable scenario) represented by Exhibit 5–2. Because this less optimistic sales forecast implies a less robust economy than assumed in the base case (perhaps no real growth and a 3% inflation rate), the analyst now assumes that chemical producers will have no opportunity to increase their gross margins over the preceding year. Keeping the other assumptions intact, the revised projections show smaller increases in net income, shareholders' equity, and funds provided by operations than the base case indicates. Long-term debt declines more slowly under the new assumptions.

Utilizing Exhibit 5–10's revised statements, the analyst can recalculate Exhibit 5–9's credit quality measures as shown in Exhibit 5–11. Under the more pessimistic assumptions regarding sales growth and gross margins, projected funds provided by operations as a percentage of total debt measure 56.6%, representing a smaller increase over 1994 than the 60.8% figure projected in the base case. Interestingly, though, total debt as a percentage of total capital is unaffected by the changed assumptions, measuring 26.7% in both the base case and the pessimistic cases. Although the addition to retained earnings (and hence growth in shareholders' equity) is smaller in the pessimistic case, so is the need for new working capital to support increased sales. The borrowing need is therefore reduced, offsetting the slower growth in equity.

To complete the analysis, an investor or lender will also want to project financial statements on an optimistic, or best-case, scenario. Sample assumptions for a three-scenario sensitivity analysis might be:

	Assumed Sales Growth	Assumed Gross Margin
Optimistic case (best realistic scenario)	8%	36%
Base case (most likely scenario)	6%	34%
Pessimistic case (worst realistic scenario)	3%	33%

Note that the assumptions need not be symmetrical. That is, the optimistic case in this instance assumes sales only two percentage points

EXHIBIT 5–10   Sensitivity Analysis Projected Financial Statements

Colossal Chemical Corporation
Year Ended December 31, 1995
($000,000 omitted)

Reduce Base Case (Exhibit 5-2) Sales Growth Assumption from 6% to 3%
(No improvement in gross margin over preceding year)

Income Statement		Statement of Cash Flow	
Sales	$2,051	Sources:	
Cost of goods sold	1,374	Net income	$ 90
Selling, general and		Depreciation	121
administrative expense	308	Deferred income taxes	25
Depreciation	121	Working capital changes, ex-	
		cluding cash and borrowings	(26)
Research and development	82	Cash provided by operations	210
		Uses:	
Total costs and expenses	1,885	Additions to property, plant,	
Operating Income	166	and equipment	165
		Dividends	30
Interest expense	34	Repayment of current maturities	
Interest (income)	(5)	of long-term debt	32
		Cash used by operations	227
Earnings before Income Taxes	137	Net cash provided (used) by	
Provision for Income Taxes	47	operations	(17)
		Increase in long-term debt	17
Net Income	$ 90	Net change in cash	$ 0

Balance Sheet

Cash and marketable securities	$ 69	Notes payable	$ 21
Accounts receivable	451	Accounts payable	267
		Current portion of long-term	
Inventories	369	debt	27
Total Current Assets	889	Total Current Liabilities	315
Property, Plant, and			
Equipment	939	Long-Term Debt	369
	$1,828	Deferred Income Taxes	95
		Shareholders' Equity	1,049
			$1,828

EXHIBIT 5–11   Trend of Credit Quality Comparison

Colossal Chemical Corporation
Year Ended December 31, 1995 (Projected)
($000,000 omitted)

	Pessimistic Case*		Base Case**	
Total Debt				
Notes payable	$ 21		$ 42	
Current portion of long-term debt	27		27	
Long-term debt	369		352	
		417		421
Deferred Income Taxes		95		95
Shareholders' Equity				
Total Capital		1,049		1,062
Total Debt as a Percentage of		$1,561		$1,578
Total Capital		26.7%		26.7%
Funds Provided by Operations				
(Before Working Capital Changes)		236		256
Total Debt				
Cash Provided as a Percentage		417		421
of Total Debt		56.6%		60.8%

*From Exhibit 5–10.
**From Exhibit 5–9.

higher than the base case, while the pessimistic case reduces base case sales by three percentage points. The analyst simply believes that the most likely scenario embodies more downside than upside.

Other assumptions can be modified as well, recognizing the interaction among the various accounts. For instance, Colossal Chemical may have considerable room to cut its capital spending in the short run if it suffers a decline in funds provided by operations. A projection that ignored this financial flexibility could prove overly pessimistic. Conversely, the assumption that a company will apply any surplus funds generated to debt reduction may produce an unrealistic projected capital structure. Particularly in a multiyear projection for a strong cash generator, the ratio of debt to capital may fall in the later years to a level that the company would consider excessively conservative. In such cases, it may be appropriate to alter the assumption from debt retirement to maintenance of a specified leverage ratio. Surplus cash will thus be applied to stock repurchase to the extent that not doing so would cause the debt component of capital to fall below a specified percentage.

In addition to creating a range of scenarios, sensitivity analysis can also enable the analyst to gauge the relative impact of changing the various assumptions in a projection. Contrast, for example, the impact of a 1% change in gross margins with the impact of a 1% change in the tax rate on Colossal Chemical's income statement. Exhibit 5–12 shows the effects of these two changes in assumptions on the projected income statement in Exhibit 5–2, holding all other assumptions constant. The sensitivity of net income to a 1% change in gross margins is $14 million ($110 million minus $96 million), all other things being equal. A 1% change in the tax rate, on the other hand, affects net income by just $2 million, all other things again being equal.

This type of analysis is quite popular among investors. They may, for example, estimate the impact on a mining company's stock price (which, as with most stocks, is presumed to be a function of earnings)

EXHIBIT 5–12   Sensitivity Analysis: Impact of Changes in Selected Assumptions on Projected Income Statement

<table>
<tr><td colspan="4" align="center">**Colossal Chemical Corporation**
Year Ended December 31, 1995
($000,000 omitted)</td></tr>
<tr><td></td><td>**Base Case**</td><td>**1% Decline in Gross Margin**</td><td>**1% Rise in Tax Rate**</td></tr>
<tr><td>Sales</td><td>$2,110</td><td>$2,110</td><td>$2,110</td></tr>
<tr><td>Cost of goods sold</td><td>1,393</td><td>1,414</td><td>1,393</td></tr>
<tr><td>Selling, general and administrative expense</td><td>317</td><td>317</td><td>317</td></tr>
<tr><td>Depreciation</td><td>121</td><td>121</td><td>121</td></tr>
<tr><td>Research and development</td><td>84</td><td>84</td><td>84</td></tr>
<tr><td>Total costs and expenses</td><td>1,915</td><td>1,936</td><td>1,915</td></tr>
<tr><td>Operating Income</td><td>195</td><td>174</td><td>195</td></tr>
<tr><td>Interest expense</td><td>34</td><td>34</td><td>34</td></tr>
<tr><td>. Interest (income)</td><td>(5)</td><td>(5)</td><td>(5)</td></tr>
<tr><td>Earnings before Income Taxes</td><td>166</td><td>145</td><td>166</td></tr>
<tr><td>Provision for Income Taxes</td><td>56</td><td>49</td><td>58</td></tr>
<tr><td>Net Income</td><td>$ 110</td><td>$ 96</td><td>$ 108</td></tr>
</table>

of a 10-cent rise in the price of a pound of copper. Another application is to identify which companies will respond most dramatically to some expected economic development such as a drop in interest rates. A rate decline will have limited impact on a company for which interest costs represent a small percentage of expenses. The impact will be greater on a company with a large interest cost component and with much of its debt at floating rates (assuming the return on its assets is not similarly rate-sensitive).

Alluring though it may be, sensitivity analysis is a technique that must be used with caution. As previously suggested, it generally isolates a single assumption and proceeds on the basis that all other things remain equal. In the real world, this is rarely the case. When sales fall, so often do gross margins, as declining capacity utilization puts downward pressure on prices. Rising interest rates affect not only interest expense and interest income but also the level of investment in the economy, which can eventually depress the company's sales.

PROJECTING FINANCIAL FLEXIBILITY

Just as projected statements can reveal a company's probable future financial profile, they can also indicate the likely direction of its financial flexibility, a concept discussed in Chapter 4. For example, the projected statement of cash flows shows by how comfortable a margin the company will be able to cover its dividend with internally generated funds. Likewise, the amount by which debt is projected to rise determines the extent to which nondiscretionary costs (in the form of interest charges) will increase in future income statements.

To assess one important aspect of financial flexibility—continuing compliance with loan covenants—projections are indispensable. As Exhibit 5–13 illustrates, debt covenants may require the borrower to maintain a specified level of financial strength as measured either by absolute dollar amounts of certain items of by ratios. (A less restrictive type of covenant merely prohibits incurrence of new debt or payment of dividends that would cause financial measures to deteriorate below a targeted level. No violation occurs if, for example, net worth declines as a result of operating losses.) Sanctions against an issuer that commits a "technical default" (violation of a covenant, as opposed to the failure to pay interest or principal on time) can be severe. The issuer may be barred from paying further dividends or compelled to repay a huge loan at a time

EXHIBIT 5–13　Sample Debt Restriction Disclosures

"The 1992 Credit Agreement contained various restrictions and conditions including a fixed charge coverage ratio, current ratio, leverage ratio and cash flow coverage ratio. In addition, the 1992 Credit Agreement limited or restricted purchases of Coltec's common stock, payment of dividends, capital expenditures, the incurrence of additional indebtedness, mergers, asset acquisitions and dispositions, investments, prepayment of other debt and transactions with affiliates. At December 31, 1993, Coltec was in compliance with the above covenants."

(Coltec Industries Inc.
1993 Annual Report)

"Under the covenants of our 10 ³/₈% Senior Notes, we can pay future dividends on our common stock, among certain other restrictions, only if such cumulative dividends do not exceed the aggregate net cash proceeds from the sale of capital stock plus 50% of a consolidated net income and minus 100% of a consolidated net loss since the second quarter of 1993, excluding certain restructuring charges. The amount available at December 31, 1993 under this covenant was $39 million."

(Bethlehem Steel Corporation
1993 Annual Report)

"[The bank credit facilities] provide that, so long as advances are outstanding, the Company will be required to maintain a Consolidated Debt to Net Worth Ratio, as defined therein, not to exceed 55:45. At December 31, 1993, the Consolidated Debt to Net Worth Ratio was 39:61."

(Inco Ltd., 1993 Annual Report)

when refinancing may be difficult. Curing the default may necessitate unpleasant actions such as a dilution of shareholders' interests by the sale of new equity at less than book value. Alternatively, the borrower can request that its lenders waive their right to accelerate payment of the debt, but the lenders are likely to demand some quid pro quo along the lines of reducing management's freedom to act without consulting them.

Analysts can anticipate this sort of loss of financial flexibility by applying covenanted tests of net worth, leverage, and fixed charge coverage to projected balance sheets and income statements. General descriptions of the tests can be found in the Notes to Financial Statements. These descriptions may omit some subtleties involving definitions of terms, but since the projections are by their nature also prone to imprecision, the objective is not in any case absolute certainty regarding a possible breach of covenants. Rather, the discovery that a company is likely to be bumping up against covenanted limits a year or two into the future means it is time to ask management how it plans to preserve its financial flexibility.

If the answers prove unsatisfactory, the effort of having made the projections and run the tests may be rewarded by a warning, well in advance, of serious trouble ahead.

PRO FORMA FINANCIAL STATEMENTS

Another way in which the analyst can look forward with financial statements is to construct pro forma statements that reflect significant developments, prior to reflection of those developments in subsequent published statements. It is unwise to base an investment decision on historical statements that antedate a major financial change such as a stock repurchase, write-off, acquisition, or divestment. By the same token, it can be important to determine quickly whether news that flashes across a news monitor will have a material effect on a company's financial condition. For instance, for the company in question, will the just-announced repurchase of 3.5 million shares materially increase financial leverage? To answer the question, the analyst must adjust the latest balance sheet available, reducing shareholders' equity by the product of 3.5 million and an assumed purchase price per share, then reducing cash and/or increasing debt as the accounting offset.

Exhibit 5–14 presents a pro forma income statement for a more complex transaction, the 1988 leveraged buyout of Fort Howard Corporation, a manufacturer of paper and plastic products. The accompanying Notes to Pro Forma Condensed Consolidated Statements of Income explain the adjustments that result in the company's 1987 reported net income of $147.7 million turning into a $164.3 million loss on a pro forma basis.

The most important pro forma adjustment is an increase of $437.7 million in interest expense, reflecting the issuance of debt to finance the acquisition of Fort Howard by FH Acquisition Corp., the LBO vehicle. Note that the calculation of new interest expense in Footnote b closely resembles the method employed in Exhibit 5–5.

Aside from the substantial increase in interest expense, the only adjustment to pretax income is a rise of $61.4 million in cost of sales, composed of higher depreciation and a net increase in goodwill amortization, as detailed in Footnote a.

The combined increases in interest expense and cost of sales reduce 1987 pretax income from $287.5 million to a $256.7 million loss on a pro forma basis. As a consequence of the pro forma loss, Fort Howard changes

EXHIBIT 5–14   Pro Forma Condensed Consolidated Statement of Income

Fort Howard Corporation
($000,000 omitted)
Year Ended December 31, 1987

	The Company Historical	Pro Forma Adjustments	The Company Pro Forma
Net Sales	$1,757,728		$1,757,728
Cost of sales	1,233,273	$ 61,458	1,294,731
Gross Income	524,455	(61,458)	462,997
Selling, general and administrative	193,787		200,616
Amortization of costs in excess of net assets acquired	11,130	47,095	58,225
Operating Income	319,538	(115,382) (a)	204,156
Interest expense	(30,997)	(437,743) (b)	(468,740)
Other expense, net	(1,080)		(1,080)
Income (Loss) before Taxes	287,461	(553,125)	(256,664)
Income taxes (credit)	128,523	(229,849) (c)	(101,326)
Net Income (Loss before Adjustment for Accounting change	158,938	(323,276)	(164,338)
Adjustment for adoption of SFAS 96	(11,241)	11,241 (d)	
Net Income (Loss)	$ 147,697	$(312,035)	$(164,338)

Notes to Pro Forma Condensed Consolidated Statements of Income

(a) The pro forma adjustments to cost of sales, selling, general and administrative expenses, and amortization of costs in excess of net assets acquired are comprised of the following (in thousands):

	Year Ended December 31, 1987
Depreciation of property, plant, and equipment[1]	$68,287
Amortization of costs in excess of net assets acquired[2]	58,225
Elimination of the historical amortization of costs in excess of net assets acquired	(11,130)
Total	$115,382

[1]The valuation of property, plant, and equipment is based upon preliminary estimates of the fair values of such assets and is subject to change. Depreciation is computed using an estimated remaining life of 10 years.

[2]The amortization of the preliminary purchase cost in excess of net assets acquired is based on an assumed life of 40 years. The allocation of such excess will differ from that set forth herein upon finalization of detailed valuations and other studies. The amount of the amortization is an estimate and is subject to change upon finalization of the allocation of such excess. It is not expected that the final allocation of the purchase cost will differ materially from that presented herein.

(Continued)

EXHIBIT 5–14 *(Continued)*

Fort Howard Corporation
($000,000 omitted)
Year Ended December 31, 1987

(b) Increased interest expense is based upon the pro forma consolidated debt of the Company following consummation of both the Merger and the Financing at the interest rates set forth on the cover page of this Prospectus as if the transaction had been consummated as of the beginning of the periods presented, as follows (in thousands):

	Year Ended December 31, 1987
Term Loan ($1,800,000 at 11%)[1]	$198,000
Revolving Credit Facility ($230,000 at 11%)[1]	25,300
Senior Subordinated Notes ($383,910 at 12⅜%)	47,509
Subordinated Debentures (383,910 at 12⅝%)	48,469
Junior Discount Debentures ($364,633 at 14⅛%)[2]	53,323
Junior Debentures ($352,709 at 14⅝%)[2]	53,470
Adjustment to interest expense from assumed retirement of existing indebtedness	(11,341)
Annual financing fees and other expenses	7,234
Amortization of debt issuance costs[3]	15,779
Total	$437,743

[1]An increase in the interest rate of one-quarter percent would change interest expense, loss before taxes, and deficiency of earnings available to cover fixed charges, as follows (in thousands):

	Year Ended December 31, 1987
Term Loan	$4,500
Revolving Credit Facility	575
Total	$5,075

The Bank Credit Agreement requires the Company to enter into interest rate agreements which effectively fix the interest cost to the Company of Eurodollar rate loans at an effective rate that does not exceed 12% per annum plus the Company's borrowing margin on Eurodollar rate loans (which ranges from 2.25% down to 1.5% if certain financial criteria are met). The interest rate agreements are required with respect to an aggregate amount of not less than $450 million for a weighted average life of not less than five years and an additional aggregate amount of not less than $450 million for a weighted average life of three years.

[2]Interest is compounded on a semiannual basis.

[3]Debt issuance costs are amortized over the life of the related debt, ranging from 8 to 16 years. The pro forma statements of income do not include a charge of approximately $27.8 million representing amortization of debt issuance costs associated with the Bridge Financing to be repaid with the proceeds of the Securities.

(c) Reflects the elimination of federal, state, and local taxes from income tax expense as a result of the pro forma adjustments described in these notes. In addition, tax benefits have been calculated on the pro forma domestic losses of the Company to the extent of net operating losses available for carryback.

(Continued)

EXHIBIT 5–14   *(Continued)*

Fort Howard Corporation
($000,000 omitted)
Year Ended December 31, 1987

(d) Reflects the elimination of a charge related to period prior to January 1, 1987, resulting from the adoption of SFAS 96, "Accounting for Income Taxes."

(e) For purposes of these computations, earnings consist of historical or pro forma income (loss) before taxes plus fixed charges (excluding capitalized interest). Fixed charges consist of interest on indebtedness (including capitalized interest and amortization of debt issuance costs) plus that portion of lease rental expense representative of the interest factor (deemed to be one-fourth of lease rental expense).

(f) Reflects the elimination of nonrecurring fees and expenses incurred by the Company in connection with Acquisition prior to the Offer.

Source: Fort Howard Corporation Prospectus dated October 25, 1988.

from a taxpayer to a tax credit recipient, as detailed in Footnote c. Elimination of the historical adjustment for an accounting change (Footnote d) produces the bottom-line $164.3-million loss. (As discussed in Chapter 4, this result is consistent with the objectives of a leveraged buyout, where the investors' primary concern is cash flow rather than reported earnings.)

Fort Howard's balance sheet undergoes significant pro forma changes, too, as depicted in Exhibit 5–15. The adjustments come in three stages, detailed under the columns headed "Offer and Merger," "Valuation," and "Issuance of Securities."

"Offer and Merger" adjustments reflect the purchase of Fort Howard for $3.7 billion (including related fees) by FH Acquisition, which was subsequently merged into Fort Howard. FH Acquisition finances the purchase with equity of $450 million and four forms of borrowings—a bank bridge loan ($400 million), a subordinated bridge loan ($1.04 billion), a revolving credit facility ($186.4 million), and a term loan ($1.8 billion). In the process, FH Acquisition also extinguishes existing Fort Howard borrowings, including $23.7 million of notes payable and $146.7 million of its long-term debt. (Often, in LBO transactions, some or all of the acquired company's existing debt is liquidated in order to eliminate loan covenants that might interfere with the creation of new credit agreements.) Other, minor, "Offer and Merger Adjustments" are described in the Notes to Exhibit 5–15.

EXHIBIT 5-15 Pro Forma Condensed Consolidated Balance Sheet

Fort Howard Corporation
($000 omitted)
June 30, 1988

	The Company Historical	Pro Forma Adjustments			The Company Pro Forma
		Offer and Merger (a)	Valuation (b)	Issuance of Securities (c)(d)	
Assets					
Current Assets					
Cash and short-term investments	$ 7,760	$ (7,000)			$ 760
Receivables—net	189,825				189,825
Inventories	276,896		$20,083		296,979
	474,481	(7,000)	20,083		487,564
Property, plant and equipment—net	1,268,337		646,052		1,914,389
Funds held by trustee for plant additions	21,694				21,694
Other assets	29,437		107,700	$72,057	209,194
Costs in excess of net assets acquired, net of amortization	409,258		1,919,735		2,328,993
Purchase cost		3,694,291	(3,694,291)		
	$2,203,207	$3,687,291	$(1,000,721)	$72,057	$4,961,834

Liabilities and Shareholders' Equity

Current Liabilities					
Notes payable	$23,672	$(23,672)			
Accounts payable	85,400				$85,400
Current portion of long-term debt	2,942				2,942
Income taxes	15,117	(4,543)			10,574
Other current liabilities	111,633				111,633
Deferred income taxes			$22,363		22,363
	238,764	(28,215)	22,363		232,912
	392,789	(146,737)			246,052
Existing Long-Term Debt					
Bank Bridge Loan		400,000		$(400,000)	
Subordinated Bridge Financing		1,040,000		(1,040,000)	
Revolving Credit Facility		186,405		43,595	230,000
Term Loan		1,800,000			1,800,000
Senior Subordinated Notes				383,910	383,910
Subordinated Debentures				383,910	383,910
Junior Discount Debentures				364,633	364,633
Junior Debentures				352,709	352,709
Deferred Income Taxes	220,800		175,868		396,668
Other Liabilities	21,391		120,000		141,391
Shareholders' Equity					
Common stock	68,546	45	(68,546)		45
Additional paid-in capital	418,236	449,955	(421,887)		446,304
Retained earnings	866,965	(14,162)	(852,803)		
Treasury stock, at cost	(24,284)		24,284	(16,700)	(16,700)
	1,329,463	435,838	(1,318,952)	(16,700)	429,649
	$2,203,207	$3,687,291	$(1,000,721)	$72,057	$4,961,834

(Continued)

147

EXHIBIT 5-15 (Continued)

Fort Howard Corporation
($000 omitted)
June 30, 1988

Notes to Pro Forma Condensed Consolidated Balance Sheet

(a) Pro forma adjustments related to the Offer and Merger are summarized in the following table (in thousands):

	Fees[1]	Equity, Bridge and Bank Financing[2]	Acquisition of Shares[3]	Cancellation of Options[4]	Total Pro Forma Adjustments
Cash	$(132,000)	$3,705,996	$(3,569,291)	$(11,705)	$ (7,000)
Purchase Cost	125,000		3,569,291		
Income Taxes	(2,800)			(1,743)	(4,543)
Notes Payable		(23,672)			(23,672)
Bank Bridge Loan		400,000			400,000
Existing Long-Term Debt		(146,737)			(146,737)
Subordinated Bridge Financing		1,040,000			1,040,000
		186,405			186,405
Facility					
Term Loan		1,800,000			1,800,000
Common Stock		45			45
Additional Paid in Capital		449,955			449,955
Retained Earnings (Deficit)	(4,200)			(9,962)	(14,162)

[1] Assumed payment of FH Acquisition of $125 million and by the Company of $7 million for legal and financial advice and other fees associated with the Offer and Merger.

[2] Issuance of debt in the aggregate amount of $3,426.4 million and Common Stock in the amount of $450 million.

[3] Acquisition of 67,345,122 shares of Company Common Stock at a price of $53 per Share in cash.

[4] Amount to be paid by the Company on the cancellation of 43,077 stock equivalents at $53 per Share in cash and 377,012 options at a price equal to the difference between $53 per share and the exercise prices of such options and recognition by the Company of the related tax benefits.

(b) The Merger will be accounted for by the Company using the purchase method of accounting and the total purchase cost will be allocated first to assets and liabilities of the Company based upon their respective fair values, with the remainder allocated to costs in excess of net assets acquired. The historical shareholders' equity of the Company will be eliminated on the Company's balance sheet. The aggregate purchase cost and its preliminary allocation to the historical assets and liabilities of the Company are as follows (in thousands):

Purchase cost, including related fees:

Acquisition of 67,345,122 shares of Company Common Stock	$3,569,291
Fees and expenses incurred in connection with the acquisition	125,000
Total purchase cost	$3,694,291

Preliminary allocation of purchase cost:

Net assets acquired at historical cost[1]		$1,329,463
Add (deduct): Cancellation of 377,012 stock options and 43,077 stock equivalents	(11,705)	
Tax benefit on cancellation of stock options and equivalents	1,743	
Fees and expenses incurred by the Company net of tax benefit	(4,200)	
		$1,315,301
Revaluation of the Company's property, plant, and equipment and inventories to estimated fair values		666,135
Elimination of historical goodwill		(409,258)
Debt issuance costs associated with the Offer and Merger		117,000
Post employment benefit obligations		(120,000)
Carryover of the cost basis in Company Common Stock to the new common stock of the Company for the investing senior management group		3,651
Deferred income tax provision associated with revaluation of the Company's assets and liabilities		(207,531)

(Continued)

EXHIBIT 5-15 *(Continued)*

Fort Howard Corporation
($000 omitted)
June 30, 1988

Costs in excess of net assets acquired	2,328,993
Total cost allocated	$3,694,291

ᵃThe allocation of the purchase cost reflects the revaluation of the Company's assets and liabilities to their estimated fair values based on preliminary estimates. Accordingly, the allocation is likely to differ from the final allocation.

(c) The pro forma adjustments reflect (i) the issuance of the Underwritten Securities and Direct Investor Securities of $1,948 million, less original issue discount of $463 million, (ii) the repayment of $400 million of Bank Bridge Loan and $1,040 million of Subordinated Bridge Financing and (iii) the payment of $57.4 million in underwriting commissions and related fees. The pro forma adjustments reflect $31.4 million in proceeds from the Financing as other assets which will be used to pay interest accruing on the Subordinated Bridge Financing subsequent to June 30, 1988, and a charge to retained earnings of approximately $16.7 million (net of income tax effect) representing debt issuance costs associated with the Subordinated Bridge Financing.

(d) Includes the acquisition by the Direct Investors of $28,910,000 principal amount of Senior Subordinated Notes, $28,910,000 principal amount of Subordinated Debentures, $124,000,000 principal amount of Junior Discount Debentures and $52,709,000 principal amount of Junior Debentures. See "The Acquisition—Bridge Financing— Direct Investor Purchase of Bridge Notes."

Source: Fort Howard Corporation prospectus dated October 25, 1988.

150

"Valuation" adjustments reflect the allocation of the $3.7-billion purchase price and elimination of Fort Howard's historical shareholders' equity. After Fort Howard's inventories, property, plant, and equipment and other assets have been revalued to their estimated fair values, fully $2.3 billion remains that must be attributed, under the purchase method of accounting, to goodwill ("Cost in excess of net assets acquired"). As shown in the Notes (Item b), this figure is netted against the $409 million of existing goodwill (so as to avoid "double-counting" an already-existing intangible asset) to produce the $1.9-billion adjustment recorded.

Finally, the permanent financing for the LBO produces one more set of adjustments ("Issuance of Securities"). Four new debt instruments— senior subordinated notes ($384 million), subordinated debentures ($384 million), junior discount debentures ($365 million), and junior debentures ($353 million)—replace the interim financing (the bank bridge and the subordinated bridge). The excess, along with an additional $44 million drawdown of the revolving credit facility, less $17 million of debt issuance costs associated with the subordinated bridge, shows up in other assets, $31.4 million of which will be used to pay interest on the subordinated bridge (see Note c).

Summarizing the balance sheet effect of the LBO, Fort Howard's capital structure changes from total debt (short- and long-term) of $419 million and shareholders' equity of $1.3 billion, to debt of $3.8 billion and equity of $430 million. Although the transaction does not entail the acquisition of any new fixed assets, the writeup to fair market value raises the property, plant, and equipment on Fort Howard's balance sheet from $1.3 billion to $1.9 billion. Unallocated costs of the acquisition raise goodwill from $409 million to $2.3 billion. Clearly, financial risk has increased (through a greater reliance on debt). The acquiring shareholders hope to use this increased leverage to raise the returns above the level that could have been earned on the previous, larger equity base. In part, the success of this buyout will depend on the correctness of the investors' determination that they are acquiring genuine (albeit intangible) value for the $1.9 billion they paid over and above the amounts that could be allocated to fixed assets and inventions. (Know-how and brand names are among the items represented by the $1.9 billion outlay for goodwill.) As a final observation, the 51% writeup of property, plant, and equipment is an indication of the magnitude of the disparities that can occur over time between historical-cost-derived asset values and fair market values.

MULTIYEAR PROJECTIONS

Although this chapter has up until this point focused on pro forma adjustments to current financial statements and one-year projections, such exercises represent nothing more than the foundation of a complete projection. A fixed-income investor buying a 30-year bond is certainly interested in the issuer's financial prospects beyond a 12-month horizon. Similarly, a substantial percentage of the present value of future dividends represented by a stock's price lies in years beyond the coming one. Even if particular investors plan to hold the securities for one year or less, they have an interest in estimating longer-term projections. Their ability, 6 or 12 months hence, to sell at attractive prices will depend on other investors' views at the time of the issuers' prospects.

Unfortunately, the volatile economic environment in which companies must operate nowadays makes long-term projections a perilous undertaking. In the late 1970s, for example, forecasters generally expected then-prevailing tightness in energy supplies to persist and to worsen, causing continued escalation of oil prices. The implications of this scenario included large profits for oil producers and boom conditions for manufacturers of oil exploration supplies, energy-conservation products, and alternative-energy equipment. By the early 1980s, the energy picture had changed from scarcity to glut, and many companies that had expected prosperity instead suffered bankruptcy. Considering as well other extreme discontinuities of the 1990s—the savings and loan crisis, the end of the Cold War, the wave of leveraged buyout bankruptcies—it is difficult to have high confidence in projections covering periods even as short as five years.

Notwithstanding their potential for widely missing the mark, multiyear projections are essential to the financial analysis of certain situations. For example, certain capital-intensive companies such as paper manufacturers have long construction cycles. They add to their capacity not in steady, annual increments but through large, individual plants that take several years to build. While a plant is in construction, the company must pay interest on the huge sums borrowed to finance it. This increased expense depresses earnings until the point—several years out—when the new plant comes onstream and begins to generate revenues. To get a true picture of the company's long-range financial condition, the analyst must somehow factor in the admittedly difficult-to-predict fourth- or fifth-year income statement, as well as its more easily forecasted first- or second-year earnings, which reflect cyclical peak borrowings and interest costs.

In recent times, radical financial restructurings—leveraged buyouts, megamergers, and massive stock buybacks—have expanded the need for multiyear projections. The short-term impact of these transactions is to increase financial risk sharply. Often, leverage increases to a level investors are comfortable with only if they believe the company will be able, from cash flow and possibly from proceeds of asset sales, to reduce debt to more customary levels within a few years. Analysts must make projections to determine whether the plan for debt retirement rests on realistic assumptions. A lender cannot prudently enter into this type of transaction without making some attempt—notwithstanding the uncertainties inherent in the process—to project results over several years.

Fortunately for analysts, the rising popularity of radical financial restructuring has been accompanied by vastly increased availability of data processing capacity via personal computers. Rapid advances in software have made it feasible to run projections on proposed transactions, even as the terms change from day to day, testing a variety of economic assumptions. Once the company's financial structure becomes definitive, the analyst can input the numbers and begin to monitor the restructured company's progress, quarter by quarter, comparing actual results with projections.

Lest the reader think that the greater ease of constructing projections brought about by personal computers is relevant only in the context of highly risky balance sheets, the truth is that it is likewise a boon to analyzing conventionally capitalized firms. In analyzing companies with already-strong balance sheets, however, analysts should not assume in their projections that all excess cash flow will be directed toward debt retirement. In most cases, a conservatively capitalized firm will not seek to reduce financial leverage below some specified level, instead using surplus funds to repurchase stock or make acquisitions.

Essentially, multiyear projections involve the same sorts of assumptions described in the one-year Colossal Chemical projection (Exhibits 5–1 through 5–12). When looking forward by as much as five years, though, the analyst must be especially cognizant of the impact of the business cycle. Many companies' projected financial statements look fine so long as sales grow "like a hockey stick" (sloping uninterruptedly upward), but less solid when sales turn downward for a year or two.

EXHIBIT 5–16

Hovnanian Enterprises, Inc.
Multiyear Financial Projections
for the Fiscal Years Ended February 28
($000,000 omitted)

	Actual		Projected		
	1990	**1991**	**1992**	**1993**	**1994**
Revenues	$410.4	$275.4	$315.0	$390.0	$450.0
Cost of Goods Sold	289.0	212.2	249.0	300.0	341.0
Selling, General, and Administrative	46.0	42.0	43.0	50.0	54.0
Earnings before Interest and Taxes	75.4	21.2	23.0	40.0	55.0
Interest Expense	26.5	23.7	21.0	24.0	26.0
Adjusted Net Income	28.2	(1.3)	2.0	12.0	20.0
Adjustments (a)	(6.4)	(13.9)	0.0	0.0	0.0
Reported Net Income	21.8	(15.2)	2.0	12.0	20.0
Financial Ratios					
EBITDA/Interest Expense (x)	2.97	1.02	1.24	1.79	2.27
Total Debt/Invested Capital (b) (%)	64.7	68.4	63.6	62.1	59.5
Total Debt/EBITDA (x)	3.3	11.2	9.5	5.9	4.3

(a) Nonrecurring items and capitalized interest.
(b) Total invested capital includes short-term debt, long-term debt, minority interest, and common equity.

Source: Duff & Phelps/MCM Investment Research Co., February 12, 1992.

Notwithstanding the many uncertainties that confront the financial forecaster, carefully constructed projections can prove fairly accurate. The results can be satisfying even when the numbers are strongly influenced by hard-to-predict economic variables.

Exhibit 5–16 is a condensed forecast of the financial results of homebuilder Hovnanian Enterprises. Prepared by Brian E. Bogart, an analyst with the firm of Duff & Phelps/MCM Investment Research,[1] it was published on February 12, 1992. At that time, the analyst was fairly optimistic about Hovnanian's prospects. The opinion was based partly on the company's market share gains at the expense of smaller firms that left the business. In addition, Bogart pointed to proposed tax incentives for first-time home buyers, as well as a favorable economic outlook.

[1] Later Duff & Phelps Investment Research Co.

A comparison of the analyst's February 1992 forecast with actual results (Exhibit 5–17) shows that his vision of the future was not unduly blurred. For example, in fiscal 1992, Hovnanian's revenues were just 1% above the projected level. The excess of actual over projected revenues rose to 10% ($429.3 million vs. $390.0 million) in the second year of the forecast (fiscal 1993). Even though precision diminished somewhat with the length of the forecast period, the projected financial ratios were uncannily accurate. EBITDA covered interest expense by 1.92 times in fiscal 1993, not far off the ratio of 1.79 times shown in the forecast. Even more nearly on target were the ratios of total debt to invested capital (63.0% actual vs. 63.6% projected) and total debt to EBITDA (6.0 times vs. 5.9 times).

Exhibits 5–16 and 5–17 also illustrate the ongoing nature of financial forecasting. By February 16, 1994, the Duff & Phelps analyst was even more optimistic about Hovnanian's business outlook than he had been

EXHIBIT 5–17

Hovnanian Enterprises, Inc.
Actual and Projected Financial Results
for the Fiscal Years Ended February 28
($000,000 omitted)

	Actual		Projected		
	1992	**1993**	**1994**	**1995**	**1996**
Revenues	$318.5	$429.3	$575.0	$677.0	$749.0
Cost of Goods Sold	249.8	332.2	448.0	526.0	578.0
Selling, General, and Administrative	44.4	57.1	78.0	91.0	99.0
Earnings before Interest and Taxes	24.3	40.0	49.0	60.0	72.0
Interest Expense	22.5	22.3	25.0	30.0	35.0
Adjusted Net Income	1.6	11.8	15.0	18.0	22.0
Adjustments (a)	0.9	2.0	3.0	5.0	5.0
Reported Net Income	2.5	9.8	18.0	23.0	27.0
Financial Ratios					
EBITDA/Interest expense (x)	1.21	1.92	2.08	2.10	2.17
Total Debt/Invested Capital (b) (%)	61.1	63.0	64.4	64.2	63.0
Total Debt/EBITDA (x)	8.2	6.0	5.9	5.6	5.0

(a) Nonrecurring items and capitalized interest.
(b) Total invested capital includes short-term debt, long-term debt, minority interest, and common equity.

Source: Duff & Phelps Investment Research Co., February 16, 1994.

two years earlier. On the other hand, he observed that the company was incurring higher lumber costs. Margins were being constrained further by increased selling, general and administrative expenses. Accordingly, Bogart's fiscal 1994 revenue forecast was up (from $450.0 million to $575.0 million), but projected earnings before interest and taxes were down (from $55 million to $49 million).

Projected financial ratios were likewise mixed, by comparison with the earlier forecast. The analyst now expected EBITDA coverage to be a touch lower than he had formerly predicted (2.27 times vs. 2.08 times). He also projected a higher level of debt, relative to both invested capital and EBITDA. This was based on his belief that the company would increase its inventories to accommodate rising sales, thereby necessitating borrowing.

Viewed with the benefit of hindsight, the Duff & Phelps forecast suggests that financial projections may prove extremely accurate for a year or two out. After that, the crystal ball begins to grow clouded. It is nevertheless worthwhile, indeed in some instances imperative, to project results five years out or more. For example, companies in capital-intensive industries tend to have long operating cycles. There is typically an extended delay between the commencement of a plant's construction and its initial generation of revenue. In such a case, analysts have little choice but to appraise, as best they can, the company's very long-term prospects.

At the same time, forecasters must not become wedded to their projections. They must update their numbers frequently. Realistically, the object of a financial forecast is not to predict, with great precision, the state of affairs several years in the future. Rather, it is to maintain compatibility between the projected numbers and all relevant information that is currently available.

CONCLUSION

Of the various types of analysis of financial statements, projecting future results and ratios requires the greatest skill and produces the most valuable findings. Looking forward is also the riskiest form of analysis, since there are no correct answers until the future statements appear. Totally unforeseeable events may invalidate the assumptions underlying the forecast; economic shocks or unexpected changes in a company's financial strategies may knock all calculations into a cocked hat.

The prominence of the chance element in the forecasting process means that analysts should not be disheartened if their predictions miss the mark—even widely—on occasion. They should aim not for absolute prescience but rather for a sound probabilistic model of the future. The model should logically incorporate all significant evidence, both within, and external to, the historical statements. An analyst can then judge whether a company's prevailing valuations (e.g., stock price, credit rating) are consistent with the possible scenarios and their respective probabilities.

By tracking the after-the-fact accuracy of a number of projections, an analyst can gauge the effectiveness of these methods. Invariably, there will be room for further refinement, particularly in the area of gathering information on industry conditions. No matter how refined the methods, however, perfection will always elude the modeler since no business cycle precisely recapitulates its predecessor. That is what ultimately makes looking forward with financial statements such a challenging task and also what makes it so important to investors. When betting huge sums in the face of massive uncertainty, it is essential that they understand the odds as fully as they possibly can.

6

CREDIT ANALYSIS

CREDIT ANALYSIS IS one of the most common uses of financial statements, reflecting the many forms of debt that are essential to the operation of a modern economy. Merchants who exchange goods for promises to pay need to evaluate the reliability of those promises. Commercial banks that lend the merchants the funds to finance their inventories likewise need to calculate the probability of being repaid in full and on time. The banks must in turn demonstrate their creditworthiness to other financial institutions that lend to them by purchasing their certificates of deposit and bonds. In all of these cases, analysis of financial statements can significantly influence a decision to extend or not to extend credit.

As important as financial statements are to the evaluation of credit risk, however, the analyst must bear in mind that other procedures also play a role. Financial statements tell much about a borrower's *ability* to repay a loan, but disclose little about the equally important *willingness* to repay. Accordingly, a thorough credit analysis may have to include a check of the subject's past record of repayment, which is not part of a standard financial statement. Moreover, to assess the creditworthiness of the merchant in this example, the bank must consider along with his balance sheet and income statement the competitive environment and strength of the local economy in which he operates. Lenders to the bank will in turn consider not only the bank's financial position, but also public policy. Believing that a sound banking system benefits the economy as a whole, the government has empowered the Federal Reserve System to intervene in the marketplace, resulting in a smaller number of bank failures than would occur with pure unrestrained competition.

An even more basic reason why analyzing a company's financial statements may not be sufficient for determining its credit quality is that the borrower's credit may be supported, formally or informally, by another entity. For example, many municipalities obtain cost savings on their financings by having their debt payments guaranteed by bond insurers with premier credit ratings. For holders of these municipal bonds, the insurer's creditworthiness, not the municipality's financial condition, is the basis for determining the likelihood of repayment. Corporations, too, sometimes guarantee the debt of weaker credits. Even when the stronger company does not take on a legal obligation to pay in the event that the weaker company fails on its debt, "implicit support" may affect the latter's credit quality. For instance, if a company is dependent on raw materials provided by a subsidiary, there may be a reasonable presumption that it will stand behind the subsidiary's debt, even in the absence of a formal guarantee.

Keeping in mind that the final judgment may be influenced by other types of information as well, the would-be analyst can begin to extract from the financial statements the data that bear on credit risk. Each of the basic statements—the balance sheet, income statement, and statement of cash flows—yields valuable insights when studied through ratio analysis techniques, as well as when used in the evaluation of fixed-income securities. In each case, the analyst must temper any enthusiasm generated by a review of historical statements with caution based on a consideration of financial ratios derived from projected statements for future years.

BALANCE-SHEET RATIOS

The most immediate danger faced by a lender is the risk that the borrower will suffer illiquidity—an inability to raise cash to pay its obligations. This condition can arise for many different reasons, one of which is a loss of ability to borrow new funds to pay off existing creditors. Whatever the underlying cause, however, illiquidity manifests itself as an excess of current cash payments due, over cash currently available. The current ratio gauges the risk of this occurring by comparing the claims against the company that will become payable during the current operating cycle (current liabilities) with the assets that are already in the form of cash or that will be converted to cash during the current operating cycle (current assets). Referring to Texas Instruments' balance sheet

(Exhibit 6–1), the company's current ratio as of December 31, 1993, was 1.66. (Note that dollar figures are in millions):

$$\text{Current ratio} = \frac{\text{Current assets}}{\text{Current liabilities}} = \frac{\$3,314}{\$2,001} = 1.66$$

Analysts also apply a more stringent test of liquidity by calculating the quick ratio, or acid test, which considers only cash and current assets that can be most quickly converted to cash (marketable securities and receivables). Texas Instruments' quick ratio on December 31, 1993, was 1.05.

$$\text{Quick ratio} = \frac{\text{Quick assets}}{\text{Current liabilities}} = \frac{\$2,106}{\$2,001} = 1.05$$

Besides looking at the ratio between current assets and current liabilities, it is also useful, when assessing a company's ability to meet its near-term obligations, to consider the difference between the two, which is termed working capital. Referring once again to Exhibit 6–1, working capital is $1.31 billion.

$$\text{Working capital} = \text{Current assets} - \text{Current liabilities}$$
$$\$1,313 \quad = \quad \$3,314 \quad - \quad \$2,001$$

Analysis of current assets and current liabilities provides warnings about impending illiquidity, but lenders nevertheless periodically find themselves saddled with loans to borrowers who are unable to continue meeting their obligations and are therefore forced to file for bankruptcy. Recognizing that they may one day find themselves holding defaulted obligations, creditors wish to know how much asset value will be available for liquidation to pay off their claims.[1] The various ratios that address this issue can be grouped as measures of financial leverage.

A direct measure of asset protection is the ratio of total assets to total liabilities, which in the example shown in Exhibit 6–1 comes to:

$$\frac{\text{Total assets}}{\text{Total liabilities}} = \frac{\$5,993}{\$3,678} = 1.63$$

---

[1]In practice, the United States Bankruptcy Code encourages companies to reorganize, rather than simply liquidate, if they become insolvent. Typically, a reorganization results in settlement of creditors' claims via distribution of securities of a firm that has been rehabilitated through forgiveness of a portion of its debt. Determination of the value of securities awarded to each class of creditor is related to asset protection, however, so the analysis that follows applies equally to a reorganization as to a liquidation.

EXHIBIT 6–1

Texas Instruments, Inc. and Subsidiaries Balance Sheet
($000,000 omitted)
December 31, 1993

Assets

Current Assets

Cash and cash equivalents	$ 404
Short-term investments	484
Accounts receivable, less allowance for losses of $42	1,218
Inventories (net of progress billings)	822
Prepaid expenses	55
Deferred income taxes	331
	3,314
Property, Plant, and Equipment-at cost	4,620
Less accumulated depreciation	(2,417)
	2,203
Deferred Income Taxes	237
Other Assets	239
	$5,993

Liabilities and Stockholders' Equity

Current Liabilities

Loans payable and current portion of long-term debt	$ 211
Accounts payable and accrued expenses	1,495
Income taxes payable	120
Accrued retirement and profit-sharing contributions	158
Dividends payable	17
	2,001
Long-Term Debt	694
Accrued Retirement Costs	739
Deferred Credits and Other Liabilities	244
Stockholders' Equity	
Common stock	91
Paid-in capital	932
Retained earnings	1,307
Less treasury common stock at cost	(5)
Other	(10)
	2,315
	$5,993

Source: Texas Instruments 1993 Annual Report.

(Total liabilities can be derived quickly by subtracting stockholders' equity from total assets.)

Put another way, Texas Instruments' assets of $5.993 billion could decline in value by 38.6% before proceeds of a liquidation would be inadequate to satisfy lenders' $3,678 billion of claims. The greater the amount by which asset values could deteriorate, the greater the "equity cushion" (equity is by definition total assets minus total liabilities), and the greater the creditor's sense of being protected.

Lenders also gauge the amount of equity "beneath" them (junior to them in the event of liquidation) by comparing it with the amount of debt outstanding. For finance companies, where the ratio is typically greater than 1.0, it is convenient to express the relationship as a debt-equity ratio:

$$\frac{\text{Total debt}}{\text{Total equity}}$$

Many industrial corporations nowadays carry debt several times as large as their equity, but harking back to an era when this was uncommon, the convention is still to express these companies' financial leverage in terms of a total-debt-to-total-capital ratio:

$$\frac{\text{Total debt}}{\text{Total debt} + \text{Minority interest} + \text{Total equity}}$$

Banks' "capital adequacy" is commonly measured by the ratio of equity to total assets:

$$\frac{\text{Total equity}}{\text{Total assets}}$$

Many pages of elaboration could follow on the last few ratios mentioned. Their calculation is rather less simple than it might appear. The reason is that aggressive borrowers frequently try to satisfy the letter of a maximum leverage limit imposed by lenders, without fulfilling the conservative spirit behind it. The following discussion of definitions of leverage ratios addresses the major issues without laying down absolute rules about "correct" calculations. As explained later in the chapter, ratios are most meaningful when compared across time and across borrower. Consequently, the precise method of calculation is less important than the consistency of calculation throughout the sample being compared.

What Constitutes Total Debt?

At one time, it was appropriate to consider only long-term debt in leverage calculations for industrial companies, since short-term debt was generally used for seasonable purposes, such as financing Christmas-related inventory. A company might draw down bank lines or issue commercial paper to meet these funding requirements, then completely pay off the interim borrowings when it sold the inventory. Even today, a firm that "zeros out" its short-term debt at some point in each operating cycle can legitimately argue that its "true" leverage is represented by the permanent (long-term) debt on its balance sheet. Many borrowers have long since subverted this principle, however, by relying heavily on short-term debt that they neither repay on an interim basis nor fund (replace with long-term debt) when it grows to sufficient size to make a bond offering cost-effective. Such short-term debt must be viewed as permanent and included in the leverage calculation. (Current maturities of long-term debt should also enter into the calculation of total debt, based on a conservative assumption that the company will replace maturing debt with new long-term borrowings.)

As an aside, the just-described reliance on short-term debt is not necessarily as dangerous a practice as in years past, although it should still raise a caution flag for the credit analyst. There are two risks inherent in depending on debt with maturities of less than one year. The first is potential illiquidity. If substantial debt comes due at a time when lenders are either unable to renew their loans (because credit is tight) or unwilling to renew (because they perceive the borrower as less creditworthy than formerly), the borrower may be unable to meet its near-term obligations. This risk may be mitigated, however, if the borrower has a revolving credit agreement, which is a longer-term commitment by the lender to lend (subject to certain conditions such as maintaining prescribed financial ratios and refraining from significant changes in the business). The second risk of relying on short-term borrowings is exposure to interest-rate fluctuations. That is, if a substantial amount of debt is about to come due, and interest rates have risen sharply since the debt was incurred, the borrower's cost of staying in business may skyrocket overnight. In this sense, relying on short-term debt is still riskier than using long-term, fixed-rate debt with maturities spaced out over a number of years. Analysts must not assume, however, that all of a company's long-term debt is at a fixed rate, as might have been the case prior to the period of increased volatility in interest rates in the late

1970s. Long-term, floating-rate debt does not insulate the borrower from interest-rate fluctuations any more than short-term debt does, except in the following instances:

1. The loan is "capped" (has in its terms a maximum interest rate that will prevail, no matter how high the benchmark rate rises).
2. The borrower has converted the floating-rate loan to a fixed-rate loan through a financial derivative known as an interest-rate swap.

Borrowers sometimes argue that the total debt calculation should exclude debt that is convertible, at the lender's option, into common equity. Hardliners on the credit analysis side respond: "It's equity when the holders convert it to equity. Until then, it's debt." Realistically, though, if the conversion value of the bond rises sufficiently, most holders will in fact convert their securities to common stock. This is particularly true if the issuer has the option of calling the bonds for early retirement, which results in a loss for holders who fail to convert. Analysts should remember that the ultimate objective is not to calculate ratios but to assess credit risk. Therefore, the best practice is to count convertible debt in total debt, but to consider the possibility of conversion when comparing the borrower's leverage with its peer group's.

Preferred stock[2] is a security that further complicates the leverage calculation. From a legal standpoint, preferred stock is clearly equity; in a liquidation, preferred stock ranks junior to debt. It pays a dividend rather than interest, and failure to pay the dividend does not constitute a default. On the other hand, preferred dividends, unlike common dividends, are contractually fixed in amount. An issuer can omit its preferred dividend, but not without also omitting its common dividend. Furthermore, a preferred dividend is typically cumulative, meaning that the issuer must repay all preferred dividend arrearages before resuming common stock dividends. Furthermore, not all preferred issues have the permanent character of common stock. A preferred stock may have a sinking fund provision, much like the provision typically found in bonds, that requires redemption of a substantial portion of the outstanding par amount prior to final maturity. Such a provision implies less financial flexibility than is the case for a perpetual preferred stock, which requires no principal repayment at any time. Another preferred security,

[2]The comments on preferred stock in this paragraph also apply generally to preference stock, which is similar to preferred stock in form but junior to it in the capital structure.

exchangeable preferred stock, can be transformed into debt at the issuer's option. Treating it purely as equity for credit analysis purposes would understate financial risk. In general, the credit analyst must recognize the heightened level of risk implied by the presence of preferred stock in the capital structure. One formal way to take this risk into account is to calculate the ratio of total fixed obligations to total capital:[3]

$$\frac{\text{Total debt} + \text{Preferred stock} + \text{Preference stock}}{\text{Total debt} + \text{Minority interest} + \text{Preferred stock} + \text{Preference stock} + \text{Common equity}}$$

Off-balance-sheet lease obligations, like preferred stock, enable companies to obtain many of the benefits of debt financing without violating covenanted limitations on debt incurrence. Accounting standards have partially brought these debtlike obligations out of hiding by requiring capital leases to appear on the balance sheet, either separately or as part of long-term debt. Credit analysts should complete the job. In addition to including capital leases in the total debt calculation, they should also take into account the off-balance-sheet liabilities represented by contractual payments on operating leases, which are reported (as "rental expense") in the Notes to Financial Statements. The rationale is that although the accounting rules distinguish between capital and operating leases, the two financing vehicles frequently differ little in economic terms. Indeed, borrowers have used considerable ingenuity in structuring capital leases to qualify as operating leases under GAAP, the benefit being that they will consequently be excluded from the balance sheet and, it is hoped, from credit analysts' scrutiny. Analysts should not fall for this ruse, but should instead capitalize the current year rental payments shown in the Notes to Financial Statements. The most common method is to multiply the payments by seven or eight, a calculation that has been found to be reasonably accurate when actual figures on capitalized value of leases have been available for comparison.

Other Off-Balance-Sheet Liabilities

In their quest for methods of obtaining the benefits of debt without suffering the associated penalties imposed by credit analysts, corporations

---

[3]Note that in this and subsequent definitions of total capital, minority interest is included. This item should be viewed as equity in leverage calculations, since it involves no contractual payment and ranks junior to debt.

have by no means limited themselves to the use of leases. Like leases, the other popular devices may provide genuine business benefits, as well as the cosmetic benefit of disguising debt. In all cases, the focus of credit quality determination must be economic impact, which may or may not be reflected in the accounting treatment.

A corporation can employ leverage yet avoid showing debt on its consolidated balance sheet by entering joint ventures or forming partially owned subsidiaries. At a minimum, the analyst should attribute to the corporation its proportionate liability for the debt of such ventures, thereby "matching" the cash flow benefits derived from the affiliates. (Note that cash flow is generally reduced by unremitted earnings—the portion not received in dividends—of non-fully-consolidated affiliates.) In some cases, the affiliate's operations are critical to the parent's operations, as in the case of a jointly owned pulp plant that supplies a paper plant wholly owned by the parent. There is a strong incentive, in such instances, for the parent to keep the jointly owned operation running by picking up the debt service commitments of a partner that becomes financially incapacitated, even though it may have no legal obligation to do so. (In legal parlance, this arrangement is known as a "several" obligation, in contrast to a "joint" obligation in which each partner is compelled to back up the other's commitment.) Depending on the particular circumstances, it may be appropriate to attribute to the parent more than its proportionate share—up to 100%—of the debt of the joint venture or unconsolidated subsidiary.

Surely one of the most ingenious devices for obtaining the benefits of debt without incurring balance sheet recognition was described by *The Independent* in 1992. According to the British newspaper, the Faisal Islamic Bank of Cairo had provided $250 million of funding to a troubled real estate developer, Olympia & York. As an institution committed to Islamic religious principles, however, the bank was not allowed to charge interest. Instead, claimed *The Independent,* Faisal Islamic Bank in effect had acquired a building from Olympia & York, along with an option to sell it back. The option was reportedly exercisable at $250 million plus an amount equivalent to the market rate of interest for the option period. Because the excess was not officially classified as interest, said *The Independent,* the $250 million of funding did not show up as a loan on Olympia & York's balance sheet.

The Independent noted a denial by an Olympia & York spokesperson that "any such *loan* existed" (emphasis added). If, however, the account was substantially correct, then the religious-prohibition-of-interest gambit succeeded spectacularly in diverting attention from a transaction that had all the trappings of a loan. Barclays Bank, one of Olympia & York's most important lenders, commented that it had never heard of the Faisal Islamic Bank transaction.[4]

Of a somewhat different character within the broad category of off-balance-sheet liabilities are employee benefit obligations. Under SFAS 87, balance sheet recognition is now given to pension liabilities related to employees' service to date. Similarly, SFAS 106 requires recognition of postretirement health care benefits as an on-balance sheet liability. Projected future wage increases are still not recognized, however, although they affect the calculation of pension expense for income statement purposes. Unlike some other kinds of hidden liabilities, these items arise exclusively in furtherance of a business objective (attracting and retaining capable employees), rather than as a surreptitious means of leveraging shareholders' equity.

Generally speaking, pension obligations that have been fully funded (provided for with investment assets set aside for the purpose) present few credit worries for a going concern. Likewise, a modest underfunding that is in the process of being remediated by an essentially sound company is no more than a small qualitative factor on the negative side. On the other hand, a large or growing underfunded liability can be a significantly negative consideration—albeit one that is hard to quantify explicitly—in assessing a deteriorating credit. In bankruptcy, it becomes essential to monitor details of the Pension Benefit Guaranty Corporation's efforts to assert its claim to the company's assets, which, if successful, reduce the settlement amounts available to other creditors.

Are Deferred Taxes Part of Capital?

Near the equity account on many companies' balance sheets appears an account labeled "Deferred Income Taxes." This item represents the cumulative difference between taxes calculated at the statutory rate and taxes actually paid. The difference reflects the tax consequences, for future years, of the differences between the tax bases of assets and liabilities and their carrying amounts for financial reporting purposes.

Many analysts argue that net worth is understated by the amount of the deferred tax liability, since it will in all likelihood never come due

---

[4]Nick Fielding, Richard Thomson, and Larry Black, "Undisclosed Debt Worries Hang over O&Y," *The Independent* (May 10, 1992).

and is therefore not really a liability at all. (As long as the company continues to pay taxes at less than the statutory rate, the deferred tax account will continue to grow.) Proponents of this view adjust for the alleged understatement of net worth by adding deferred taxes to the denominator in the total-debt-to-total-capital calculation, thus:

$$\frac{\text{Total debt}}{\text{Total debt} + \text{Deferred taxes} + \text{Minority interest} + \text{Total equity}}$$

In general, this practice is sound. Analysts must, however, keep in mind that the precise formula for calculating a ratio is less important than the assurance that it is calculated consistently for all companies being evaluated. The caveat is that a number of different factors can contribute to deferred taxes, and not all of them imply a permanent deferral. A defense contractor, for instance, can defer payment of taxes related to a specific contract until the contract is completed. The analyst would not want to add to equity the taxes deferred on a contract that is about to be completed, although in such situations specific figures may be hard to obtain.

INCOME-STATEMENT RATIOS

Although an older approach to credit analysis places primary emphasis on liquidity and asset protection, both of which are measured by balance-sheet ratios, the more contemporary view is that profits are ultimately what sustain liquidity and asset values. High profits keep plenty of cash flowing through the system and confirm the value of productive assets such as plant and equipment. In line with this latter view, the income statement is no longer of interest mainly to the equity analyst, but is essential to credit analysis as well.

A key income-statement focus for credit analysis is the borrower's profit margin (profit as a percentage of sales). The narrower the margin, the greater is the danger that a modest decline in selling prices or a modest increase in costs will produce losses, which will in turn begin to erode such balance-sheet measures as total-debt-to-total-capital by reducing equity.

Profit can be measured at several levels of the income statement—before or after deducting various expenses to get to the bottom-line, net income. The most commonly used profit margins are the following:

$$\text{Gross margin} \quad = \frac{\text{Sales} - \text{Cost of goods sold}}{\text{Sales}}$$

$$\text{Operating margin} = \frac{\text{Operating income}}{\text{Sales}}$$

$$= \frac{\text{Net income} + \text{Income taxes} + \text{Interest expense} - \text{Interest income} - \text{Other income}}{\text{Sales}}$$

$$\text{Pretax margin} \quad = \frac{\text{Net income} + \text{Income taxes}}{\text{Sales}}$$

$$\text{Net margin} \atop \text{(Return on sales)} = \frac{\text{Net income}}{\text{Sales}}$$

Applying these definitions to Texas Instruments' income statement (Exhibit 6–2), the company's profit margins in 1993 were:

$$\text{Gross margin} \quad = \frac{\$8{,}523 - 6{,}274}{\$8{,}523} \quad = 26.4\%$$

$$\text{Operating margin} = \frac{\$472 + 220 + 47 - 15}{\$8{,}523} = \ 8.5\%$$

$$\text{Pretax margin} \quad = \frac{\$472 + 220}{\$8{,}523} \quad = \ 8.1\%$$

$$\text{Net margin} \quad = \frac{\$472}{\$8{,}523} \quad = \ 5.5\%$$

Note that the approach of adding from the bottom up to derive the numerators in the pretax and operating margins produces a slightly different number from the one derived by working from the top down. For example, the sum of net income and provision for income taxes is $692 million, slightly less than the $696 million that appears in the income statement. The discrepancy arises from an aftertax nonoperating item, a cumulative effect of accounting changes.

The various margin measures reflect different aspects of management's effectiveness. Gross margin, which is particularly important in analyzing retailers, measures management's skill in buying and selling at advantageous prices. Operating margin shows how well management has run the business—buying and selling wisely, controlling selling and administrative expenses—before taking into account financial policies,

EXHIBIT 6–2

Texas Instruments, Inc. and Subsidiaries
Consolidated Statement of Income
($000,000 omitted)

	1993
Net Revenues	$8,523
Operating Costs and Expenses	
Cost of revenues	6,274
General, administrative, and marketing	1,247
Employees' retirement and profit-sharing plans	274
	7,795
Profit from Operations	728
Other income (expense) net	15
Interest on loans	47
Income before Provision for Income Taxes and Cumulative Effect	
of Accounting Changes	696
Provision for income taxes	220
Income before Cumulative Effect of Accounting Changes	476
Cumulative Effect of Accounting Changes	(4)
Net Income	$ 472

Source: Texas Instruments 1993 Annual Report.

which largely determine interest expense, and the tax rate, which is outside management's control.[5] These last two factors are sequentially added to the picture by calculating pretax margin and net margin, with the latter ratio reflecting all factors, whether under management's control or not, that influence profitability.

In calculating profit margins, analysts should eliminate the effect of extraordinary gains and losses to determine the level of profitability that is likely to be sustainable in the future.

Fixed-charge coverage is the other income-statement ratio of major interest to credit analysts. It measures the ability of a company's earnings to meet the interest payments on its debt, the lender's most direct concern. In its simplest form, the fixed-charge coverage ratio indicates the multiple by which operating earnings suffice to pay interest charges:

$$\text{Fixed-charge coverage} = \frac{\text{Net income} + \text{Income taxes} + \text{Interest expense}}{\text{Interest expense}}$$

[5]Technically speaking, the effective tax rate is somewhat manageable, even though the statutory rate is not. It is nevertheless useful to calculate the operating margin separately from the pretax margin, to measure management's operating prowess separately from its financial acumen.

This basic formula requires several refinements, however. As with profit margins, extraordinary items should be eliminated from the calculation to arrive at a sustainable level of coverage. The other main adjustments involve capitalized interest and payments on operating leases.

Capitalized Interest

Under SFAS 34, companies may be required to capitalize, rather than expense, a portion of their interest costs. The underlying notion is that like the actual bricks and mortar purchased to construct a plant, the cost of the money borrowed to finance the purchase provides benefits in future periods and therefore should not be entirely written off in the first year. Regardless of whether it is expensed or capitalized, however, all interest accrued must be covered by earnings and should therefore appear in the denominator of the fixed-charge coverage calculation. Accordingly, the basic formula can be rewritten to include not only the interest expense shown on the income statement, but also capitalized interest, which may appear either on the income statement or else in the Note to Financial Statements. (If the amount is immaterial, capitalized interest will not be shown at all, and the analyst can skip this adjustment.) The numerator should not include capitalized interest, however, for the amount is a reduction to total expenses and consequently reflected in net income. Including capitalized interest in the numerator would therefore constitute double counting:

$$\text{Fixed-charge coverage (adjusted for capitalized interest)} = \frac{\text{Net income} + \text{Income taxes} + \text{Income expense}}{\text{Interest expense} + \text{Capitalized interest}}$$

Lease Expense

As mentioned in the preceding section, off-balance-sheet operating leases have virtually the same economic impact as on-balance-sheet debt. Just as credit analysts should take into account the liabilities represented by these leases, they should also factor into coverage calculations the annual fixed charges associated with them. One approach simply adds the total current-year rental expense from Notes to Financial Statements to both the numerator and denominator of the fixed-charge coverage calculation. An alternate method includes one-third of rentals (as shown in the following calculation), on the theory that one-third of a lease payment typically represents interest that would be paid if the assets had been purchased with borrowed money, and two-thirds is equivalent to principal repayment:

$$\text{Fixed-charge coverage (adjusted for capitalized interest and operating leases)} = \frac{\text{Net income + Income taxes + Interest expense + }\frac{1}{3}\text{ Rentals}}{\text{Interest expense + Capitalized interest + }\frac{1}{3}\text{ Rentals}}$$

Two complications arise in connection with incorporating operating lease payment into the fixed-charge coverage calculation. First, the SEC does not require companies to report rental expense in quarterly statements. The analyst can therefore only estimate where a company's fully adjusted coverage stands, on an interim basis, in relation to its most recent full-year level. (Capitalized interest, by the way, presents the same problem, although a few companies voluntarily report capitalized interest on an interim basis.) Second, retailers in particular often negotiate leases with rents that are semifixed, tied in part to revenues of the leased stores. Some argue that the variable portion—contingent rentals—should be excluded from the fixed-charge coverage calculation. That approach, however, results in a numerator that includes income derived from revenues in excess of the threshold level, while omitting from the denominator charges that were automatically incurred when the threshold was reached. A better way to recognize the possible avoidance of contingent lease payments is by capitalizing only the mandatory portion when calculating the balance-sheet ratio of total-debt-to-total-capital.

Interest Income

A final issue related to fixed-charge coverage involves interest income. Companies sometimes argue that the denominator should include only net interest expense, that is, the difference between interest expense and income derived from interest-bearing assets, generally consisting of marketable securities. They portray the two items as offsetting, with operating earnings having to cover only the portion of interest expense not "automatically" paid for by interest income. Such treatment can be quite deceptive, however, when a company holds a large but temporary portfolio of marketable securities. In this situation, fixed-charge coverage based on net interest expense in the current year can greatly overstate the level of protection that may be expected in the succeeding year, after the company has invested its funds in operating assets. If, however, a company's strategy is to invest a substantial portion of its assets indefinitely in marketable securities (as some pharmaceutical manufacturers do, to capture certain tax benefits), analysts should consider the associated liquidity as a positive factor in their analysis.

STATEMENT OF CASH FLOWS RATIOS

Ratios related to sources and uses of funds measure credit quality at the most elemental level—a company's ability to generate sufficient cash to pay its bills. These ratios also disclose a great deal about financial flexibility; a company that does not have to rely on external financing can take greater operating risks than one that would be forced to retrench if new capital suddenly became scarce or prohibitively expensive. In addition, trends in sources-and-uses ratios can anticipate changes in balance-sheet ratios. Given corporations' general reluctance to sell new equity, which may dilute existing shareholders' interest, a recurrent cash shortfall is likely to be made up with debt financing, leading to a rise in the total-debt-to-total-capital ratio.

For capital-intensive manufacturers and utilities, a key ratio to watch is cash flow to capital expenditures:

$$\frac{\text{Cash flow from operations}}{\text{Capital expenditures}}$$

The higher this ratio, the greater the financial flexibility implied. It is important, though, to examine the reasons underlying a change in the relationship between internal funds and capital outlays. It is normal for a capital-intensive industry to go through a capital-spending cycle, adding capacity by constructing large-scale plants that require several years to complete. Once the new capacity is in place, capital expenditures ease for a few years until demand growth catches up and another round of spending begins. Over the cycle, the industry's ratio of cash falls. By definition, the downleg of this cycle does not imply long-term deterioration in credit quality. In contrast, a company that suffers a prolonged downtrend in its ratio of cash flow to capital expenditures is likely to get more deeply into debt, and therefore become financially riskier with each succeeding year. Likewise, a rising ratio may require interpretation. A company that sharply reduces its capital budget will appear to increase its financial flexibility, based on the cash-flow-to-capital-expenditures ratio. Cutting back on outlays, however, may impair the company's long-run competitiveness by sacrificing market share or by causing the company to fall behind in technological terms.

While the most recent period's ratio of cash flow to capital expenditures is a useful measure, the credit analyst is always more interested in the future than in the past. One good way of assessing a company's ability to sustain its existing level of cash adequacy is to calculate depreciation as a percentage of cash flow:

$$\frac{\text{Depreciation}}{\text{Cash flow from operations}}$$

Unlike earnings, depreciation is essentially a programmed item, a cash flow assured by the accounting rules. The higher the percentage of cash flow derived from depreciation, the higher is the predictability of a company's cash flow, and the less dependent its financial flexibility on the vagaries of the marketplace.

Finally, among the ratios derived from the statement of cash flows is the ratio of capital expenditures to depreciation:

$$\frac{\text{Capital expenditures}}{\text{Depreciation}}$$

A ratio of less than 1.0 over a period of several years raises a red flag, since it suggests that the company is failing to replace its plant and equipment. Underspending on capital replacement amounts to gradual liquidation of the firm. By the same token, though, the analyst cannot necessarily assume that all is well simply because capital expenditures consistently exceed depreciation. For one thing, persistent inflation means that a nominal dollar spent on plant and equipment today will not buy as much capacity as it did when the depreciating asset was acquired. (Technological advances in production processes may mitigate this problem because the cost in real terms of producing one unit may have declined since the company purchased the equipment now being replaced.) A second reason to avoid complacency over a seemingly strong ratio of capital expenditures to depreciation is that the depreciation may be understated, with respect either to wear and tear or to obsolescence. If so, the adequacy of capital spending will be overstated by the ratio of capital spending to depreciation. Finally, capital outlays may be too low even if they match in every sense the depreciation of existing plant and

equipment. In a growth industry, a company that fails to expand its capacity at roughly the same rate as its competitors may lose essential
economies of scale and fall victim to a shakeout.

COMBINATION RATIOS

Each of the financial ratios discussed so far in this chapter is derived
from numbers collected from just one of the three basic financial statements. In financial analysis, these rudimentary tools are analogous to the
simple machines—the wedge, the lever, the wheel, and the screw—that
greatly increased the productivity of their prehistoric inventors. How
much more remarkable an advance it was, however, when an anonymous
Chinese combined two simple machines, a lever and a wheel, to create a
wheelbarrow! In similar fashion, combining numbers from different financial statements unleashes vast new analytical power.

Rate-of-Return Measures

One of the most valuable types of combination ratios combines earnings
with balance-sheet figures. Such ratios measure the profit that an enterprise is generating relative to the assets employed or the capital invested
in it. This kind of measure provides a link between credit analysis and the
economic concept of productivity of capital.

   To illustrate, consider Companies A, B, and C below, all of which are
debt-free. If we look only at net margin, a ratio derived solely from the
income statement, Company A is superior to both its direct competitor,
Company B, and Company C, which is in a different business. Looking at
the combination ratio of return on equity, however, we find that Company C ranks highest, notwithstanding that sales margins tend to be narrower in its industry:

	Company A	Company B	Company C
Sales	$1,000,000	$1,000,000	$2,000,000
Net Income	50,000	40,000	60,000
Equity	500,000	500,000	500,000
Net Margin $\left(\dfrac{\text{Net Income}}{\text{Net Sales}}\right)$	5.0%	4.0%	3.0%
Return on Equity $\left(\dfrac{\text{Net Income}}{\text{Equity}}\right)$	10.0%	8.0%	12.0%

To an economist, this result suggests that investors earning 8% to 10% in Company A and Company B's industry will seek to shift their capital to Company C's industry, where 12% returns are available. The credit implication of this migration of capital is that Companies A and B will have greater difficulty raising funds and therefore less financial flexibility. The credit impact on Company C, conversely, is favorable.

There are several variants of the rate-of-return combination ratio, each with a specific analytical application. Return on equity, which has already been alluded to, measures a firm's productivity of equity and therefore provides an indication of its ability to attract a form of capital that provides an important cushion for the debtholder:

$$\text{Return on equity} = \frac{\text{Net income}}{\text{Common equity} + \text{Preferred equity}}$$

In calculating this ratio, analysts most commonly use as the denominator equity as of the final day of the year in which the company earned the income shown in the numerator. This method may sometimes produce distortions. For example, a company might raise a substantial amount of new equity near the end of the year. The denominator in the return on equity calculation would consequently be increased, but the numerator would not reflect the benefit of a full year's earnings on the new equity, since it was employed in the business for only a few days. Under these circumstances, return on equity will compare unfavorably (and unfairly) with that of a company that did not abruptly expand its equity base.

The potential for distortion in the return-on-equity calculation can be reduced somewhat by substituting for end-of-year equity so-called average equity:

$$\text{Return on average equity} = \frac{\text{Net income}}{(\text{Equity at beginning of year} + \text{Equity at end of year}) \div 2}$$

(Some analysts prefer this method to the year-end-based calculation, even when sudden changes in the equity account are not an issue.)

Another limitation of combination ratios that incorporate balance-sheet figures is that they have little meaning if calculated for portions of years. Suppose, for example, that in 1993 a company earns $6 million on year-end equity of $80 million, for a return on equity of 7.5%. During the first half of 1994 its net income is $4 million, of which it pays out $2 million in dividends, leaving it $82 million in equity at June 30, 1994.

With the company having earned in half a year two-thirds as much as it did during all of 1993, it is illogical to conclude that its return on equity has fallen from 7.5% to 4.9% ($4 million ÷ $82 million).

To derive a proper return on equity, it is necessary to annualize the earnings figure. Merely doubling the first half results can introduce some distortion, though, since the company's earnings may be seasonal. Even if not, there is no assurance that the first-half rate of profitability will be sustained in the second half. Accordingly, the best way to annualize earnings is to calculate a trailing 12-months' figure.

$$\frac{\text{Net income for second half of 1993} + \text{Net income for first half of 1994}}{\text{Equity at June 30, 1994}}$$

If the analyst is working with the company's 1993 annual report and 1994 second-quarter statement, 1993 second-half earnings will not be available without some backing out of numbers. For ease of calculation, the numerator in the preceding ratio can be derived as follows:

Net income for full year 1993
Less: Net income for first half of 1993
Plus: Net income for first half of 1994

For the credit analyst, return on equity alone may be an insufficient, or even a misleading, measure. The reason is that a company can raise its return on equity by increasing the proportion of debt in its capital structure, a change that reduces credit quality. In Exhibit 6–3, Company Y produces a higher return on equity than the more conservatively capitalized Company X, even though both have equivalent operating margins. Note that Company Y enjoys its edge despite having to pay a higher interest rate on account of its riskier financial structure.

Income statement ratios such as net margin and fixed-charge coverage, which point to higher credit quality at Company X, serve as a check against return on equity, which ranks Company Y higher. A later section of this chapter will explore systematic approaches to reconciling financial ratios that give contradictory indications about the relative credit quality of two or more companies. The more immediately relevant point, however, is that other combination ratios can also be used as checks against an artificially heightened return on equity. Using the same figures for Companies X and Y, the analyst can calculate return on total capital, which equalizes for differences in capital structure. On

EXHIBIT 6–3

Effect of Debt on Return on Equity
($000,000 omitted)

	Company X				Company Y			
	12/31/92		12/31/93		12/31/92		12/31/93	
Total Debt	$25.0	25.0%	$25.0	23.5%	$50.0	50.0%	$50.0	47.5%
Total Equity	75.0	75.0%	81.4	76.5%	50.0	50.0%	55.3	52.5%
Total Capital	$100.00	100.0%	$106.4	100.0%	$100.0	100.0%	$105.3	100.0%

1993 Results	Company X	Company Y
Sales	$125.0	$125.0
Operating Expenses	108.5	108.5
Operating Income	16.5	16.5
Interest Expense	2.0*	4.5**
Pretax Income	14.5	12.0
Income Taxes	4.9	4.1
Net Income	9.6	7.9
Dividends	3.2	2.6
Addition to Retained Earnings	6.4	5.3
Operating Margin	$\dfrac{16.5}{125.0} = 13.2\%$	$\dfrac{16.5}{125.0} = 13.2\%$
Net Margin	$\dfrac{9.6}{125.0} = 7.7\%$	$\dfrac{7.9}{125.0} = 6.3\%$
Return on Equity	$\dfrac{9.6}{81.4} = 11.8\%$	$\dfrac{7.9}{55.3} = 14.3\%$
Fixed-Charge Coverage	$\dfrac{9.6 + 4.9 + 2.0}{2.0} = 8.3\text{x}$	$\dfrac{7.9 + 4.1 + 4.5}{4.5} = 3.7\text{x}$

*At 8%.
**At 9%.

this basis, Company Y enjoys only a negligible advantage related to its slower growth in retained earnings (and hence in capital):

$$\text{Return on total capital} = \frac{\text{Net income} + \text{Income taxes} + \text{Interest expense}}{\text{Total debt} + \text{Total equity}}$$

Company X   **Company Y**

$$\frac{9.6 + 4.9 + 2.0}{25.0 + 81.4} = \frac{16.5}{106.4} = 15.5\% \qquad \frac{7.9 + 4.1 + 4.5}{50.0 + 55.3} = \frac{16.5}{105.3} = 15.7\%$$

Total debt in this calculation includes short-term debt, current maturities of long-term debt, and long-term debt, for reasons described earlier under "What Constitutes Total Debt?" Similarly, total equity includes both preferred and preference stock. If there is a minority interest, the associated income statement item should appear in the numerator, and the balance sheet amount in the denominator.

Turnover Measures

In addition to measuring return on investment, a particular type of combination ratio known as a turnover ratio can provide valuable information about asset quality. The underlying notion of a turnover ratio is that a company requires a certain level of receivables and inventory to support a given volume of sales. For example, if a manufacturer sells its goods on terms that require payment within 30 days, and all customers pay exactly on time, accounts receivable on any given day (barring seasonality in sales) will be 30 ÷ 365, or 8.2% of annual sales. Coming at the question from the opposite direction, the analyst can calculate the average length of time that a receivable remains outstanding before it is paid (the calculation uses the average amount of receivables outstanding during the year):

$$\text{Average days of receivables} = \frac{(\text{A/R beginning of yr.} + \text{A/R end of yr.}) \div 2}{\text{Annual sales}} \times 365$$

This ratio enables the analyst to learn the company's true average collection period, which may differ significantly from its stated collection period.

By inverting the first portion of the average days of receivables calculation, one can determine how many times per year the company turns over its receivables:

$$\text{Receivables turnover} = \frac{\text{Annual sales}}{(\text{ARBY} + \text{AREY}) \div 2}$$

where ARBY = Accounts receivable at beginning of year
AREY = Accounts receivable at the end of year

As long as a company continues to sell on the same terms, its required receivables level will rise as its sales rise, but the ratio between the two should not change. A decline in the ratio may signal that the company's customers are paying more slowly because they are encountering financial difficulties. Alternatively, the company may be trying to increase its sales by liberalizing its credit standards, allowing its salespeople to do more business with less financially capable customers. Either way, the ultimate collectibility of the accounts receivable shown on the balance sheet has become less certain. Unless the company has reflected this fact by increasing its allowance for doubtful receivables, it may have to write off a portion of receivables against income at some point in the future. The analyst should therefore adjust the company's total-debt-to-total-capital ratio for the implicit overstatement of equity.

Another asset quality problem that can be detected with a combination ratio involves unsalable inventory. A fashion retailer's leftover garments from the last season or an electronics manufacturer's obsolete finished goods can be worth far less than their balance-sheet values (historical cost). If the company is postponing an inevitable write-off, it may become apparent through a rise in inventory without a commensurate rise in sales, resulting in a decline in inventory turnover:

$$\text{Inventory turnover} = \frac{\text{Annual sales}}{(\text{IBY} + \text{IEY}) \div 2}$$

A drop in sales is another possible explanation of declining inventory turnover. In this case, the inventory may not have suffered a severe reduction in value, but there are nevertheless unfavorable implications for credit quality. Until the inventory glut can be worked off by cutting back production to match the lower sales volume, the company may have to borrow to finance its unusually high working capital, thereby increasing its financial leverage. Profitability may also suffer as the company cuts its selling prices, accepting a lower margin to eliminate excess inventory.

One objection to the preceding inventory-turnover calculation involves the variability of selling prices. Suppose, for example, that the price of a commodity chemical suddenly shoots up as the result of a temporary shortage. A chemical producer's annual sales—and hence its inventory turnover—may rise, yet the company may not be physically moving its inventory any faster than before. Conversely, a retailer may respond to a drop in consumer demand and cut its prices to avoid a buildup of inventory. The shelves and back room have no more product than previously, yet the ratio based on annual sales indicates that turnover has declined.

To prevent such distortions, the analyst can use the following variant ratio:

$$\text{Inventory turnover} = \frac{\text{Annual cost of goods sold}}{(\text{IBY} + \text{IEY}) \div 2}$$

This version should more closely capture the reality of a company's physical turnover. Cost of goods sold and inventory are both based on historical cost, whereas selling prices fluctuate with market conditions, causing a mismatch between the numerator and denominator of the turnover calculation.

Total-Debt-to-Cash-Flow Ratio

A final combination ratio that is invaluable in credit analysis is the ratio of total debt to cash flow:

$$\text{Total debt to cash flow} = \frac{\substack{\text{Short-term debt} + \text{Current maturities} \\ + \text{Long-term debt}}}{\text{Cash flow from operations}}$$

This ratio expresses a company's financial flexibility in a most interesting way. If, for the sake of illustration, a company has total debt of $60 million and cash flow from operations of $20 million, it has the ability to liquidate all its debt in three years by dedicating 100% of its cash flow to that purpose. This company clearly has greater financial flexibility than a company with $80 million of debt and a $10-million annual cash flow, for an eight-year debt-payback period. In the latter case, flexibility would be particularly limited if the company's debt had an average maturity of significantly less than eight years, implying the possibility of significant refinancing pressure under tight credit conditions.

All very interesting, one might say, but in reality how many companies dedicate 100% of their cash flow to debt retirement? The answer is "very few," but total debt to cash flow is still a good ratio to monitor for credit quality. It enjoys distinct advantages over some of the more frequently invoked credit-quality measures, which are derived from the balance sheet or income statement alone. The total-debt-to-total-capital ratio has the inherent flaw that equity may be understated or overstated relative to its economic value, since the accounting rules do not permit a writeup of assets unless they are sold, nor require a writedown until someone makes the often subjective determination that they have fallen in value. In comparison, total debt is an objective number, a dollar amount that must contractually be repaid. Fixed-charge coverage, too, has a weakness, for it is based on earnings, which are subject to considerable manipulation. Cash flow eliminates one major opportunity for manipulation—underdepreciation. If a company inflates its reported earnings by writing down its fixed assets more slowly than economic reality dictates, it is merely taking money out of one cash flow pocket and putting it into the other. Cash flow, then, puts companies on equal footing, whatever their depreciation policies.

Built from two comparatively hard numbers, the ratio of total debt to cash flow provides one of the best single measures of credit quality. Analysts should not worry about whether its literal interpretation—the period required for a total liquidation of debt—is realistic, but instead focus on its analytical value.

RELATING RATIOS TO CREDIT RISK

The discussion of financial ratios up to this point has sidestepped an obvious and critical question: How does an analyst who has calculated a ratio know whether it represents good, bad, or indifferent credit quality? Somehow, the analyst must relate the ratio to the borrower's propensity to pay interest and principal in full and on schedule. In practice, this is accomplished by testing financial ratios as predictors of the borrower's propensity *not* to pay (to default). After identifying the factors that create high default risk, the analyst can use ratios to rank all borrowers on a relative scale of propensity to default. All other things being equal, for instance, a company with high financial leverage is more likely to default than one with low leverage. Similarly, high fixed-charge coverage implies less default risk than low coverage.

For many credit analysts, ratio analysis is conducted within an established ranking framework. Individuals employed at processing loan applications, for instance, may be provided with criteria based on the lending institution's experience over many years in recognizing the financial characteristics that lead to timely payment or to default. In the securities field, bond ratings (see Exhibits 6–4 and 6–5) provide a structure for analysis. Because much credit work is done in the context of established standards, the text will first explain how companies can be ranked by ratios on a relative scale of credit quality—specifically using bond ratings as the standard. Then this chapter will explore the methods underlying the construction of standards, that is, the process of relating financial ratios directly to default risk.

EXHIBIT 6–4   Moody's Bond Ratings

Moody's ratings indicate gradations of investment quality. In the generic rating classifications from Aa to B, Moody's applies numerical modifiers. For example, A1 quality ranks in the higher end of the A category, A2 in the middle range, and A3 in the lower end of the A category.

Definitions

Aaa	Best quality. Large or exceptionally stable margin of protection for interest payments and secure principal.
Aa	High quality by all standards, but somewhat riskier long-term than Aaa, based on smaller margins or more widely fluctuating margins of protection.
A	Upper medium grade. Security of principal and interest is adequate but susceptible to change in the future.
Baa	Medium grade. Security of principal and interest appears adequate for present, but certain protective elements may be lacking or unreliable over time. Some speculative characteristics.
Ba	Speculative elements. Protection of interest and principal may be very moderate and not well safeguarded for the future.
B	Generally lacking in characteristics of the desirable investment. May have small assurance of interest and principal payments over long periods.
Caa	Poor standing. May be in default or have elements of danger regarding principal or interest.
Ca	Highly speculative. May be in default.
C	Lowest rated. Poor prospects of ever attaining any real investment standing.

Source: Moody's Investors Service.

The analysis presented in this section focuses primarily on determining whether a borrower is likely to pay interest and repay interest on schedule and in full, rather than the percentage of principal that the lender is likely to recover in the event of default. Certainly, the latter consideration is significant in the decision to extend or deny credit, as well as in the valuation of debt securities. Bankruptcy analysis, however, is a huge topic in its own right. Its proper practice depends on a detailed knowledge of the relevant legislation and a thorough understanding of the dynamics of the negotiations between creditors and the management of a company in Chapter 11 reorganization proceedings. Such matters are beyond the scope of the present work. Furthermore, the percentage of potential recovery tends to be a comparatively minor valuation factor for

EXHIBIT 6–5   Standard & Poor's Bond Ratings

Standard & Poor's ratings are current assessments of the creditworthiness of an obligor with respect to a specific obligation. For the ratings from AA to CCC, Standard & Poor's may add a plus (+) or minus (−) modifier to show relative standing within the major categories.

Definitions

AAA   Extremely strong capacity to pay interest and repay principal.

AA   Very strong capacity to pay interest and repay principal.

A   Strong capacity to pay interest and repay principal, but somewhat more susceptible to adverse changes in circumstances and economic conditions than higher rated issues.

BBB   Adequate capacity to pay interest and repay principal.

Predominantly Speculative Categories

BB   Less vulnerable to default in near term than lower categories, but faced with ongoing uncertainties or exposed to conditions that could lead to inadequate capacity for timely interest and principal payments. Also used for debt subordinated to senior debt with an actual or implied BBB − rating.

B   Currently has capacity to meet interest payments and principal repayments but with greater vulnerability to default than BB category. Also used for debt subordinated to senior debt with an actual or implied BB or BB − rating.

CCC   Has a currently identifiable vulnerability to default. Dependent on favorable conditions to meet timely payment of interest and repayment of principal. Also used for debt subordinated to senior debt with an actual or implied B or B − rating.

CC   Usually applied to debt subordinated to senior debt with an actual or implied CCC rating.

C   Usually applied to debt subordinated to senior debt with an actual or implied CCC − rating. May indicate that a bankruptcy petition has been filed but debt-service payments are continuing.

C1   Reserved for income bonds (which pay interest only if earned) on which no interest is being paid.

D   In default on payments. Used even if grace period for interest payments has not expired, unless Standard & Poor's believes that such payments will be made during the grace period. Also used upon filing of bankruptcy petition if debt service payments are jeopardized.

Source: Standard & Poor's.

securities of highly rated companies, for which the probability of bankruptcy over the short to intermediate term is ordinarily small.

While the reader will not find a complete guide to bankruptcy analysis in these pages, Chapter 7 is relevant from the standpoint of determining the failed firm's equity value, a key step in the process of reorganizing or liquidating the company. In addition, the Bibliography includes books that discuss aspects of bankruptcy in extensive detail.

Comparative Ratio Analysis

The basic technique in assigning a relative credit ranking is to compare a company's ratio with those of a peer group.

An essential qualification for belonging to a credit quality peer group is for the groups to be of comparable size. Of two firms with similar financial ratios, a manufacturer with $1 billion in annual sales will ordinarily be a better credit risk than one with $5 million in sales. As a generalization, bigger companies enjoy manufacturing economies of scale and greater leverage with suppliers because of their larger purchasing power. A big firm can spread the risks of obsolescence and competitive challenges over a wide range of products and customers, whereas a smaller company's sales are likely to be concentrated on a few products and customers. Particularly vulnerable is a company with just a single manufacturing facility; an unexpected loss of production could prove fatal. Lack of depth in management is another problem commonly associated with smaller companies. Statistical models of default risk confirm the expectations created by these qualitative considerations, notwithstanding that some very large companies have failed and that there is ample evidence of inefficiency in large, bureaucratic organizations. Therefore, it is not surprising that the bond rating agencies effectively create size-based peer groups.

In an analysis I conducted in 1986, for example, Standard & Poor's Compustat database listed more than 250 industrial companies with investment grade (BBB− or higher) ratings. Of these, only two had shareholders' equity of less than $100 million, and one of the two exceptions was rated BBB− only on the strength of the implicit support of a larger parent. The inference—corroborated by statements from Standard & Poor's—was that companies with less than $100 million of net worth were placed in a separate peer group for rating purposes, namely, the speculative grade (BB+ and lower) group.

Line of business is another basis for defining a peer group. Because different industries have different financial characteristics, ratio comparisons across industry lines may not be valid.

For example, a machinery manufacturer's sales may fluctuate substantially over the capital goods cycle. In contrast, a packaged food company derives its revenues from essential products that are in demand year in and year out. The food processor therefore has greater predictability of earnings and cash flow. It can tolerate a higher level of fixed charges, implying a larger proportion of debt in its capital structure, than the machinery manufacturer. The rating agencies may assign Double-A ratings to a food company with a 28% ratio of total debt to total capital, whereas a machinery maker with a similar ratio might be rated no higher than Single-A.

A ratio comparison between a packaged food producer and a machinery manufacturer sheds little light. The latter company can look "good" in comparison with the former, yet still be too highly leveraged in view of the operating risks in its industry. Comparability problems become even more pronounced when ratio analysis crosses boundaries of broadly defined sectors of the economy (e.g., industrial, financial, utility, and transportation).

Carrying this principle to its logical conclusion, however, requires a peer group consisting of companies with virtually identical product lines, for operating risk varies to some extent even among closely allied businesses. Strictly speaking, a producer of coated white paper is not comparable to a producer of kraft linerboard, nor a producer of facial tissue to a producer of fine writing paper. Too zealous an effort to create homogeneous peer groups, though, narrows the field to such an extent that ratio comparisons begin to suffer from having too few data points. At the extreme, a comparison with only one other peer company is not terribly informative. The company being evaluated may rank above its lone peer, but the analyst does not know whether the peer is strong or weak. In contrast, suppose a company ranks fourth on a particular financial ratio among a peer group of 10 companies, with 8 in the group tightly distributed around the median and with 1 outlier each at the high and low ends. A statement that the company in question has average risk within its group (based on one particular ratio) is reasonably well supported in this case.

There are two techniques for resolving the tradeoff between strict comparability and sufficient sample size. By employing both, the analyst can achieve a satisfactory assessment of relative credit risk.

One technique is to compare the company within a narrowly defined industry peer group, as in Exhibit 6–6. The credit analyst can use this type of analysis to "slot" a company within an industry.

Note that the ratios in the sample comparison are averages, computed over three years. Averaging minimizes the impact of highly atypical results that any company may report in a single year. Observe as well that the peer group includes only oil companies and is further restricted to the major and integrated competitors. (An integrated company produces, transports, refines, and markets petroleum, whereas an independent company typically is engaged in only one of those processes.)

Texaco has the median ratios (number 5 out of 9) in all three categories shown—pretax interest coverage, funds flow as a percentage of total debt, and total debt as a percentage of capital. It is therefore appropriately rated exactly in the middle range of its peer group. That is, Texaco's A+ Standard & Poor's rating is midway between the industry's highest (AAA) and lowest (BBB) ratings.

Exhibit 6–6 also brings out an important characteristic of financial ratios, namely, their interrelatedness. Not only Texaco, but the other major and integrated oil companies as well tend to be ranked similarly on each of the ratios shown. This is not surprising, since it would be difficult for a company to have, for example, both a comparatively high ratio of debt to capital and a comparatively high level of interest coverage. It can happen, through some combination of unusually low-cost debt and exceptionally high return of capital, but is hardly a common occurrence. More often, companies with high financial leverage have low fixed charge coverage.

An important implication of this observation is that beyond a certain point, calculating and comparing a still greater number of financial ratios adds little additional understanding. Each new ratio essentially represents a new way of expressing information already contained in the analysis. Analysts should avoid the trap of adding ratios without adding understanding. Instead, they should use a limited number of ratios to extract the bulk of the information that can be derived through this mode of analysis. Remaining time and energy can be put to best use by searching for other pertinent facts, both inside and outside the financial statements.

A second comparative ratio analysis technique is to rank a company within a rating peer group. As already noted, it is not appropriate to compare companies in different economic sectors, such as industrials and utilities. A rating peer group can, however, legitimately include a variety of companies within the industry sector. Using the larger sample made

EXHIBIT 6-6

Comparative Ratio Analysis of Major and Large Integrated Oil Companies Annual Average 1990–1992

	Pretax Interest Coverage			Funds Flow as a Percentage of Total Debt			Total Debt as a Percentage of Capital		
	Standard & Poor's			Standard & Poor's			Standard & Poor's		
Rank	Rating	Company	Times	Rating	Company	Percentage	Rating	Company	Percentage
1	AAA	EXXON	6.37	AAA	EXXON	71.7	AAA	EXXON	29.2
2	AA	Chevron	5.81	AAA	Amoco	59.6	AAA	Amoco	31.6
3	AAA	Amoco	5.78	AA	Mobil	51.7	AA	Mobil	34.9
4	AA	Mobil	5.66	AA	Chevron	50.7	AA	Chevron	36.0
5	A+	Texaco	3.51	A+	Texaco	46.0	A+	Texaco	41.3
6	A+	Atlantic Richfield	3.13	A+	Atlantic Richfield	34.9	A+	Atlantic Richfield	54.9
7	BBB	Phillips Petroleum	2.58	BBB	Phillips Petroleum	30.7	BBB	Phillips Petroleum	58.6
8	BBB*	Unocal	1.90	BBB*	Unocal	27.0	BBB*	Unocal	61.9
9	BBB	Occidental Petroleum	1.27	BBB	Occidental Petroleum	14.9	BBB	Occidental Petroleum	64.7

*Rating of Union Oil of California subsidiary.

available through this approach, the analyst can fine-tune the slotting achieved with the industry group technique.

Instead of showing ratios for all 125 industrial companies rated Single-A by Standard & Poor's, Exhibit 6–7 lists the medians for the Single-A group. As a further aid in slotting companies, the table includes the cutoff points for the upper and lower quartiles in the rankings of Single-A companies.

Texaco's rating at the high end (A+) of the Single-A peer group is consistent with its ranking on the measure of funds from operations as a percentage of total debt. At 46.0%, Texaco is above the median of 37.0%. The company is also slightly above the median (41.3% vs. 40.3%) on the measure of total debt as a percentage of capitalization, but in that case, a lower ratio is desirable. As for pretax interest coverage, Texaco falls below the Single-A median (3.51x vs. 4.14x), although not as low as the bottom quartile (3.20x).

Does Texaco's overall showing imply that the company is overrated by Standard & Poor's? In some cases, this sort of result provides a clue that a downgrading may indeed be expected before long. At other times, a seeming mismatch of ratings and ratios merely points out certain subtleties of the ratio comparison process. The most important of these is the influence of the direction, as opposed to the level, of a ratio.

Ratio Trend Analysis

Comparative ratio analysis is an effective technique for assessing relative credit risk, yet it leaves the analyst exposed to a major source of error. Suppose two companies in the same industry posted an identical

EXHIBIT 6–7

**Average Ratios for Standard & Poor's Single-A Industrials
1990–1992**

	Pretax Interest Coverage	Funds from Operations as a Percentage of Total Debt	Total Debt as a Percentage of Capitilization (Including Short-Term Debt)
Upper Quartile	6.37	54.5	49.3
Medium	4.14	37.0	40.3
Lower Quartile	3.20	27.1	30.9

Source: Standard & Poor's Creditstats, October 27, 1993.

fixed-charge coverage of 3.5 times last year. On a ratio comparison, the two appear to be equally risky. What if, however, one company had coverage of 5.0 times five years ago and has steadily declined to 3.5 times, while the other has improved over the same period from 2.0 times to 3.5 times? If further analysis suggests that the two companies' trends are likely to continue, then the coincidence that they are both currently at 3.5 times should have little bearing on one's credit assessment. The better risk is the company that will have stronger coverage in the future.

A further complication is that improving or deteriorating financial ratios can have different implications for different companies. In some cases, a declining trend over several years signals that a company has genuinely fallen to a new, lower level of credit quality. For other companies, negative year-over-year comparisons merely represent the downlegs of their normal operating cycles.

Certain industries enjoy fairly stable demand, year in and year out. Small-ticket nondurables such as food, beverages, and beauty aids are not items that consumers cease to buy during recessions. At most, they trade down to cheaper goods within the same categories. In contrast, people tend to postpone purchases of big-ticket durable goods when credit is tight or when they have misgivings about economic conditions. Producers of automobiles, houses, and major appliances are among the businesses that experience wide swings in demand between peaks and troughs in the economy. Profits typically fluctuate even more dramatically in these industries, due to the high fixed costs entailed in capital-intensive production methods.

In evaluating the long-range creditworthiness of cyclical companies, the bond rating agencies focus on cycle-to-cycle, rather than year-to-year trends. A cycle-to-cycle pattern of similar highs and similar lows (Exhibit 6–8) does not imply any impairment of financial strength. Deterioration is indicated only when a company displays a trend of successively lower highs and lower lows (Exhibit 6–9).

As a practical matter, it can be difficult to distinguish a normal, cyclical decline from more permanent deterioration, without the benefit of hindsight. It may be that the company is genuinely incurring a nonrecurring loss at a point at which its earnings are already at a cyclically depressed level. On the other hand, management may be attempting to portray a permanent reduction in profitability as a standard cyclical slump. The analyst must look beyond the financial statements to make an informed judgment about the truth of the matter.

During 1988–1990, both Data General and International Paper showed erosion in coverage of interest charges (Exhibit 6–10). Only Data General

EXHIBIT 6-8   Cycle-to-Cycle Stability (Similar highs and lows)

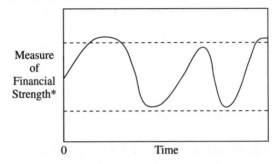

*Examples: Operating margin, fixed charge coverage, ratio of cash flow to total debt.

suffered a downgrading by Moody's during the period, however. The computer maker's senior debt rating fell from Baa3 to Ba1 in 1989, then dropped to B2 in 1990. International Paper, in contrast, remained at A3 throughout the period. As a matter of fact, the paper producer's rating held steady even in 1991, when its interest coverage finally bottomed out at 2.89 times.

Part of the difference, no doubt, was the greater magnitude of Data General's decline between 1988 and 1990 (3.20 times to −5.10 times vs. 8.07 times to 4.74 times). Furthermore, International Paper, unlike Data General, did not go into the red. On the other hand, Data General began the period at a lower rating than International Paper, which would be

EXHIBIT 6-9   Cycle-to-Cycle Deterioration (Successively lower highs and lower lows)

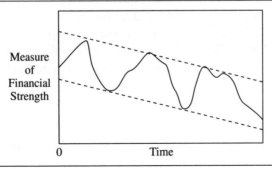

EXHIBIT 6–10   Comparative Trend in Interest Coverage (Times)

	1988	1989	1990
Data General	8.07	7.45	4.74
International Paper	3.20	−3.30	−5.10

Source: Moody's Investors Service.

consistent with an expectation of wider swings in profit over the course of a cycle.

There was a larger reason, however, for the paper company's retention of its rating, even as the computer manufacturer was moving steadily lower on the Moody's scale. The rating agency judged, at least in the period 1988–1990, that International Paper and its industry were not undergoing fundamental, long-range deterioration. Coverage was moving down, but not toward a meaningfully lower low than in previous cycles, according to Moody's.

The agency viewed Data General very differently. In the computer company's case, Moody's perceived extreme competitiveness in an industry characterized by "dismal" conditions. At the source of the problem, argued the agency, were swift advances in computer technology and a move toward open systems. In the agency's view, proprietary mainframe and minicomputer systems had been rendered obsolete by these changes, forcing companies such as Data General to adapt quickly, simply to survive.[6]

In view of the fundamental turn for the worse in Data General's business, Moody's interpreted the short-term erosion in coverage as evidence of a cycle-to-cycle downtrend. Even considering the red ink, however, the agency's interpretation was not a foregone conclusion. Only by looking at the business fundamentals, rather than the numbers alone, was Moody's justified in taking the rating down twice during the period.

A final method of putting credit-quality ratios into context is to compare them with averages for specified rating categories. Exhibit 6–11 provides median ratios, by ratings, for industrial companies over the period 1990–1992. Viewing figures of this type over a multiyear period normalizes the data to some extent for fluctuations in the general level of business activity.

---

[6]Juanita Mayr, "Data General Corporation," Moody's Investors Service, February 19, 1993.

EXHIBIT 6–11

Median Ratios by Bond Rating Category
(Industrials, 1990–1992)

	AAA	AA	A	BBB	BB	B	CCC
Pretax interest coverage (x)	16.7	9.31	4.41	2.30	1.31	0.77	(0.06)
Pretax interest coverage including rents (x)	6.77	4.83	2.93	1.80	1.23	0.88	0.54
EBITDA interest coverage (x)	20.12	12.67	6.42	4.02	2.36	1.51	0.57
Funds from operations/total debt (%)	128.5	72.7	43.1	27.7	16.1	9.2	4.8
Free operating cash flow/total debt (%)	34.8	30.6	13.3	4.1	1.3	(1.9)	2.7
Pretax return on permanent capital employed (%)	28.2	19.2	14.9	9.8	10.0	6.1	(0.4)
Operating income/sales (%)	21.6	16.0	13.9	12.3	10.3	9.7	9.8
Long-term debt/capitalization (%)	11.1	17.0	29.7	40.4	53.0	56.8	74.8
Total debt/capitalization including short-term debt (%)	21.9	26.4	37.2	46.5	59.7	65.9	84.6
Total debt/capitalization including short-term debt (including 8 times rents) (%)	33.0	37.8	48.1	58.5	72.7	75.1	87.1

Source: Standard & Poor's Creditstats, October 27, 1993.

Default Risk Models

As noted previously, comparative ratio analysis and ratio trend analysis are techniques for placing companies on a relative scale of credit quality. Many analysts have no need to look more deeply into the matter, but it is impossible to cover the topic of credit analysis satisfactorily without discussing two more fundamental issues. First, there is the question of how to set up a ranking scheme such as bond ratings in the first place. Second, there is the problem of conflicting indicators. How, for example, should an analyst evaluate a company that ranks well on fixed-charge coverage but poorly on financial leverage? A rigorous approach demands something more scientific than an individual analyst's subjective opinion that coverage should, for example, be weighted twice as heavily as leverage, or vice versa.

The solution to both of these problems lies in establishing a statistical relationship between financial ratios and default. This requires, first of all, collecting data on the default experience in a given population. Next, statistical methods are employed to determine which financial ratios have most reliably predicted defaults. Using a model derived from the best predictors, the analyst can then rank companies on the basis of how closely their financial profiles resemble the profiles of companies that defaulted.

One example of the various models that have been devised to predict defaults is Edward I. Altman's Z-Score model, which takes the following form:

$$Z = 1.4x_1 + 1.2x_2 + 3.3x_3 + 0.6x_4 + 1.0x_5$$

where x_1 = Working capital/Total assets (%, e.g., .20, or 20%)
x_2 = Retained earnings/Total assets (%)
x_3 = Earnings before interest and taxes/Total assets (%)
x_4 = Market value of equity/Total liabilities (%)
x_5 = Sales/Total assets (number of times, e.g., 2.0 times)

In this model, scores below 1.81 signify serious credit problems, while a score above 3.0 indicates a healthy firm.

A refinement of the Z-Score model, the Zeta model developed by Altman and his colleagues,[7] achieved greater predictive accuracy by using the following variables:

---

[7]See Edward I. Altman, Robert G. Haldeman, and Paul Narayanan, "Zeta Analysis: A New Model to Identify Bankruptcy Risk of Corporations," *Journal of Banking and Finance* (June 1977): 29–54.

x_1 = Earnings before interest and taxes (EBIT)/Total assets

x_2 = Standard error of estimate of EBIT/Total assets (normalized) for 10 years

x_3 = EBIT/Interest charges

x_4 = Retained earnings/Total assets

x_5 = Current assets/Current liabilities

x_6 = Five-year average market value of equity/Total capitalization

x_7 = Total tangible assets, normalized

Quantitative models such as Zeta, as well as others that have been devised using various mathematical techniques, have several distinct benefits. First, they are developed by objectively correlating financial variables with defaults. They consequently avoid guesswork in assigning relative weights to the variables. Second, the record of quantitative models is excellent from the standpoint of classifying as troubled credits most companies that subsequently defaulted. In addition, the scores assigned to nondefaulted companies by these models correlate fairly well with bond ratings. This suggests that although Moody's and Standard & Poor's originally developed their rating methods along more subjective lines, their conclusions are at least partially vindicated by statistical measures of default risk. Therefore, the credit analyst can feel comfortable about using methods such as ratio trend analysis to slot companies within the ratings framework. Although one can quarrel with the rating agencies' assessments of particular companies or particular industries, there is statistical support for the notion that in the aggregate, ratings provide a valid, if rough, assessment of default risk.[8]

Useful as they are, though, quantitative default models cannot entirely replace human judgment in credit analysis.

For one thing, quantitative models tend to classify as troubled credits not only most of the companies that eventually default, but also many that do not default. Often, firms that fall into financial peril bring in new management and are revitalized without ever failing in their debt service. If faced with a huge capital loss on the bonds of a financially distressed company, an institutional investor might wish to assess the probability of a turnaround—an inherently difficult-to-quantify prospect—instead of selling purely on the basis of a default model.

---

[8]See, for example, K. Scott Douglass and Douglas J. Lucas, "Historical Default Rates of Corporate Bond Issuers 1970–1988," Moody's Investors Service (July 1988). The study found that for periods of as much as 15 years after issuance, the incidence of default rose with each letter-grade reduction in credit quality.

By the same token, the credit analyst must bear in mind that companies can default for reasons that a model based on reported financial data cannot pick up. In recent years, several major corporations have filed for bankruptcy despite the absence of clear indications of imminent insolvency. A. H. Robbins filed for bankruptcy in 1985, when it faced the prospect of paying massive damages in litigation related to injuries linked to one of its products, the Dalkon Shield intrauterine device. Smith International's 1986 bankruptcy was also related to litigation, specifically, a patent infringement suit brought by Hughes Tool. Texaco defaulted in 1987 as a consequence of a multibillion-dollar judgment awarded to Pennzoil in a dispute over Texaco's acquisition of Getty Oil. U.S. Brass entered Chapter 11 proceedings in 1994 in an effort to resolve litigation involving defective plastic-plumbing systems that it had manufactured. In none of these cases did the defaulting company's balance sheet or income statement signal an impending collapse. U.S. Brass's parent company, Eljer Industries, specifically indicated that the bankruptcy filing did not result from a cash flow shortfall. The problems were apparent in the firm's Notes to Financial Statements, but quantitative default models do not deal with contingent liabilities. (One could conceivably attempt to factor these items into a model. Subjective judgment would, however, be required to determine the probability that huge claims—which are commonplace in financial reports—might actually result in solvency-threatening outlays.)

CONCLUSION

Ultimately, then, default risk models can provide a solid foundation for credit analysis but must be complemented by the analyst's judgment on matters too complex to be modeled. Much the same applies to all of the quantitative techniques discussed in this chapter. A lender should not provide credit before first "running the numbers." By the same token, one should never build a case based solely on the numbers in order to avoid a difficult decision. This can take the form either of rejecting a reasonable risk by too rigidly applying quantitative criteria, or of approving a credit against one's better judgment while counting on technically satisfactory financial ratios as a defense against criticism if the loan goes bad. As other chapters in this book demonstrate, financial statements are vulnerable to manipulation, much of which is perfectly legal. Often, those doing the manipulation are specifically trying to outfox credit analysts who mechanically calculate ratios without pausing to consider whether the purposes underlying the ratios have been undone by accounting ruses. Another danger in relying too heavily on quantitative analysis is that (as described more fully in Chapter 2) a company may radically alter its capital structure to finance an acquisition or to defend itself against a hostile takeover. Such action can render ratio analysis on even the most recent financial statements largely irrelevant. In the end, credit analysts must equip themselves with all the tools described in this chapter, yet not be made complacent by them.

7

EQUITY ANALYSIS

COUNTLESS BOOKS HAVE been written on the subject of "picking stocks." The approaches represented in their pages range from technical analysis, which seeks to establish the value of a common equity by studying its past price behavior, to expounding of the Efficient Market Hypothesis, which implies that no sort of analysis whatsoever can identify values not already recognized and properly discounted by the market.

This chapter does not attempt to summarize or criticize all the methods employed by the legions who "play the market." Rather, the discussion that follows focuses primarily on the use of financial statements in fundamental analysis, which is the attempt to determine whether a company's stock is fairly valued, based on its financial characteristics.

Note that certain elements of fundamental analysis do *not* utilize information found in the financial statements. For example, a company may seem like a good candidate for a "bust-up"—a hostile takeover premised on selling portions of the company to realize value not reflected in its stock price. As discussed later in this chapter, the analyst can estimate the firm's ostensible breakup value by studying its annual report. The feasibility of a hostile raid, however, may hinge on the pattern of share ownership, the availability of financing for a takeover, and applicable laws relating to tender offers. All these factors lie outside the realm of financial-statement analysis but may have a major bearing on the valuation process.

A final point regarding the following material is that it should be read in conjunction with Chapter 5. A company's equity value lies wholly in its future performance, with historical financial statements aiding the analysis only to the extent that they provide a basis for projecting future results.

Into the formulas detailed in this chapter, the analyst must plug earnings and cash flow forecasts derived by the techniques described in Chapter 5.

THE DIVIDEND-DISCOUNT MODEL

Several different methods of fundamental common stock analysis have been devised over the years, but few match the intuitive appeal of regarding the stock price as the discounted value of expected future dividends. This approach is analogous to the yield-to-maturity calculation for a bond and therefore facilitates the comparison of different securities of a single issuer. Additionally, the method permits the analyst to address the uncertainty inherent in forecasting a noncontractual flow[1] by varying the applicable discount rate.

To understand the relationship between future dividends and present stock price, consider the following fictitious example: Tarheel Tobacco's annual common dividend rate is currently $2.10 a share. Because the company's share of a nonexpanding market is neither increasing nor decreasing, it will probably generate flat sales and earnings for the indefinite future and continue the dividend at its current level. Tarheel's long-term debt currently offers a yield of 10%, reflecting the company's credit rating and the prevailing level of interest rates. Based on the greater uncertainty of the dividend stream relative to the contractual payments on Tarheel's debt, investors demand a risk premium of four percentage points—a return of 10% + 4% = 14%—to own the company's common stock rather than its bonds.

The stock price that should logically be observed in the market, given these facts, is the price at which Tarheel's annual $2.10 payout equates to a 14% yield, or algebraically:

$$P = \frac{D}{K}$$

$$P = \frac{\$2.10}{.14}$$

$$P = \$15.00$$

---

[1]Dividends, unlike interest payments on debt, are payable at the discretion of the board of directors, rather than in fulfillment of a contractual obligation. They are consequently subject to greater variability—through reduction, increase, or suspension—than bond coupons or scheduled principal payments.

where P = Current stock price
      D = Current dividend rate
      K = Required rate of return

If the analyst agrees that 14% is an appropriate discount rate, based on a financial comparison between Tarheel and other companies with similar implicit discount rates, then any price less than $15 a share indicates that the stock is undervalued. Alternatively, suppose the analyst concludes that Tarheel's future dividend stream is less secure than the dividend streams of other companies to which a 14% discount rate is being applied. The analyst might then discount Tarheel's stream at a higher rate, say 15%, and recalculate the appropriate share price as follows:

$$P = \frac{\$2.10}{.15}$$

$$P = \$14.00$$

A market price of $15 a share would then indicate an overvaluation of Tarheel Tobacco.

Dividends and Future Appreciation

When first introduced to the dividend-discount model, many individuals respond by saying, "Dividends are not the only potential source of gain to the stockholder. The share price may rise as well. Shouldn't any evaluation reflect the potential for appreciation?"

It is in responding to this objection that the dividend-discount model displays its elegance most fully. The answer is that there is no reason for the stock price to rise in the future unless the dividend rises. In a no-growth situation such as Tarheel Tobacco, the valuation will look the same five yeras hence (assuming no change in interest rates and risk premiums) as today. There is consequently no fundamental reason for a buyer to pay more for the stock at that point. If, on the other hand, the dividend payout rises over time (the case that immediately follows), the stock *will* be worth more in the future than it is today. The analyst can, however, incorporate the expected dividend increases directly into the present-value calculation to derive the current stock price, without bothering to determine and discount back the associated future price appreciation. By thinking through the logic of the discounting method, the analyst will find that value always comes back to dividends.

Valuing a Growing Company

No-growth companies are simple to analyze, but in practice most public corporations strive for growth in earnings per share, which, as the ensuing discussion will demonstrate, leads to gains for shareholders. In analyzing growing companies, a somewhat more complex formula must be used to equate future dividends to the present stock price:

$$P = \frac{D(1 + g)^1}{(1 + K)^1} + \frac{D(1 + g)^2}{(1 + K)^2} + \cdots \frac{D(1 + g)^n}{(1 + K)^n}$$

where P = Current stock price
D = Current dividend rate
K = Required rate of return
g = Growth rate

A number of dollars equivalent to *P,* if invested at an interest rate equivalent to *K,* will be equal, after *n* periods, to the cumulative value of dividends paid over the same interval, assuming the payout is initially an amount equivalent to *D* and increases in each period at a rate equivalent to *g.*

Fortunately, from the standpoint of ease of calculation, if *n*—the number of periods considered—is infinite, the preceding formula reduces to the simpler form:

$$P = \frac{D}{K - g}$$

In practice, this is the form ordinarily used in analysis, since companies are presumed to continue to operate as going concerns, rather than to liquidate at some arbitrary future date.

Figures projected from the financial statements of the fictitious Wolfe Food Company (Exhibit 7–1) illustrate the application of the dividend-discount model. Observe that the company is expected to pay out 33⅓% of its earnings to shareholders in the current year:

$$\text{Dividend-payout ratio} = \frac{\text{Dividends to common shareholders}}{\text{Net income available to common shareholders}}$$

$$= \frac{\$15,000,000}{\$45,000,000}$$

$$= 33\tfrac{1}{3}\%$$

EXHIBIT 7–1   Selected Financial Data

Wolfe Food Company

Net income available to common shareholders	$45,000,000
Dividends to common shareholders	$15,000,000
Common shares outstanding	10,000,000
Expected annual growth in earnings	10 %
Investors' required rate of return, given predictability of Wolfe's earnings	13 %

If Wolfe maintains a constant dividend-payout ratio, it follows that the growth rate of dividends will equal the growth rate of earnings, which is expected to be 10% annually. On a per-share basis, the initial dividend comes to $1.50:

$$\text{Dividend rate} = \frac{\text{Dividends to common shareholders}}{\text{Common shares outstanding}}$$

$$= \frac{\$15,000,000}{10,000,000}$$

$$= \$1.50 \text{ per share}$$

With these numbers, the analyst can now use the valuation formula to derive a share price of $50 for Wolfe:

$$P = \frac{D}{K - g}$$

$$P = \frac{\$1.50}{.13 - .10}$$

$$P = \frac{\$1.50}{.03}$$

$$P = \$50$$

The execution of this model rests heavily on the assumptions underlying the company's projected financial statements. To estimate the future growth rate of earnings, the analyst must make informed judgments both about the growth of the company's markets and about the company's ability to maintain or increase its share of those markets. Furthermore, the company's earnings growth rate may diverge from its sales growth due to changes in its operating margins—changes that may or may not reflect industrywide trends.

Because of the uncertainties affecting such projections, the analyst should apply to equity valuation the same sort of sensitivity analysis discussed in connection with financial forecasting (Chapter 5). For instance, if Wolfe Foods ultimately falls short of the 10% growth rate previously projected, then the $50 valuation will prove in retrospect to have been $12.50 too high:

$$P = \frac{D}{K - g}$$

$$P = \frac{\$1.50}{.13 - .09}$$

$$P = \$37.50$$

Therefore, an analyst whose forecast of earnings growth has a one-percentage-point margin of error should not put a strong "Buy" recommendation on Wolfe when it is trading at $45 a share. By the same token, a price of $25—which implies a 7% growth rate—can safely be regarded as an undervaluation, if other assumptions are valid.

Earnings or Cash Flow?

Intuitively appealing though it may be, the relating of share price to future dividends via projected earnings growth does not jibe perfectly with reality. In particular, highly cyclical companies do not produce steady earnings increases year in and year out, yet the formula $P = D/K - g$ demands a constant rate of growth. If, as assumed previously, the company's dividend-payout ratio remains constant, the pattern of its dividends will plainly fail to fit neatly into the formula.

What saves the dividend-discounting approach from irrelevance is that companies generally do not strive for a constant dividend-payout ratio at all costs. More typically, they attempt to avoid cutting the amount of the payout, notwithstanding declines in earnings. A company that aims to pay out 25% of its earnings over a complete business cycle might record a payout ratio of 15% in a peak year and 90% or 100% in a trough year. For a few years at least, a company that records net losses may maintain its dividend at the established level, resulting in a meaningless payout-ratio calculation. (If losses persist, however, financial prudence will usually dictate cutting or eliminating the dividend in the interest of conserving cash.) Even though a cyclical company will not ordinarily increase its dividend on a regular, annual basis, it will raise its payout over the longer term. The $P = D/K - g$ formula will work reasonably well as a valuation tool, with adjustments to the discount rate (K) serving to reflect the uncertainty implicit in an irregular pattern of dividend increases.

While the dividend-discount model can accommodate earnings' cyclicality, however, the analyst must pay close attention to the method by which a company finances the maintenance of its dividend at an established rate. A chronically money-losing company that borrows to pay dividends is simply undergoing slow liquidation. (That is, it is replacing its equity—eventually all of it—with liabilities.) In such circumstances, it becomes impossible to sustain the assumption that dividends will continue for an infinite number of periods (the condition that led to the derivation of the $P = D/K - g$ formula). On the other hand, a cyclical company may sustain losses at the bottom of a business cycle but never reach the point at which its funds from operations, net of capital expenditures required to maintain long-term competitiveness, fail to cover the dividend. Maintaining the dividend under these circumstances poses no financial threat.

On this basis, many analysts argue that cash flow, rather than earnings, is the true determinant of dividend-paying capability and therefore should—more than earnings-per-share forecasts—be the focus of equity analysis. Certainly, analysts need to be acutely conscious of changes in a company's cash-generating capability that are not paralleled by changes in earnings. For example, a company may for a time maintain a given level of profitability even though its business is becoming more capital-intensive. Rising plant and equipment requirements might transform the company from a self-financing entity into one that is dependent on external financing. Return on equity will not reflect the change until cumulatively, after several years, the resulting rise in borrowing costs (or increase in the equity base required to support a given level of operating earnings) becomes large enough to be noticeable. Furthermore, as detailed in Chapter 3, reported earnings are subject to considerable manipulation, a flaw that helped to popularize the use of cash flow analysis in the first place. Cash generated from operations, generally a more reliable number than earnings, can legitimately be viewed as the preferred measure of future dividend-paying capability.

Notwithstanding these arguments, earnings-per-share forecasts remain the focal point of equity research on Wall Street and elsewhere. For many companies, the other components of cash flow—depreciation typically being the largest—are highly predictable over the near term. By accurately forecasting earnings—the more variable component—an investor can best hope to identify a misvaluation. To some extent, too, the unflagging focus on earnings probably reflects institutional inertia. Business reporters ask for earnings forecasts, brokerage firms use them to evaluate the accuracy of their analysts' forecasts, and corporations base executive compensation on earnings per share, whether achieved through effective management or through clever accounting tricks. For good and not-so-good reasons, then, the earnings forecast is simply what is expected of an analyst. Fortunately, a mechanism is available for adjusting a stock evaluation when the quality of the forecasted earnings is questionable, namely, reducing the earnings multiple, as explained in the following section.

THE PRICE-EARNINGS RATIO

Although the dividend-discount model is an intuitively satisfying approach to valuing a common stock, it is not the most convenient method of comparing one stock's value with another's. Better suited to that task is the price-earnings ratio, alternately known as the P/E ratio or earnings multiple:

$$\text{Price-earnings ratio} = \frac{\text{Stock price}}{\text{Earnings per share}}$$

Based on this formula, Wolfe Food Company (see preceding section) has a price-earnings ratio of:

Stock price	$50
Net income available to common shareholders	$45,000,000
Common shares outstanding	10,000,000
$\text{Earnings per share} = \dfrac{\$45,000,000}{10,000,000}$	$4.50
$\text{Price-earnings ratio} = \dfrac{\$50}{\$4.50}$	= 11.1X

To understand how the price-earnings ratio may be used to compare companies with another, consider a competitor of Wolfe Food Company, Grubb & Chao (Exhibit 7–2). Grubb & Chao has the same expected earnings growth rate as Wolfe (10%) and is assigned the same required rate of

EXHIBIT 7–2   Selected Financial Data

Grubb & Chao	
Net income available to common shareholders	$45,000,000
Dividends to common shareholders	$15,000,000
Common shares outstanding	10,000,000
Expected annual growth in earnings	10 %
Investors' required rate of return, given predictability of Wolfe's earnings	13 %
Current stock price	$48.75

return (13%). Its price-earnings ratio, however, is higher than Wolfe's (13.5X vs. 11.1X):

$$\text{Price-earnings ratio} = \frac{\text{Stock price}}{\text{Earnings per share}}$$

$$= \frac{\$48.75}{\$54,000,000 \div 15,000,000}$$

$$= \frac{\$48.75}{\$3.60}$$

$$= 13.5X$$

Based on the information provided, an investor would regard Wolfe as a better value than Grubb & Chao. This conclusion proceeds from applying the dividend-discount model to the latter's numbers:

$$P = \frac{D}{K - g}$$

$$P = \frac{\$18,000,000 \div 15,000,000}{.13 - .10}$$

$$P = \frac{\$1.20}{.03}$$

$$P = \$40$$

The price thus derived is lower than the actual price of $48.75, implying an overvaluation by the market. Observe as well that the "correct" price for Grubb & Chao produces the same price-earnings ratio as calculated for Wolfe Food Company:

$$\text{Price-earnings ratio} = \frac{\$50}{\$3.60}$$

$$= 11.1X$$

P/E-based value comparisons can go well beyond this sort of company-to-company matchup. The analyst can rank all the companies within an industry (Exhibit 7–3), then judge whether the variations in price-earnings ratios appear justified, or whether certain companies seem misranked. Note that the table ranks companies on the basis of estimated current-year earnings, rather than on the past year's earnings.

Why P/E Multiples Vary

Justifications for differences in earnings multiples derive from the variables of the preceding valuation formulas. Consider the following two equations:

$$P = \frac{D}{K - g} \text{ and } P/E = \frac{P}{EPS}$$

EXHIBIT 7–3   Companies within an Industry Ranked by Price-Earnings Ratio

Cosmetics and Personal Care Industry—August 1994	
Company	Share Price Divided by Estimated 1994 Earnings per Share
Gillette	21.4
Perrigo	19.8
International Flavors	19.5
INBRAND	19.1
Maybelline	17.7
Helene Curtis	16.4
Avon Products	15.0
Tambrands	14.8
Alberto-Culver	13.1
Paragon Trade	9.9
Playtex Products	9.9

Source: Merrill Lynch Capital Markets.

where   P = Current stock price
         D = Current dividend rate
         K = Required rate of return
         g = Growth rate
         P/E = Price-earnings ratio
         EPS = Current earnings per share (annual)

Substituting $D/K - g$, which equals P, for the P in the other equation, produces the following expanded form:

$$P/E = \frac{\left(\dfrac{D}{K - g}\right)}{EPS}$$

Using this expanded equation permits the analyst to see quickly that an increase in the expected growth rate of earnings produces a premium multiple. For example, both Wolfe Food Company and Grubb & Chao have 10% growth factors, and both stocks currently trade at 11.1 times earnings. Suppose another competitor, Eatmore & Co., can be expected to enjoy 11% growth, by virtue of concentration in faster-growing segments of the food business. A substantially higher multiple results from this modest edge in earnings growth:

$$P/E = \frac{\left(\dfrac{D}{K - g}\right)}{EPS}$$

$$P/E = \frac{\left(\dfrac{\$1.60}{.13 - .11}\right)}{\$4.80}$$

$$P/E = 16.7X$$

Eatmore & Co.'s earnings will not, however, command as big a premium (16.7X versus 11.1X for its competitors) if the basis for its higher projected growth is subject to unusually high risks. For example, Eatmore's strategy may emphasize expansion in developing countries, where the rate of growth in personal income is higher than in the more mature economy of the United States. If so, Eatmore may be considerably more exposed than Wolfe or Grubb & Chao to the risks of nationalization, new restrictions on repatriation of earnings, protectionist trade policies, and adverse fluctuations in exchange rates. If so, the market will raise its discount rate (K) on Eatmore's earnings. An increase of just one-half percentage point (from 13.0% to 13.5%) wipes out more than half the premium in Eatmore's multiple, dropping it from 16.7X to 13.3X:

$$P/E = \frac{\left(\dfrac{D}{K - g}\right)}{EPS}$$

$$P/E = \frac{\left(\dfrac{\$1.60}{.135 - .11}\right)}{\$4.80}$$

$$P/E = 13.3X$$

In effect, the ability to vary the discount rate, and therefore to assign a lower or higher multiple to a company's earnings, is the equity analyst's defense against the sort of earnings manipulation by management described in Chapter 3. A company may use liberal accounting practices and skimp on long-term investment spending, yet expect the resulting artificially inflated earnings per share to be valued at the same multiple as its competitor's more legitimately derived profits. Indeed, the heart of many management presentations to analysts is a table showing that the presenting company's multiple is low by comparison with its peers. Typically, the chief executive officer cites this table as proof that the company is undervalued. The natural corollary is that in time investors will become aware of the discrepancy and raise the multiple, and therefore the price of shares owned by those who are astute enough to buy in at today's dirt-cheap level.

These stories are sometimes persuasive, yet one must wonder whether such "discrepancies" in earnings multiples are truly the result of inattention by analysts. In the case of a large-capitalization company, it is probable that hundreds of Wall Street and institutional analysts are making the comparison on their own. If so, they are fully aware of the below-average multiple but consider it justified for one or more reasons, including the following:

- The company's earnings are more cyclical than those of its peer group.
- The company has historically been prone to earnings "surprises," which raise suspicions that the reported results reflect an exceptionally large amount of "earnings management."
- Management has a reputation for erratic behavior (e.g., abrupt changes in strategy, ill-conceived acquisitions) that makes future results difficult to forecast.

Analysts may be mistaken in these perceptions, and may genuinely be undervaluing the stock, but the low multiple is a conscious judgment, not a function of neglect. Even a small-capitalization company, which can more credibly claim that its stock is "underfollowed" by Wall Street, may have the multiple it deserves, despite the fact that its competitors sport higher P/E ratios. It is entirely proper to assign an above-average discount factor to the earnings of a company that competes against larger, better-capitalized firms and suffers the disadvantages of lack of depth in management and concentration of its production in one or two plants.

Recognizing that qualitative factors may depress their multiples, companies often respond in kind, arguing that their low valuations are based on misperceptions. For example, a company in a notoriously cyclical industry may argue that it is an exception to the general pattern of its peer group. Thus, a manufacturer of automotive components may claim that its earnings are protected from fluctuations in new car sales by a heavy emphasis on selling replacement parts. Whether or not consumers are buying new cars, the reasoning goes, they must keep their existing vehicles in good repair. In fact, sales of replacement parts should rise if the existing fleet ages because fewer individuals buy new autos. Similarly, a building-materials manufacturer may claim to be cushioned against fluctuations in housing starts because of a strong emphasis in its product line on the remodeling and repair markets.

These arguments may be valid, but investors should not accept them on faith. Instead of latching on to the "concept" as a justification for immediately pronouncing the company's multiple too low, an analyst should independently establish whether an allegedly countercyclical business has in fact fit that description in past cycles. It is also important to determine whether the supposed source of earnings stability is truly large enough to offset a downturn of the magnitude that can realistically be expected in the other areas of the company's operations.

A good practice is to remember that a company can more easily create a new image than it can recast its operations. Analysts should be especially wary of companies that have tended to jump on the bandwagon of "concepts" associated with the hot stocks of the moment. During the late 1970s, for instance, skyrocketing oil prices led directly to higher expected earnings growth (g), and hence higher P/E multiples and stock prices for oil producers. Suddenly, chemical companies, capital-goods producers, and others began presenting themselves as "energy plays." Some did so by acquiring oil properties, but others simply began publicizing their existing—and sometimes tangential—links to the oil business in markets that might conceivably have benefited from rising petroleum prices. A few years later, when oil prices collapsed, these same companies deleted from their annual reports the glowing references and photographs playing up their energy-relatedness. Around the same time, as the economic boom ended in Houston and other cities that had benefited from surging oil prices, national retailing chains became less vocal about their concentration in the Sunbelt, which had for several years been synonymous with high growth and therefore high P/E ratios.

Normalizing Earnings

Because companies have strong incentives to gain increases, however modest, in their earnings multiples, even at the cost of stretching the facts to the breaking point (or beyond), a conservative bias in calculating appropriate multiples is generally wise. In addition to upping the discount rate (K) when any question about the quality of earnings arises, the analyst should normalize the earnings-per-share trend when its sustainability is doubtful.

Suppose, for example, that the fictitious PPE Manufacturing Corporation's earnings per share over the past five years are as shown in Exhibit 7–4. PPE has customarily commanded a multiple in line with the overall market, which is at present trading at 12 times estimated current-year earnings. By this logic, a price of 12 times $2.67, or approximately 32, seems warranted for PPE stock.

Exhibit 7–5 shows, however, that the current-year earnings estimate is well above PPE's historical trend line, making the sustainability of the current level somewhat suspect. As it turns out, the $2.67 estimate is bloated by special conditions that will probably not recur in the near future. Specifically, the customers for PPE's major product are stepping up their purchases in anticipation of an industry-wide strike later in the year.

EXHIBIT 7–4

PPE Manufacturing Corporation Earnings History Table	
Year	**Earnings per Share**
1991	$1.52
1992	$1.63
1993	$1.86
1994	$2.04
1995	$2.67 (Estimated)

EXHIBIT 7–5 PPE Manufacturing Corporation Earnings History Graph

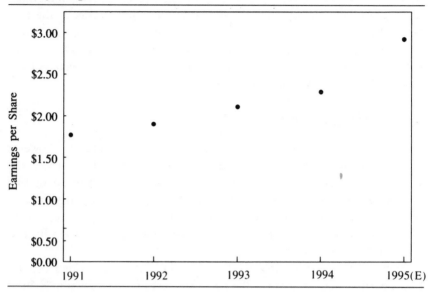

A temporary shortage has resulted, causing buyers to raise their bids. With its plants running flat out (reducing unit costs to the minimum) and its price realizations climbing, PPE is enjoying profit margins that it has never achieved before—and probably never will again.

It hardly seems appropriate to boost PPE's valuation from 24½ (12 times last year's earnings per share) to 32, a 31% increase, solely on the basis of an EPS hiccup that reflects no change in PPE's long-term earnings power. Accordingly, the analyst should normalize PPE's earnings by projecting the trend line established in preceding years. Exhibit 7–6 shows such a projection, using the least-squares method. The formula for this method is as follows:

$$y = a + m(x - \bar{x})$$

$$a = \bar{y}$$

$$m = \frac{\Sigma xy - n\bar{x}\bar{y}}{\Sigma x^2 - n\bar{x}^2}$$

$$\bar{x} = \frac{0 + 1 + 2 + 3}{4} = 1.5$$

$$\bar{y} = \frac{1.52 + 1.63 + 1.86 + 2.04}{4} = 1.7625$$

$\Sigma xy = (0 \times 1.52) + (1 \times 1.63) + (2 \times 1.86) + (3 \times 2.04) = 11.47$

$n\bar{x}\bar{y} = 4 \times 1.5 \times 1.7625 = 10.575$

$\Sigma x^2 = 0^2 + 1^2 + 2^2 + 3^2 = 14$

$n\bar{x}^2 = (4) \times (1.5)^2 = 9$

$$m = \frac{11.47 - 10.575}{14 - 9} = 0.179$$

$y = 1.7625 + 0.179(x - 1.5)$

Solving for $x = 4$, we derive a current-year trend-line value of $2.21. Applying the market multiple of 12 produces an indicated stock price of 26½. Some modest upward revision from this point may be warranted, for if nothing else the company can reinvest its windfall profit in its business and generate a small, incremental earnings stream. By no means, though, should the company be evaluated on the basis of an earnings level that is not sustainable.

EXHIBIT 7–6   PPE Manufacturing Corporation Earnings Trend—Least-Squares Method

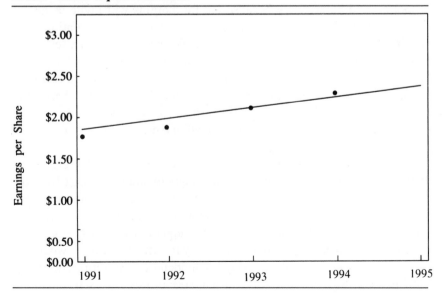

Sustainable Growth Rate

Sustainability is an issue not only in connection with unusual surges in earnings, but also when it comes to determining whether a company's historical rate of growth in earnings per share is likely to continue. The answer is probably "no" if the growth has been fueled by anything other than additions to retained earnings per share.

Consider the following derivation of earnings per share:

$$\begin{array}{c}\text{Asset turnover} \times \text{Return on sales} \\ \times \text{Leverage} \times \text{Book value per share}\end{array} = \text{Earnings per share}$$

Or:

$$\frac{\text{Sales}}{\text{Assets}} \times \frac{\text{Net income}}{\text{Sales}} \times \frac{\text{Assets}}{\text{Net worth}} \times \frac{\text{Net worth}}{\text{Shares outstanding}} = \frac{\text{Net income}}{\text{Shares outstanding}}$$

Earnings per share will not grow merely because sales increase. Any such increase will be canceled out in the preceding formula, since sales appears in the denominator of return on sales as well as in the numerator of asset turnover. Only by an increase in one of the four terms on the left side of the equation will the product (earnings per share) rise. Aggressive management may boost asset turnover, but eventually the assets will reach the limits of their productive capacity. Return on sales, likewise, cannot expand indefinitely because too-fat margins will invite competition. Leverage also reaches a limit, since lenders will not continue advancing funds beyond a certain point as financial risk increases. This leaves only book value per share, which can rise unceasingly through additions to retained earnings, as a source of sustainable growth in earnings per share. As long as the amount of equity capital invested per share continues to rise, more income can be earned on that equity, and (as the reader can demonstrate by working through the preceding formula) earnings per share can increase.

A company's book value per share will not rise at all, however, if it distributes 100% of its earnings in dividends to shareholders. (This, by the way, is why an immediate increase in the dividend-payout ratio will not ordinarily cause a direct, proportionate rise in the stock price, as might appear to be the implication of the equation $P = D/K - g$.) Assuming the company can earn its customary return on equity on whatever profits it reinvests internally, raising its dividend-payout ratio reduces its growth in earnings per share (g). Such a move proves to be self-defeating as both the numerator and the denominator (D and $K - g$, respectively) rise and P remains unchanged.

To achieve sustainable growth in earnings per share, then, a company must retain a portion of its earnings. The higher the portion retained, the more book value is accumulated per share and the higher can be the EPS growth rate. By this reasoning, the following formula is derived:

$$\frac{\text{Sustainable}}{\text{growth rate}} = (\text{Return on equity}) \times (\text{Income reinvestment rate})$$

where Income reinvestment rate $= 1 -$ Dividend payout ratio

THE DU PONT FORMULA

The preceding section introduced a formula that provided insight into earnings per share by disaggregating it into several simple financial ratios. Disaggregation can be applied in other beneficial ways in equity analysis, most notably in a technique known as the Du Pont Formula. (The idea is generally credited to Donaldson Brown, who developed the formula while at E.I. du Pont de Nemours, then applied it during the 1920s as vice president of finance at General Motors.) With the aid of the Du Pont Formula, the analyst can more readily perceive the sources of a firm's return on assets:

$$\text{Asset turnover} \times \text{Return on sales} = \text{Return on assets}$$

$$\frac{\text{Sales}}{\text{Assets}} \times \frac{\text{Income}}{\text{Sales}} = \frac{\text{Income}}{\text{Assets}}$$

Like most ratio analysis, the Du Pont Formula is valuable not only for the questions it answers but also for the new ones it raises. If a company raises its return on assets by finding ways to reduce working capital without impairing competitiveness (thereby improving asset turnover), then it is likely to be able to perform at the higher level. On the other hand, cutting back on necessary capital expenditures will also have a positive effect—in the short run—on return on assets. Not only will the denominator decline in the asset turnover factor as a result of depreciation, but return on sales will rise as future depreciation charges are reduced by lower capital outlays in the current year. Underspending will eventually hurt competitiveness, and therefore the company's long-run return on assets, so analysts must probe to determine the true nature of shifts in these ratios.

The Modified Du Pont Formula

Carrying the disaggregation technique a step further, the Modified Du Pont Formula analyzes the sources of return on shareholders' investment:

Return on assets × Financial leverage = Return on equity

$$\frac{\text{Income}}{\text{Assets}} \quad \times \quad \frac{\text{Assets}}{\text{Equity}} \quad = \quad \frac{\text{Income}}{\text{Equity}}$$

As noted earlier, the stock market will ordinarily value earnings at lower multiples than they would otherwise command if the earnings were subject to unusual risks. Financial risk, as signified by financial leverage, is one consideration that may penalize a company's P/E ratio. Generally speaking, an analyst will respond more favorably to a firm that raises its return on equity by increasing its return on assets than one that does so by leveraging its equity more aggressively. Besides introducing greater volatility into the rate of return, adding debt to the balance sheet demonstrates no management skill in improving operations. Furthermore, a company that has already fully utilized its debt capacity has no additional potential for increasing its return on equity by the same means. A somewhat under-borrowed company, on the other

EXHIBIT 7–7

Du Pont Analysis of Food Processing Industry's 1993 Results*

	Asset Turnover (×)	×	Return on Sales (%)	=	Return on Assets (%)	×	Financial Leverage (×)	=	Return on Equity (%)
ConAgra	2.15		1.82		3.92		4.14		16.24
CPC International	1.33		6.75		8.98		2.86		25.69
Dole Foods	1.01		2.27		2.30		3.22		7.40
Gerber	1.36		3.29		4.45		2.60		11.60
Heinz (H.J)	1.04		5.58		5.81		2.94		17.07
Hershey Foods	1.22		5.54		6.77		2.02		13.69
Kellogg	1.49		10.81		16.07		2.47		39.73
McCormick & Co.	1.19		4.70		5.57		2.81		15.66

*Calculations are subject to rounding error.

hand, has hidden profitability potential that may be exploited (with concomitant benefits to shareholders) at a later point. The Modified Du Pont Formula, in summary, enables investors to judge the quality of a company's return on equity in much the same way that other financial tests can be applied to the quality of earnings.

Exhibit 7–7 confirms the value of taking a closer look at shareholder returns. Judged by the sole criterion of return on equity, McCormick & Co. outperformed Hershey Foods in 1993 (15.66% vs. 13.69%). A more detailed inspection, however, reveals that Hershey surpassed McCormick on the Du Pont Formula's two measures of operating skill—asset turnover and return on sales. The high ROE at McCormick, while by no means artificial or illusory, was less solidly supported by evidence of competitive strength than Hershey's lower figure.

VALUATION VIA RESTRUCTURING POTENTIAL

Not as immediately apparent in the analysis presented in Exhibit 7–7 is the companies' potential for restructuring. Whether initiated internally or imposed from outside, major revisions in operating and financial strategies can dramatically increase the price of a corporation's common shares. The Modified Du Pont Formula helps to identify the type of restructuring that can unlock hidden value in a particular instance.

During the early 1990s, much of the restructuring of U.S. corporations came about in response to increased shareholder activism. Large institutional shareholders exerted pressure to reform corporations, sometimes precipitating the ouster of senior management if they could not otherwise break the inertia. The institutions' behavior contrasted with their past tendency to support management. Formerly, when they were seriously dissatisfied with a company's performance, institutions sold their shares and reinvested the proceeds in other stocks. Increasingly, though, some of the largest pension funds began to recognize the influence they could wield, by virtue of their vast share holdings. Boards of directors realized that if they did not induce management to improve return on assets, they might be voted out by coalitions of large institutions. Suddenly, companies became less reluctant to reduce their workforces and divest unprofitable operations, steps typically advocated by dissident slates of directors.

The shareholder activism of the early 1990s flourished in an environment of comparatively high price-earnings ratios. Additionally, the period was characterized by a backlash against the previous decade's trend toward increased financial leverage. Conditions, in short, were not conducive to the sort of borrow-and-acquire transactions that drove much of the corporate restructurings of the 1980s.

In that era, the prototypical deal consisted of gaining control of a company by buying its stock at a depressed price, then adding debt to the capital structure. Opportunities of this sort were abundant, not only because of low prevailing price-earnings ratios, but also because many corporations carried far less debt than their cash flows could support. At least in the early stages, before some raiders became overly aggressive in their financial forecast assumptions, it was feasible to extract value without creating undue bankruptcy risk, simply by increasing the ratio of debt to equity. The hostile takeover artists, in other words, focused on the second factor in the Modified Du Pont Formula, financial leverage.

By releasing the potential embedded in a relatively debt-free balance sheet, the corporate raiders of the 1980s did more than pursue large profits. More important to the subject matter at hand (although not to the raiders), their activities seriously undermined the earnings multiple as a basis for valuing companies.

Consider, for example, the fictitious Sitting Duck Corporation (Exhibit 7–8). Under conventional assumptions, and given a prevailing earnings multiple of 11 on similar companies, Sitting Duck's equity will be valued at $715 million, about 1.7 times its book value of $413 million.

Corporate raiders, however, would approach the valuation much differently. Their focus would not be on earnings, but rather on cash flow. After paying out approximately one-third of its earnings in dividends and more than offsetting depreciation through new expenditures for plant and equipment, Sitting Duck generated $30 million of cash in 1994. Present management used this cash to reduce an already conservative (36%) total-debt-to-total-capital ratio and to add to the company's existing portfolio of marketable securities. To a takeover artist, a more appropriate use would be to finance a premium bid for the company. The arithmetic goes as follows: Assume commercial banks are currently willing to lend to sound leveraged-buyout projects that can demonstrate EBITDA coverage of 1.5 times. (The lenders do not care about the company's book profits, but rather about its ability to repay debt. Cash generation is a key determinant of that ability.) Sitting Duck's operating income of $186 million, with $38 million of depreciation added back, produces EBITDA of $224 million. The amount of interest that $224 million can cover by 1.5 times is $149 million, an increase of $130 million

EXHIBIT 7–8   Financial Statement

Sitting Duck Corporation
Year Ended December 31, 1994
($000,000 omitted)

Balance Sheet		Statement of Cash Flows	
Current Assets	$ 594	Net Income	$ 65
Property, Plant, and Equipment	406	Depreciation	38
Total Assets	$1,000	Cash Generated by Operations	103
Current Liabilities	$ 350	Dividends	22
Long-Term Debt	237	Capital Expenditures	41
Shareholders' Equity	413	Increase in Working Capital	10
Total Liabilities and Equity	$1,000	Cash Used in Operations	73
		Net Cash Available	30

Income Statement

Sales	$1,253	Reduction of Long-Term Debt	25
Cost of Goods Sold	972	Increase in Cash and Equivalents	$ 5
Selling, General and Administrative Costs	95		
Operating Income	186		
Interest Expense	19		
Pretax Income	167		
Income Taxes	102		
Net Income	$ 65		

over Sitting Duck's present interest expense. Assuming a blended borrowing cost of 13% on the LBO financing, a raider can add $1 billion of debt to the existing balance sheet. If prevailing lending standards require equity of at least 10% in the transaction, the raider must put up an additional $111 million, for a total capitalization of $1.111 billion. By this arithmetic, the takeover artist can pay a 55% premium ($1.111 billion divided by $715 million) over Sitting Duck's present market capitalization. The purchase price equates to a multiple of 17 times earnings, rather than the 11-times figure currently assigned by the market. (Note, however, that the raider got to this number via cash flow, not via earnings. The *cash flow* multiple of the bid is 5.0 times.)

Stepping back from these calculations, one is bound to wonder whether the raider can truly expect to earn a high return on investment after paying 55% above the prevailing price for Sitting Duck's shares. In actuality, many comparably "high-priced" takeovers of the 1980s proved quite remunerative for the equity investors. To be sure, a number of acquirers genuinely turned out to have overpaid and were subsequently unable to meet their debt servicing requirements. Part of the analyst's job in evaluating future buyouts will be to gauge the potential for adopting strategies that worked out well in past transactions. Typically, the successful acquirers achieved their gains through one (or a combination) of the following means:

1. *Profit Margin Improvement.* Through either a change in ownership, permitting a fresh look at operations, or an arrangement that gives management a significantly higher stake in the firm's success, profitability may improve dramatically. Unnecessary costs that were formerly tolerated are likely to be eliminated, and potential sales to be pursued more aggressively than in the past. Larger profit margins mean higher EBITDA, which in turn serves as the basis of a higher valuation, enabling the equity investors to realize a gain on their original stake.

2. *Asset Sales.* To the extent that the stock market values a company on the basis of its earnings, its market capitalization may be far less than the value that its assets might fetch individually. A subsidiary or division, for example, may generate negligible profits yet have considerable value in the private market (where it would be priced on a cash flow multiple). Alternatively, the business unit might be unprofitable mainly due to insufficient scale. A competitor might be willing to buy the unit and consolidate it with its own operations (antitrust rules permitting), thereby producing higher combined earnings than the two operations were able to generate independently. A raider who perceives this sort of opportunity at a company may launch a highly leveraged takeover premised on liquidating certain operations to pay off the debt. If successful, the strategy will leave the acquirer debt-free and in control of the remainder of the target company despite having invested equity equivalent to just a small fraction of the firm's value, calculated on the basis of an earnings multiple. The raider may then "cash out" by selling the company at its full value to another corporation or by taking it public again.

The second strategy—repaying acquisition debt via asset sales—would not be feasible if the stock market fully recognized the potential value of all assets of a company. In reality, though, assets sometimes command lower stock-market valuations when held within certain corporate structures than they would command if owned differently. Consider, for example, the following comment on an announcement by Gulf + Western, the parent of Paramount Pictures,[2] of its intention to sell its finance subsidiary, Associates First Capital: "Analysts said the sale of Associates is likely to push up Gulf + Western Stock, which closed Friday at $49.50 a share. Gulf + Western shares have been trading at roughly 12 times per share earnings. Entertainment stocks generally trade at roughly 16 times earnings, but the multiple has been dragged down by Associates."[3] The analysts believed, in other words, that splitting Gulf + Western into two would raise the stock market's valuation of the company's assets. As it turned out, they did not have to wait long for confirmation of this hypothesis, for the following day's *Wall Street Journal* reported that on April 10, 1989, "Gulf + Western jumped 2⅜ to 51⅞ on 1.4 million shares after a Big Board trading delay to fix an order imbalance."[4] In other words, the aggregate value of Gulf + Western's motion picture, publishing, and finance operations rose once the expectation was established that all the businesses would cease to be owned by a single corporation.

Given the substantial wealth that can be realized in this fashion, investors have in recent years paid increasing attention to a corporation's potential value in the event of its being split up. While this mode of evaluating companies has not supplanted the dividend discount and P/E methods, it has certainly taken its place alongside them in the investor's toolbox.

Breakup analysis has entered the mainstream not only in terms of its users but also in terms of the companies to which it is applied. Firms being evaluated on the basis of their separate parts do not include only one-time conglomerates like Gulf + Western—the companies generally perceived to be more readily broken up by virtue of owning several diverse, unrelated businesses. Rather, analysts are calculating breakup values even on corporations as middle-of-the-road as Du Pont—the very same company that gave birth to the Du Pont Formula discussed earlier. A *Wall Street Journal* article dated March 28, 1989, focused on Du Pont's ownership of Conoco, an integrated oil company acquired in 1981:

---

[2]In conjunction with the divestment of Associates First Capital, Gulf + Western renamed itself "Paramount Communications."
[3]Geraldine Fabricant "Divestiture Is Planned by G + W," *New York Times* (April 10, 1989), p. D1.
[4]William Power and David Wilson "Stocks Are Mixed and Lethargic but Takeover Issues Show Life," *The Wall Street Journal,* Heard on the Street (April 11, 1989), p. C2.

Du Pont is well aware of the biggest inherent problem in owning Conoco—that most investors and analysts evaluate Du Pont on the basis of its chemicals operations. In the long run, both the oil and the chemicals would be better understood if analyzed separately.

"The chemical analysts look for earnings. Petroleum companies [which have big depreciation] are cash generators," one Du Pont official says. "Petroleum analysts understand that. Chemical analysts generally don't—or at least not as well."

"Du Pont's shares ended yesterday at $101.25, about 10 times estimated 1989 earnings. Conoco's oil and gas operations should earn about $340 million this year," says Bryan Jacoboski, a Paine Webber oil analyst. "Thus," he says, "the stock market is valuing Conoco at only $3.4 billion."

He says that Conoco, if spun off, would be valued at about $6.4 billion, based on the cash flow multiples at which other oil companies trade. "In other words," he says, "holders would gain an estimated $13 a share in market valuation if the companies traded separately."[5]

Besides evaluating a company's discrete businesses on the basis of prevailing earnings or cash flow multiples, analysts can often put prices on specific assets identified in the financial statements. For example, oil companies (and companies primarily engaged in other businesses but which own some oil properties) disclose the amounts of their reserves in their annual reports. Because energy companies frequently buy and sell reserves, and because the prices of larger transactions are widely reported, current market valuations are always readily at hand. If, for instance, recent sales of reserves in the ground have occurred at prices that equate to $10 a barrel, then a company with 25 million barrels of reserves could theoretically liquidate those assets for $250 million.[6] It may be the case that adding $250 million to a price for the balance of the company, derived from an earnings multiple, produces a sum well in excess of the company's current market capitalization. If so, the "unrecognized" value of the oil reserves can be the basis of an alternative method of evaluating the company's stock. The higher stock price will not be fully achieved unless the company—or an acquirer—monetizes the asset,[7] but the potential

---

[5]Roger Lowenstein "Close Watchers of Du Pont Prefer a Spinoff of Disappointing Conoco to Selling Its Assets," *The Wall Street Journal,* Heard on the Street (March 28, 1989), p. C2.

[6]Note, however, the uncertainties associated with reserve valuations, discussed in Chapter 2 under the heading "The Value Problem."

[7]Methods of realizing the value of an unrecognized asset include selling the asset for cash; placing the asset in a separate subsidiary, then taking a portion of the subsidiary public in order to put a

for realization of true asset values will very likely raise the stock price higher than the values that more traditional methods (dividend-discount model, price-earnings ratio) would produce.

In the 1990s, the stock market has by most accounts given full value to corporate assets. With share prices generally higher than breakup value, analysts have resumed their former focus on earnings multiples. As time passes, though, the stock market will fluctuate, as will other factors in the takeover equation. These include interest rates, expectations for growth in cash flow, and the regulatory environment. With the help of memories of the huge profits made in hostile takeovers of the 1980s, breakup analysis will probably continue to set a floor under stock prices. As such, it will remain a useful item in the toolbox of users of financial statements.

CONCLUSION

As noted at the outset of this chapter, valuations derived from financial statements represent only a portion of the analyses being conducted by millions of stock buyers and sellers during each trading session. Indeed, the split-second decision making of traders on the exchange floors can scarcely be described as analysis of any kind. Rather, it amounts to a highly intuitive response to momentary shifts in the balance of supply and demand.

For the investor who takes a longer view, however, financial statement analysis constitutes a solid foundation for valuation. A stock may temporarily soar or plummet in frenzied reaction to a development of little ultimate consequence. Eventually, however, rationality tends to reassert itself, and the share price returns to a level that is justifiable on the basis of the company's long-range capacity to generate earnings and cash. The intensified focus, in recent years, on breakup values is consistent with this thesis, for the value of previously "unrecognized" assets likewise rests on earnings power and cash flow potential. Without a thorough study of the company's historical financial statements and projections of its future results, an investor cannot have great confidence in a valuation that purports to reflect a stock's fundamental merits rather than merely the market's transitory mood.

---

price on the company's residual interest; and placing the asset in a master limited partnership, interests in which are distributed to shareholders.

8

SPECIAL CATEGORIES OF ISSUERS

THE ISSUERS OF financial statements selected to illustrate points made in the preceding chapters have for the most part been publicly owned corporations based in the United States. Industrial companies have predominated within that already circumscribed sample. To omit a sampling of the variations in style and substance employed by other kinds of financial statement issuers would deny the reader an appreciation of the diversity that the practicing analyst encounters.

For starters, not every financial statement submitted to analysts is required to conform to U.S. generally accepted accounting principles. As an example, statutory accounting principles, discussed in this chapter in connection with insurance companies and municipalities, tend toward a liquidating concept, rather than a going-concern basis as contemplated under GAAP.

The accounting practices of many foreign companies, while sharing the going-concern credo, depart from U.S. GAAP in a number of other ways. Whereas U.S. accounting practice has basically remained within the orthodoxy of historical cost accounting, analysts may encounter inflation-based valuations of fixed assets when dealing with foreign financial statements. Goodwill created through corporate acquisitions is likewise treated differently outside the United States. Instead of capitalizing and then gradually writing off the portion of the purchase price not attributable to tangible assets, non-U.S. companies are generally permitted to expense the "excess amount" immediately or else to create a nonamortizing asset. Either way, the foreign company's reported earnings in subsequent years escape the annual goodwill amortization penalty suffered by U.S. firms. Cross-border comparisons may be further distorted by "hidden reserves" that can make, for example, a German balance sheet stronger than one with similar numbers issued by a U.S. company. Finally, principles of consolidation vary around the globe, meaning that certain subsidiary liabilities that would be on-balance-sheet for a U.S. company are off-balance-sheet in other countries.

As economic activity becomes increasingly integrated on a worldwide scale, "harmonization" of accounting standards will likely follow. By the same token, analysts must be aware not only of accounting principles, but also of the manner in which they are implemented. For example, the United Kingdom shares with the United States the notion of limiting the conditions under which an earnings aberration may be deemed extraordinary and recorded on an after-tax basis. As of the early 1990s, however, about half of all British companies were reporting extraordinary items in their income statements, according to the *Economist.* At that time, extraordinary items appeared on the profit and loss statement of only about 5% of U.S. companies. Analysts can safely assume that the accounting principle was being applied differently in the two countries, rather than that Great Britain was more prone to extraordinary occurrences. A more disturbing illustration of differing practices involves Latin American banks. As Moody's points out, "In many countries, an institution's outside auditors may be part of a large corporate group which own the bank, making the value of the statements questionable."[1]

It is essential to familiarize oneself with the financial reporting practices of the country in which a firm is domiciled before attempting to compare its financials with those of another company that is subject to a different set of rules. The most efficient way of doing so is probably to discuss the practices of the country in question with a certified public accountant specializing in that country. In this age of multinational corporations, there are many such individuals employed at the major accounting firms.

Even within the community of GAAP-based entities, accounting approaches can vary sufficiently to invalidate the comparison of different companies' statements unless the analyst makes sweeping adjustments.

[1]Lynn Exton, "Ratings for Latin American Banks Shaped by Volatility and Risk." *Moody's Speculative Grade Commentary* (May 1994), pp. 4–5.

Private companies, which are exempt from Securities and Exchange Commission disclosure requirements, may furnish comparatively sketchy statements. Furthermore, small, privately held businesses are unlikely to prepare separate statements for financial reporting and tax reporting. Since the single set will be examined by the Internal Revenue Service, it will probably utilize every lawful means (at least) of reporting the lowest possible profit. Where there is discretion with respect to depreciation schedules, for example, a tax-minimizing statement will incorporate shorter write-off periods than a statement prepared for shareholders and lenders. Also, to the extent that the owner-managers of a small business wish to withdraw available cash for their own needs, they have a tax incentive to pay it out in the form of compensation (which generates a deduction for the company) instead of declaring a nondeductible dividend. The IRS may disallow deductions of executive compensation that it deems unreasonable, but the line is hard to draw. Accordingly, analysts who regularly examine small businesses' statements (in connection with proposed acquisitions, for example) often presume that they understate true profit potential.

Even while recognizing this private/public contrast within the universe of GAAP-based firms, however, analysts should remember that "true profit" is an elusive notion. Chapter 3 showed that reported earnings can be manipulated through a variety of sanctioned practices. From an equity standpoint, moreover, the ability to pay further dividends (which is largely a function of cash flow) is more pertinent than accounting profits. For these and other reasons, a standard of profitability that makes sense in one context can prove highly misleading in another.

To cite a common example, the depreciation of tangible, wasting assets does not represent the same economic reality as a programmed writedown of assets that are not physically deteriorating to any great extent and may even be rising in value. A broadcasting or cable television firm typically takes a comparatively small annual depreciation charge associated with plant and equipment and writes off a much larger sum that represents the value of its franchise (the right granted by a regulatory body to serve a particular geographical area). The latter charge does not ordinarily reflect a true diminution of value, since the economic rents that can be collected by the holder of the rights will likely rise as the region's population grows. Franchise value (in nominal dollars) will probably also increase essentially in line with the general inflation rate. Accordingly, the income reported by a broadcaster or cable system operator—reduced, in accordance with GAAP, by depreciation and amortization expenses that do not represent actual economic costs—is inherently understated.[2] An analyst who compares such a company with companies in other businesses on the basis of return on sales or return on equity will draw unduly pessimistic conclusions.

Financial statements that reflect a quasi-monopoly right such as a broadcasting franchise[3] differ from other statements in one more important way. Certain kinds of nonphysical assets, such as trademarks, can decline in value even though they are not subject to wear and tear. Poor management, for instance, can diminish the marketing power of a well-regarded brand name by extending it to goods of significantly lower quality than the product it originally represented. In contrast, ill-conceived programming does not reduce the scarcity value of a radio frequency or television channel. The only brand-name loss involves the call letters used by the operator currently controlling the spot on the broadcasting spectrum. Under different management—or even under the same management but with a new programming format—the spot on the airwaves has as much revenue-generating capacity as ever.

The possession of an indestructible asset warrants an approach to liquidation value different from that used in situations where evaluating assets is inseparable from the assessment of management. An intrinsically valuable service right can be more durable than even the most imposing manufacturing plant. The latter can turn into redundant—and therefore nearly worthless-capacity if management permits itself to be outflanked or technologically leapfrogged.

All of this is not to say that media franchises are perfect storehouses of value. The markets for independent (non-network-affiliated) television stations and cable television properties have gone through speculative

---

[2]Readers should not interpret this discussion as a criticism of the accounting standards that are imposed on media companies. On theoretical grounds, a broadcasting franchise ought perhaps to be written off over time since the owner does not hold it in perpetuity and faces some risk of being denied renewal of the right to serve the territory. Since such denials are fairly uncommon, however, an analyst who is attempting to estimate the broadcaster's economic worth does not err by viewing asset value in a different light than an accountant might.

[3]The use of a broadcasting frequency can be viewed as a quasi-monopoly, even though other stations serve the same population and despite the fact that other media (newspapers, magazines) and forms of entertainment (videocassettes, motion picture theaters) compete with it. Some measure of monopoly power is afforded by the limited availability of frequencies, which creates a meaningful barrier to entry. Similarly, cable television franchises have monopolistic qualities even though they are not technically exclusive rights and notwithstanding competition from competing technologies such as satellite dishes. Once an operator has cabled a territory, achieved a high level of subscriptions among the households in it, and established a record of good service, the risk/reward ratio of "overbuilding" (constructing a new system to compete with the existing operator) generally becomes unfavorable.

phases that bid their prices up to higher levels than were realizable at later times. Declining video market share by the television networks during the late 1980s altered the perceived values of their affiliates. Nevertheless, the relative independence of franchise value from managerial competence has historically tended to establish a floor for the price that a broadcasting property will fetch.

A similar argument, by the way, can be made for natural resources. Even if present management has failed to exploit a mineral deposit efficiently, the asset remains valuable to another team that can. Like a radio or television station, a good natural-resource property tends to retain some minimum value despite price swings. (Business cycles produce wide fluctuations in the prices of industrial commodities such as copper and paper, in turn causing mines and timberland to rise and fall in value. Gold and oil prices also tend to be volatile, reflecting a variety of economic trends, including the rate of inflation.)

In general, though, an oil reserve or an ore body can become completely worthless more easily than the right to broadcast on a certain frequency can. The reason is that a sharp drop in the price of a commodity can make it uneconomical to produce from higher-cost properties. For example, it is less costly to extract natural gas that lies relatively close to the earth's surface than it is to produce "deep gas" located 15,000 feet or more underground. Similarly, the cost of extracting metal is inversely proportional to the percentage of ore content represented by the metal. The less nonvaluable mass that has to be moved to obtain a ton of valuable metal, the lower is the cost of obtaining that ton. If demand for a commodity climbs high enough, prices will rise to a level at which it becomes profitable to exploit even comparatively costly reserves. The fortunate owners of low-cost reserves will earn extraordinary profits at such times. In the volatile world of natural resources, however, prices can easily fall below the cost of producing certain reserves. Particularly vulnerable is a marginal deposit brought into production expressly to capitalize on a sudden, sharp rise in the price of a commodity. If the price then just as suddenly drops below the property's production cost, ownership of the property will cease to have any intrinsic worth. In these circumstances, there is only a speculative value related to the possibility that prices will at some point rebound to a level that once again makes high-cost reserves profitable to produce.

Analysts must read the financial statements of a venture premised on developing high-cost natural reserves with an awareness that, acting in combination with other projects conceived in response to a spike in prices, the venture may ultimately contribute to its own undoing. Often the cause of a pronounced rise in a commodity's price is the inability of producers to add capacity in the short term to meet an unexpectedly rapid growth in demand. For example, large new mines by their nature require years of construction before they can commence production. In the interim, though, incremental production may be obtainable from low-grade reserves. Similarly, high prices may make it profitable to resume mining at sites that were abandoned years ago when the highest quality ore was depleted. If comparatively quick startup sources of this sort emerge in sufficient numbers, the price surge that made them economically viable may end abruptly. The risk of a sudden end to the boom is compounded, moreover, by the possibility that the commodity's high price will induce users to switch to some substitutable material that remains plentiful and comparatively cheap. In short, financial projections that pertain to a natural-resource venture—or for that matter, to the income statement of an established resource company—may incorporate a critical but invalid assumption regarding the sustainability of prices.

Sustainability can also be an issue when the topic is volume. In the aerospace/defense sector, for example, a shrinking backlog of orders may indicate that a company's sales cannot long remain at a currently high level. Furthermore, even a seemingly fat backlog may prove deceptive, since the timing of delivery is an uncertainty. Revenues may get delayed for a few years as procurement programs get stretched out in response to budgetary pressures. In the consumer goods sector, a seemingly healthy *volume* trend—an absolute increase in unit sales—may mask a deterioration in market share. If the underlying problem is that management is losing touch with consumer preferences, the current rate of volume growth will probably not be sustained over time. The decline will be accelerated if competitors, by virtue of building their own volume more quickly, gain an advantage through economies of scale.

Whether the key to projecting sales is backlogs or market share, a thorough analysis involves considerable research beyond the company's financial statements.[4] Merely extrapolating from historical figures can lead to gross estimation errors.

Still more challenging is the situation—often encountered in the high-technology sector—in which there are essentially no sales from which to extrapolate. In an extreme case, the company may not yet have developed its first product.

---

[4]Outside of a few major categories, such as cigarettes and beer, for which companies disclose general market share data in their financial statements, analysts must rely on independent market research organizations for information on estimated sales by brand.

Ordinarily, such an early-stage firm is evaluated only by venture capitalists, who typically have acquired expertise in assessing specialized technology and the managerial ability of entrepreneurs. At times, though, companies are taken public—and therefore made objects of study by large numbers of analysts—before they have generated the sort of financial track record on which analysts usually rely.

One period in which many analysts were forced to work with little of their accustomed data was the biotechnology craze of the early 1980s. The boom began in earnest with the spectacularly successful initial public offering of Genentech, highlighted by a one-day rise of more than 50 points in the stock. Recognizing a once-in-a-lifetime opportunity, a boatload of other gene-splicing firms came to market on the strength of the public's expectations of miraculous breakthroughs in medical science. Most companies had little else on which to base their offerings, having generated no sales (much less earnings), yet by 1986 the stock market assigned the biotechnology firms an estimated aggregate value of $4 to $5 billion.[5]

On what basis did investors evaluate these stocks in the absence of standard financial measures? One of the few available ratios was the number of years that the prevailing rate of negative cash flow could continue before equity would be completely depleted. With tongue only partly in cheek, journalist Robert Teitelman listed—in a book on the genetic engineering boom—such additional valuation benchmarks as the number of Ph.D.s on the payroll and the frequency of press release issuance, the latter being considered an inverse indicator of value.[6]

Ultimately, investors found that the early-stage biotechnology firms did not submit easily to conventional analysis. The best strategy, concluded many, was to buy a selection of biotechnology stocks, knowing that the big gainers in the pack would be difficult to identify but would compensate for the equally hard-to-spot big losers.

Highly speculative firms such as the genetic engineering firms of the early 1980s help to define the limits of financial statement analysis. The usual methods can be adapted to facilitate the evaluation in a wide range of special circumstances, but in a few extreme cases they are of little value.

Away from these extremes, yet in a range that requires a great deal of adaptation, are a number of specialized kinds of issues. The balance of

[5]David Webber, "Biotechnology Firms Still Difficult to Evaluate," *Chemical & Engineering News* (February 24, 1986): 15–17.

[6]Robert Teitelman, *Gene Dreams: Wall Street, Academia, and the Rise of Biotechnology* (New York: Basic Books, Inc., 1989).

this chapter discusses four varieties that an analyst has a fairly good chance of encountering—electric utilities, commercial banks, insurance companies, and municipalities. In studying these sections, the reader should focus particularly on the economic, political, and structural determinants of financial performance and reporting methods. Similar analysis can help to demystify the statements of other specialized classes of issuers not dealt with here.

ELECTRIC UTILITIES

To an analyst who has never before studied the financial statements of an electric utility, the first encounter may not be a pleasant experience. The statements are riddled with unusual accounts, and to make matters worse, the economic events they reflect do not appear to follow the normal logic of the marketplace.

Unraveling the mysteries of electric utilities' financial reporting becomes easier once one understands two basic characteristics of the industry:

1. By virtue of its high capital-intensity in both generation and distribution, the electric power industry historically has been regarded and regulated as a natural monopoly. The business is opening up to competition, however, as government authorities grow increasingly willing to rely on market mechanisms to promote economic efficiency.
2. The long lead time required to construct a generating plant (five to eight years for a conventional, coal-fired facility) results in the current receipt of revenues for services to be rendered far in the future. Under the theory of "intergenerational equity," however, electric utility regulators seek to avoid forcing present-day ratepayers to subsidize future users of the service.

On the matter of power companies' natural monopoly character, the granting of exclusive territorial franchises has rested historically on the premise that it would be economically unsound for society to duplicate, solely to preserve competition, the massive capital investment entailed in generating electricity. As an indication of the magnitude of such outlays, the largest U.S. investor-owned utility, Pacific Gas and Electric, had net plant in service of $19.1 billion in 1993, against revenues of $10.6 billion.

It took $1.80 of fixed assets, in other words, for the utility to generate one dollar of sales. By way of comparison, Phelps Dodge—the largest competitor in copper production, which is also considered a capital-intensive business—required only 92 cents of property, plant, and equipment to generate a dollar of sales in 1993. In the same year, Crown Cork & Seal, the largest publicly held container manufacturer, generated a dollar of sales on just 38 cents of fixed assets.

Because it has long been regarded as a monopoly service, electric power by definition has not been sold (for the most part) in free, competitive markets. Accordingly, the governmental bodies (primarily the states) that grant the monopoly franchises must somehow establish "correct" prices for the service. To do so, they authorize regulatory entities (hereinafter referred to generically as "public utility commissions," or "PUCs") to set rates for the residential, commercial, and industrial users of power.

PUCs exercise their rate-making authority in accordance with a theory that appears simple at first blush. The notion is that the rates paid by customers should fully reimburse the utility for its costs. These include both operating expenses (including fuel, wage and salaries, depreciation, and property taxes) and the cost of capital (interest and dividends).

Suppose, for example, that a company's annual sales volume is 50 billion kilowatt hours and that its costs—excluding capital costs and income taxes—amount to $3 billion. The "correct" rate to charge electric utility customers is the $3 billion divided by 50 billion kilowatt hours, or $0.06 per kilowatt hour, plus a charge per kilowatt hour calculated to compensate the utility for its capital costs. To derive the capital charge, the PUC calculates the company's blended cost of capital as follows:

Type of Capital	Percentage of Total Capital		Embedded Cost		
Debt	49%	×	9.53%	=	4.67%
Preferred equity	8	×	8.61	=	0.69
Common equity	43	×	13.70	=	5.89
	100%				11.25%

The PUC applies this 11.25% blended rate to the utility's rate base, consisting of $7.367 billion of plant in service and $855 million of inventories and other current assets, for a total of $8.222 billion. The product, $925 million, is divided by the 50 billion kilowatt hours of annual volume to determine a cost of capital per kilowatt hour of $0.0185. To recapture all its costs, then, the electric company must charge $0.0785 per kilowatt hour.

$0.0185   Capital cost per kilowatt hour
+ 0.0600   Operating cost per kilowatt hour
$0.0785   Total cost per kilowatt hour

Complications in Rate Making

Conceptually simple though it seems, the rate-making process can be quite complex in practice. Rates set on the basis of projected expenses may prove inadequate or much more than adequate for full recovery of costs in a period of wildly fluctuating oil prices, for example. An automatic adjustment for fuel costs can eliminate this problem, but other expenses incurred by a utility are not so easy to quantify. The capital cost, associated with common equity, for instance, is notoriously difficult to measure. Investors' expected returns include not only the present dividend yield, which can be calculated directly from available information, but also some expectation of future dividend increases, which cannot. Simply calculating historical total returns on electric utility shares does not solve the problem, either. To some extent, at least, utility stocks compete with bonds as an investment. Yields on the latter fluctuate over time, as does the comparative riskiness of stocks and bonds, which determines the size of the expected return premium that will induce investors to substitute the equity for the debt.

Such ambiguities in the rate-making process could no doubt be resolved much more readily than they are if politics were not a factor. Unfortunately, there is considerable political pressure on a public utility commission, which is either elected directly or appointed by a governor, depending on the state. Monthly electric bills constantly remind voters of the cost of power, enabling candidates to win considerable support by promising to hold down or reverse rate increases, even though the increases may reflect unavoidable increases in a utility's costs. The political attraction of railing against the power companies is enhanced because they are large corporations. (As seven-foot-high basketball star Wilt Chamberlain once said, nobody roots for Goliath.) Further heightening the emotions surrounding electric power is the view held by many that utilities earn profits from natural resources—coal, oil, natural gas, dammable rivers—that rightly belong to society at large. Voters who believe that all power companies should be publicly owned (as some U.S. companies have been for many years) are probably inclined to view privately owned utilities' profits as less than totally legitimate and therefore expendable in the cause of reducing costs to consumers.

The highly political environment in which public utility commissions operate gives them much greater latitude to consider local and regional economic conditions (which greatly influence voter sentiment) than a simple description of the rate-making process suggests. The financial forecaster must recognize that whatever future rates and revenues might be implied by an electric company's current and projected expenditures, the actual outcome will probably not exceed the load that the service territory can bear. A cyclical downturn in the state's economy may very well result in a drop in the utility's revenues, even though demand for electricity is relatively insensitive to the business cycle and notwithstanding that the company will have to recover no less in costs than it would have if no recession had occurred.

To achieve politically expedient adjustments to rates, PUCs exploit the second basic characteristic of the utility industry—the long lead time required to construct generating capacity. As discussed in connection with that point, regulators wish to avoid imposing on present rate payers the cost of benefits to be enjoyed by rate payers many years hence. Therefore, instead of allowing companies to collect cash payments from customers to fund construction of plant and equipment that is not yet in service, the regulators require companies to finance such outlays by selling debt and equity securities. The heavy capital costs associated with these financings may likewise not be recovered through current rates. Instead, the company records a noncash income item known as allowance for funds used during construction (AFUDC) to offset its financing charges (which involve actual cash outlays). Although the presumption ought to be that the resulting cash flow mismatch will be corrected when the plant comes into service and rate payers pick up the tab, the utility is vulnerable by virtue of having paid out cash with no assurance of recovery. Its PUC can lawfully decide, with hindsight, that certain of the plant-related expenditures were imprudently incurred and disallow them (decide that they may not be passed on to rate payers). The utility can appeal the disallowance to the courts, but it will likely find that judges—who, like utility commissioners, are either elected or appointed by elected officials—are not entirely immune to the political pressures that often underlie PUC disallowances.

Exhibit 8–1 illustrates how severely a disallowance can affect a company's financial performance. Niagara Mohawk, an electric utility operating in New York State, recorded an average of $158 million of AFUDC annually during 1983 through 1986. (Note that the total figure for each year includes an income item, "Allowance for other funds used during construction," and an offset against interest charges, "Allowance for borrowed funds used during construction.") The large increase in AFUDC over previous years—from $45 million in 1978, for example— reflected construction of the Nine Mile Point 2 plant. Like many other nuclear-generating facilities, this plant incurred serious delays and massive cost overruns. Wherever the blame lay, it was not politically feasible to force rate payers to foot the entire bill. Niagara Mohawk's regulators therefore disallowed much of its Nine Mile Point 2 costs. After the Financial Accounting Standards Board ruled that all companies in similar predicaments must reverse previously accrued revenues that might never be realized in cash, Niagara Mohawk wrote off $833 million in 1987. (This figure includes the SFAS 90 current-year effect of $268 million and the cumulative effect on prior years of $615 million.) The result was a net loss of $577 million and a year-over-year decline in retained earnings from $922 million to $104 million. Because a utility's ability to pay dividends is constrained by its retained earnings, Niagara Mohawk was obliged to cut its quarterly payout from 52 cents to 30 cents per share.

Of particular interest to financial analysts in Exhibit 8–1 is the pro forma restatement of Niagara Mohawk's earnings, based on the retroactive application of SFAS 90 (as opposed to recognizing the full impact in 1987). Absent the AFUDC benefit, the company earned $0.53 and $0.13 per share in 1985 and 1986, respectively, versus the $2.88 and $2.71 reported. This large disparity dramatizes the importance of considering the quality of earnings when analyzing electric utilities. An evaluation of Niagara Mohawk common stock based on reported profits would have overlooked the fact that dividends per share far exceeded bona fide earnings per share. Accordingly, the company's accounting income grossly overstated its ability to sustain—much less increase—its dividend, a reality that was driven home in 1987.

The long delay between construction expenditures and revenue realization in the utility industry can impair balance sheets, as well as quality of earnings. Exhibit 8–2 shows a $997 million asset labeled "Deferred River Bend costs" on the December 31, 1988, balance sheet of Gulf States Utilities. This item reflects the regulatory lag between the time a plant goes into commercial operation and the time that the associated rates go into effect. During the deferral period, there is a danger that the PUC may disallow some of the expense on the grounds that the plant in question is not necessary to the public convenience. If that happens, the

EXHIBIT 8-1 Consolidated Statement of Earnings

Niagara Mohawk Power Corporation and Subsidiary Companies
($000, omitted)

	1983	1984	1985	1986	1987
Operating Revenues:					
Electric	$2,023,728	$2,134,470	$2,096,404	$2,131,833	$2,170,191
Gas	608,587	651,076	598,536	528,486	453,239
	2,632,315	2,785,546	2,694,940	2,660,319	2,623,430
Operating Expenses:					
Operation:					
Fuel for electric generation	501,328	476,040	391,382	391,834	339,382
Electricity purchased	381,703	377,052	367,406	352,126	326,152
Gas purchased	432,898	452,960	411,801	338,634	268,099
Other operation expenses	326,057	353,660	364,010	397,714	383,874
Maintenance	136,338	140,987	144,312	149,124	158,939
Depreciation and Amortization	127,390	141,150	150,627	155,311	157,631
Federal and Foreign Income Taxes	117,089	181,767	173,471	211,237	195,472
Other Taxes	254,797	269,204	280,643	295,165	308,483
	2,277,600	2,392,820	2,283,652	2,291,145	2,138,032
Operating Income	354,715	392,726	411,288	441,174	485,398

236

Other Income and Deductions:					
Allowance for funds used during construction	85,350	122,354	141,320	121,932	20,563
Federal income taxes	31,511	33,460	26,708	32,293	17,622
Current year effect of adoption of SFAS No. 90					
Disallowed plant costs	—	—	—	—	(268,400)
Retained income taxes	—	—	—	—	50,400
Other items (Net)	9,994	8,591	53,110	37,539	10,947
	126,855	164,405	221,138	191,764	(168,868)
Income before Interest Charges	481,570	557,131	632,426	632,938	316,530
Interest Charges:					
Interest on long-term debt	189,006	224,099	260,271	264,054	264,472
Other interest	12,598	12,440	6,721	14,880	4,587
Allowance for borrowed funds used during construction	(32,443)	(39,142)	(45,996)	(43,861)	(10,315)
	169,161	197,397	220,996	235,073	258,744
Income before cumulative effect of accounting change	312,409	359,734	411,430	397,865	57,786
Cumulative effect on prior years of adoption of SFAS No. 90	—	—	—	—	(615,000)
Net Income (Loss)	$312,409	$359,734	$411,430	$397,865	($557,214)

Source: Niagara Mohawk Power Corporation 1987 Annual Report.

EXHIBIT 8–2   Consolidated Balance Sheet

Gulf States Utilities Company
($000 omitted)
December 31, 1988

Assets	
Utility and other plant, at original cost	
Plant in service	$6,579,622
Less: Accumulated provision for depreciation	1,523,229
	5,056,393
Construction work in progress	7,690
Nuclear fuel, net of accumulated amortization	161,688
	5,225,771
Other Property and Investments	50,988
Current Assets	
Cash and cash equivalents	102,393
Receivables	
Customers	147,913
Other	11,289
Fuel inventories	27,387
Materials and supplies	6,005
Prepayments and other	39,703
	334,690
Deferred Charges and Other Assets	
Unamortized debt expense	22,506
Unamortized project cancellation costs	94,848
Accumulated deferred income taxes	61,899
Deferred River Bend costs	997,079
Long-term receivable	47,220
Other	23,085
	1,246,637
	$6,858,086
Capitalization and Liabilities	
Capitalization	
Common shareholders' equity	$2,088,055
Preference stock	100,000
Preferred stock	
Not subject to mandatory redemption	136,444
Subject to mandatory redemption	387,189
Long-term debt	2,603,745
	5,315,433

(Continued)

EXHIBIT 8–2 *(Continued)*

Current Liabilities	
Long-term debt due within one year	84,333
Preferred stock and long-term sinking-fund requirements	36,967
Deferred River Bend construction and continuing services commitments	29,170
Accounts payable—trade	107,465
Customer deposits	16,646
Taxes accrued	34,993
Interest accrued	86,327
Capital leases—current	79,074
Over-recovery of fuel costs	14,602
Other	41,187
	530,764
Deferred Credits and Other Liabilities	
Investment tax credits	109,907
Accumulated deferred income taxes	576,312
Capital leases—noncurrent	19,778
Deferred River Bend financing costs	135,764
Over-recovery of fuel costs	19,062
Disputed amounts	72,793
Deferred income from sale of utility plant	46,283
Other	31,990
	1,011,889
	$6,858,086

Source: Gulf States Utilities Company 1988 Annual Report.

deferral will end without revenues being recognized, causing the expense to be charged against income and ultimately against shareholders' equity. In Gulf States' case, a total charge-off would have reduced equity by 37%. The company's 49% ratio of long-term debt to long-term equity would then have risen to 60%. Given the possibility that expected revenues might not be realized, a true measure of Gulf States' financial risk at year-end 1988 probably lay in between these figures.

From the creditors' standpoint, moreover, the heightened risks that are apparent in the financial statements of Niagara Mohawk and Gulf States Utilities do not represent the maximum hazards imaginable in the electric power sector. In 1988, Public Service Company of New Hampshire, which had already defaulted on some of its debt in the preceding year, declared bankruptcy as a result of disallowances related to the Seabrook nuclear power plant. This event overthrew the conventional wisdom among bond investors that a public utility could not fail, based on the U.S. Supreme

Court's 1942 ruling (in *Federal Power Commission v. Hope Natural Gas Company*) that shareholders were entitled to a fair return on their investment. Indeed, no major investor-owned utility went bankrupt for the first 45 years following the Hope Natural Gas decision, and bondholders presumed that because PUCs were legally required to provide fair returns to shareholders, the senior securities would be serviced under any circumstances. What they overlooked was that accruals (which in Public Service Company of New Hampshire's case produced fine accounting profits) could satisfy the Supreme Court's requirement for a fair return. There was no stipulation that a utility must receive cash. Public Service Company of New Hampshire, with $2 billion of investment on which it was receiving no cash return, financed its cash shortfall as long as it could, but when creditors lost confidence that the required revenues would eventually materialize, insolvency resulted.

The industrywide deterioration in credit quality that culminated in Public Service Company of New Hampshire's bankruptcy greatly increased investors' awareness of the risks inherent in the electric power business, which was previously considered nearly ideal for conservative investors. Even today, the industry continues to benefit from inherently steady demand for its service, which tends to stabilize cash flow and thereby to justify a comparatively high degree of financial leverage. When analyzing an individual security, however, an analyst should carefully consider the following factors.

Regulatory Risk.   Paradoxically, an electric utility is subject to sudden, sharp swings in its revenues despite the fundamental stability of demand for power. A PUC, reacting to short-term political pressures, may reduce rates based on any of several different rationales. The outcome of regulatory proceedings are difficult to predict, since there are inconsistencies of approach from state to state, from company to company within a state, and even from one rate case to the next for a company operating within a single state.

Asset Concentration Risk.   Following General Public Utilities' severe nuclear power plant accident at Three Mile Island in 1979, bond investors began to assign large risk premiums to companies for which nuclear power represented a significant portion of existing generating capacity. (Coal, oil, natural gas, and hydroelectric power were considered lower risk at that point.)

As time passed, though, a more sophisticated understanding developed. A company might have a large nuclear component in its "fuel mix," but its nuclear capacity might be divided among several different plants. If so, the shutdown of one plant as the result of an accident would bar only a small portion of its rate base from earning a return. A far greater risk of revenue loss was faced by a company for which a single plant accounted for a large portion of rate base. For some companies, investment in an uncompleted plant (or pro rata portions of an uncompleted, jointly owned plant) represented a high percentage of rate base. In such a case, the risk of revenue loss was even greater than for a company with an up-and-running nuclear facility, since there was a danger that the plant would never go into commercial service.

Reflecting their concern about the risk of asset concentration, analysts nowadays view warily electric utilities with single-plant investments that represent large percentages of their rate base or of shareholders' equity. The latter measure is significant because as previously mentioned, utilities can pay dividends only out of their net worth. A write-off that wipes out a substantial portion of a company's equity can jeopardize its payout, exposing shareholders to the risk of a sudden loss of expected current income.

Service Territory Risk.   Although a utility is legally entitled to earn a fair return on investors' capital, its rate of return will, as a practical matter, reflect what its service territory can bear. PUCs are reluctant to grant rate increases in the midst of regional economic slumps, even though they may be sympathetic to the utilities and notwithstanding that such increases may be cost-justified. Accordingly, a company's ability to increase its dividend substantially and steadily over time can depend heavily on the health and diversity of its service territory's economic base.

Competitive Risk.   Having long operated in a fully regulated environment, some electric utilities are ill-prepared for the advent of competition. Companies are going through culture shock as they confront, for the first time in any serious way, the need to market their services to customers who have a genuine alternative. Analysts must look beyond the financial statements to assess senior managers' ability to control costs and encourage internal change, as well as their skills in dealing with the political and regulatory environment. Even more intangible, but no less important to the analysis, is management's strategic vision.

One final point for analysis of electric utilities' statements is that cash flow forecasts must always be done with an eye toward regulators' views on credit quality.

By being more stingy with rate relief, a PUC could save rate payers some money in the short run, but those savings could be offset over time by higher interest costs incurred by the utility as a result of declining fixed-charge coverage. For this reason, the analyst should temper a financial projection that points to severe deterioration in credit quality with the realization that the PUC may grant relief "in the nick of time," before a downgrading of the utility's bonds occurs.

At the opposite extreme, some skepticism should greet a projection that indicates substantial excess cash flow, resulting in liquidation of debt until a Triple-A capital structure is obtained. Most commissions consider an overly conservative balance sheet contrary to the interest of rate payers. The reasoning is that it is uneconomical to finance more of a company's needs than necessary with equity (which generates non-tax-deductible dividends) than with debt (interest on which produces a tax benefit). Based on this logic, a PUC may calculate the company's blended cost of capital as if it were more leveraged than it actually is. The effect is to provide less revenue than the company requires to earn a competitive return on its heavily equity-oriented capitalization. The practice of imputing a capital structure discourages companies from ever deleveraging to the point where their bond ratings would rise to the top categories. Instead, they tend to buy in shares ("homemade leverage") to prevent their equity from getting "too high."

COMMERCIAL BANKS

When assessing the financial condition of a bank, an analyst must always be conscious of the heavy hand of regulation. For better and for worse, regulators prevent normal economic forces from producing the results that a purely financial analysis might forecast.

Foremost in the regulators' minds is protection of depositors' money. Operationally, this objective is to a large extent translated into sparing the Federal Deposit Insurance Corporation (FDIC) the heavy costs that might result from having to reimburse depositors in the event of a failure. To minimize such costs, the regulators—which include the Federal Reserve System, the Comptroller of the Currency, and state banking commissions—deliberately alter the risk-sharing pattern that might otherwise prevail among depositors, lenders, shareholders, and owners of securities of the bank's holding company parent (if applicable). Given its primary mission of protecting depositors, for example, the FDIC may try to save a failed bank by selling it or by facilitating a merger with a stronger institution. If the bank's rescue happens to be achieved on terms that are unfavorable to holding company investors, the FDIC will nonetheless have fulfilled its primary mission. By the same token, investors and creditors can benefit from regulatory intervention in the affairs of a troubled bank. All classes of claim holders will generally be better off if regulators step in early enough to prevent a failure.

In pursuing their goal of protecting depositors, regulators have traditionally focused on capital as the key to preserving banks' solvency. This orientation seems somewhat misguided, since bank failures have generally not been caused by capital inadequacy, but rather by asset quality problems or loss of funding capability. Financial analysts should maintain their bearings, concentrating their credit assessment of a bank on the quality of its loan portfolio and the solidity of its funding, while regarding capital adequacy as a regulatory mandate that may affect the institution's freedom to pursue other objectives. Profitability and strategic coherence become critical in evaluating the upside in a banking company's common stock.

One additional point on banking regulation is that much of it is predicated on sociopolitical—rather than strictly economic or financial—premises. Specifically, there is a strong antibank strain in American legislative history, fed by popular fears concerning excessive concentration of power over the extension of credit. Manifestations of the desire to block the formation of a "money trust" include past and present constraints on branch banking, interstate banking, and participation by banks in nonbanking financial services such as insurance and the underwriting of registered securities. Because such regulations spring from noneconomic motives, they have helped to produce a different banking system from that which would have resulted if banks had been allowed a freer hand to rationalize their activities. Understanding this fact will help the analyst to explain otherwise puzzling aspects of banks' structure and competitive behavior.

Bank Ratio Analysis

Considered within the context of major industries, the universe of banks is large and relatively homogeneous, characteristics that tend to facilitate comparative ratio analysis as described in Chapter 6. Relative homogeneity, however, does not eliminate the need for certain distinctions within the total bank population to identify appropriate peer groups for such analysis. To begin with, ratios of U.S. banks are not comparable with those of foreign banks, which as a general rule enjoy a higher level of implicit credit support from their regulators and ministries of finance. In addition, analysts should segregate money center banks from regional banks when comparing financial ratios. The money center institutions— generally the largest banking organizations, concentrated in New York, Illinois, and California—characteristically have higher occupancy and personnel costs than the regionals. They also maintain costly foreign offices and are heavily involved in processing services. As a result, the money center banks tend to have lower returns on assets than their regional counterparts.

Subject to these caveats, ratio comparisons can be a fruitful approach to ranking banks according to credit quality and profitability. Ratio-trend analysis, by studying the pattern of a single firm's performance over time, is likewise illuminating, with the added virtue of not being dependent on identification of a perfect peer group. Reflecting the primary concerns of bank analysis, the pertinent ratios can be divided into credit quality ratios and profitability ratios, as follows:

Credit Quality Ratios

Nonperforming loans as a percentage of loans

Loan loss reserves as a percentage of loans

Annual charge-offs (net of recoveries) as a percentage of loans

(In each case, loans may be calculated as an average outstanding for the year, i.e., the mean of beginning-of-year and end-of-year balances.)

Profitability Ratios

$$\text{Net interest margin} = \frac{\text{Net interest income on a fully taxable equivalent basis*}}{\text{Average earning assets}}$$

$$\text{Return on assets} = \frac{\text{Net income}}{\text{Average total assets}}$$

$$\text{Return on equity} = \frac{\text{Net income}}{\text{Shareholders' equity}}$$

*The numerator and denominator of this fraction are both disclosed in the annual report. Earning assets include loans and securities.

Exhibit 8–3 gives some examples of supplemental disclosures that enable the analyst to gain additional insight into a bank holding company's financial and operating characteristics.

A Vital Balance

What makes bank analysis fascinating, and at the same time treacherous, is the tension between these two measures of success. By taking more credit risk in its loan portfolio, a bank can earn wider spreads (higher net interest margins), but if it takes too much risk, charge-offs may rise sharply. Sacrificing credit quality is also an easy way to generate growth in the commercial loan portfolio, which may raise the bank's return on assets. Instead of building business through effective marketing, a bank can "put assets on the books" simply by making loans that its competitors reject as being too risky—perhaps rightly so.

Growth obtained by liberalizing a bank's lending policies is a perennial trap for investors. Rapid expansion of a loan category in which a bank is relatively inexperienced (e.g., shipping, real estate, international loans) can create unacceptably high risk. Similarly dangerous is a concentration of loans in the bank's regional economy, which may be booming at present but poised for a bust a few years hence. A rising stock price that reflects growth of this variety can easily be a prelude to a sharp sell-off, as an economic downturn exposes the shaky foundations on which expansion of the lending portfolio rests.

The danger of a sudden reversal in the bank's fortunes is magnified if the institution lacks a solid deposit base. Banks that do not have sizable branch networks for gathering consumer deposit may instead rely on the sale of large certificates of deposit (CDs) to wealthy individuals and to other financial institutions. These deposits tend to include a large proportion of "hot money"—funds that are extremely sensitive to the interest rate paid and likely to be withdrawn, rather than rolled over, at maturity if the bank fails to match rates offered elsewhere. To remain competitive in a bidding war, yet continue to earn a positive spread over the high interest rates it is thereby forced to pay, the bank may in turn stretch its credit standards further and make riskier (and therefore higher-yielding) loans. If problem loans consequently begin to escalate, threatening the bank's viability, the "hot money" may flow out, leaving the bank insolvent, with no means of funding its portfolio. (Even though FDIC insurance provides protection in such cases, coverage is limited to a ceiling amount for each depositor. Very large depositors of "hot money" therefore face the possibility

EXHIBIT 8–3

Examples of Supplemental Disclosures
BankAmerica Corporation
December 31, 1993
($000 omitted)

Loan Outstandings

	December 31				
(in millions)	1993	1992	1991	1990	1989
Domestic					
Consumer:					
Secured by first mortgages					
on residential properties[a]	$ 30,306	$ 28,404	$18,897	$16,310	$11,672
Installment[b]	15,332	16,663	10,961	10,809	9,212
Credit card	7,474	8,306	7,712	7,323	6,039
Individual lines of credit[b]	8,486	8,347	5,546	4,566	3,412
Other[b]	382	354	181	186	328
	61,980	62,074	43,297	39,194	30,663
Commercial:					
Commercial and industrial	20,486	21,632	13,831	14,749	14,632
Loans secured by real estate[a]	9,251	10,123	5,366	5,718	5,673
Construction and					
development loans					
secured by real estate[a]	4,418	6,781	4,002	4,265	3,500
Loans for purchasing or					
carrying securities	3,090	987	216	255	376
Financial institutions	2,170	2,017	1,427	1,424	1,131
Lease financing	1,715	1,889	779	825	835
Agricultural	1,679	1,704	1,124	1,177	1,159
Other	1,370	1,360	497	730	624
	44,179	46,493	27,242	29,143	27,930
	106,159	108,567	70,539	68,337	58,593
Foreign					
Commercial and industrial	11,448	10,338	9,538	10,577	10,797
Governments and official					
institutions	3,429	3,513	3,557	3,934	3,374
Banks and other financial					
institutions	2,279	1,855	2,080	1,867	2,181
Other[a]	3,064	1,436	920	1,100	958
	20,220	17,142	16,095	17,478	17,310
Total loans	126,379	125,709	86,634	85,815	75,903
Less: Allowance for credit					
losses	3,508	3,921	2,420	2,912	3,373
	$122,871	$121,788	$84,214	$82,903	$72,530

(Continued)

EXHIBIT 8-3 *(Continued)*

[a]During 1993, in-substance repossessions (ISR) were reclassified to the loan portfolio as a result of regulatory clarification of the definition of an ISR. This clarification also resulted in the reclassification of corresponding prior-period amounts. ISRs reclassified to loans during 1993 were as follows: secured by first mortgages on residential properties of $2 million, loans secured by real estate of $148 million, construction and development loans secured by real estate of $411 million, and other foreign of $7 million. Loans previously reported as ISRs that were reclassified to loans were as follows: secured by first mortgages on residential properties of $14 million at December 31, 1992; loans secured by real estate of $211 million, $57 million, $28 million, and $32 million at December 31, 1992, 1991, 1990, and 1989, respectively; construction and development loans secured by real estate of $944 million, $209 million, $22 million, and $10 million at December 31, 1992, 1991, 1990, and 1989, respectively; and other foreign of $17 million at December 31, 1992.

[b]Installment loans, individual lines of credit, and other consumer loans included the following aggregate amounts that were collateralized by junior mortgages on residential real estate: $12,847 million at December 31, 1993, $13,870 million at December 31, 1992, $9,281 million at December 31, 1991, $7,857 million at December 31, 1990, and $5,600 million at December 31, 1989.

Risk-Based Capital and Risk-Based Capital Ratios

	December 31		
(dollar amounts in millions)	1993[a]	1992[b]	1991[b]
Risk-Based Capital			
Common stockholders' equity	$14,165	$12,509	$ 6,737
Perpetual preferred stock	2,979	2,979	1,326
Less: Goodwill, nongrandfathered core deposit and other identifiable intangibles, and other deductions	(5,125)[c]	(4,179)	(150)
Tier 1 capital	12,019	11,309	7,913
Eligible portion of the allowance for credit losses (exclusive of allocated transfer risk reserve)[d]	1,995	2,096	1,378
Hybrid capital instruments[e]	568	1,762	1,165
Subordinated notes and debentures[f]	4,422	4,122	1,377
Less: Other deductions	(37)	(250)	(6)
Tier 2 capital	6,948	7,730	3,914
Total Risk-Based Capital	$18,967	$19,039	$11,827
Risk-Based Capital Ratios			
Tier 1 capital	7.61%	6.82%	7.25%
Tier 2 capital	4.39	4.66	3.58
Total Risk-Based Capital Ratio	12.00%	11.48%	10.83%
Tier 1 Leverage Ratio[g]	6.64%	6.37%	6.80%

[a]This risk-based capital information is calculated in accordance with the guidelines of the federal banking regulators as they apply to the corporation beginning in 1993. Due to the adoption of SFAS No. 109 in the first quarter of 1993, CDI and other identifiable intangibles that are normally deducted from Tier 1 capital under the current guidelines were $510 million higher at December 31, 1993, with a corresponding increase in deferred taxes. The federal banking regulators have not issued final capital regulations on the adoption of SFAS No. 109 and are currently considering whether such increased intangibles should be deducted from capital. Management believes that the

(Continued)

EXHIBIT 8–3   *(Continued)*

increased amounts of CDI and other identifiable intangibles resulting from the adoption of SFASNo. 109 do not pose a risk to the corporation's capital and should not be deducted from capital in determining capital ratios. Pending final resolution of this issue by the banking regulators, such amounts have not been deducted from capital in determining the December 31, 1993 capital ratios shown above.

[b]Risk-based capital and risk-based capital ratios under guidelines effective December 31, 1992.
[c]Includes nongrandfathered CDI and other identifiable intangibles acquired after February 19, 1992 of $1,008 million and $71 million, respectively, excluding gross-ups due to the adoption of SFAS No. 109. Also, includes $35 million of the excess of the net book value over 90 percent of the fair value of purchased mortgage servicing rights and credit card intangibles.
[d]Limited to 1.25% of risk-weighted assets.
[e]Represents subordinated capital notes adjusted for certain limitations.
[f]Limited to 50% of core capital, and reduced by 20% per year during an instrument's last five years before maturity.
[g]Based on Tier 1 capital before other deductions of $37 million, $250 million, and $6 million at December 31, 1993, 1992, and 1991, respectively.

Derivative and Foreign Exchange Transactions

	December 31, 1993		
(in billions)	Contractual or Notional Amount	Credit Exposure Amount	Fair Value Amount[a]
Trading:			
Derivatives	$432.5	$5.1[b]	$0.3
Foreign exchange contracts	423.7	3.0[b]	(0.2)
Other[c]	19.6	0.1[b]	—
Asset and liability			
management derivatives	46.2	0.2[d]	1.2

[a]Fair value amounts consist of net unrealized gains and losses, accrued interest receivable or payable, and premiums paid or received.
[b]Amounts represent net unrealized gains on contracts with counterparties for whom legally enforceable master netting agreements were in place and effective at December 31, 1993 and gross unrealized gains on contracts with other counterparties.
[c]Includes amounts related to foreign currency options purchased and sold.
[d]Represents the maximum potential accounting loss related to contracts outstanding at December 31, 1993.

Source: BankAmerica 1993 Annual Report.

of losses on amounts above the ceiling. Small depositors could also suffer some delay in receiving their funds in the event of a bank failure. Therefore, while FDIC insurance can be a stabilizing influence, it will not block a runoff of deposits at a bank that lacks a firm depositor base.)

Growing Confidence

Ultimately, a bank's financial health rests on its ability to continue to fund. The ability to generate cash from operations, a key tool in analyzing industrial companies, is less useful in assessing banks. Banks can always meet their cash requirements from external sources (depositors and lenders), as long as they enjoy the confidence of the providers of funds.

Unfortunately for the analyst, confidence is both difficult to measure and subject to sudden and dramatic fluctuations. A bank that seems, based on its most recent quarterly financial statement, to be facing nothing worse than some near-term earnings problems, may suffer a loss of confidence and face a severe funding crisis before its next statement appears. The inadequate response time of an analyst who relies entirely on 10-Q reports is a function also of the limited disclosure requirements relating to problem loans. (For example, a bank can continue to accrue income on a loan upon which it is receiving no cash interest payments, until a necessarily subjective judgment is made that the borrower's ability to repay has been permanently impaired.)

To anticipate the losses on a bank's securities that accompany an evaporation of confidence, an analyst must be aware when the attitude of lenders and depositors is changing over periods shorter than the three-month reporting cycle. Religiously following trade publications, the most prominent of which is *American Banker,* represents a good start. Beyond that, the analyst who wishes to follow banks on any sort of permanent basis should invest time in developing a network of contacts. A great deal of valuable—and perfectly legal, non-inside—information can be obtained from a bank's employees, ex-employees, customers, and competitors, as well as from business people with intimate knowledge of the bank's regional economy and real estate environment. Devoting a few days each year to attending conferences can pay handsome dividends in the form of people to call when questions begin to be asked that the financial statements cannot answer.

To be sure, some rumor and misinformation will emerge from these discussions, but the analyst must learn through experience to identify which sources are most reliable. Gauging the confidence factor is an inexact science, but in some situations has more near-term importance to the investment decision maker than all the ratio analysis one can perform.

INSURANCE COMPANIES

Risk, an important determinant of value for any type of enterprise, is central to the business of insurance underwriting. Mindful of that fact, state insurance commissioners—who are charged with protecting policyholders' interests—impose rules that limit insurers' risk-taking. The regulators take the further precaution of requiring companies to establish sizable loss reserves, just in case the risk rules fail to perform as intended. As a final safeguard, insurance commissions in many states oblige underwriters to participate in risk-sharing pools, which prevent any company's failure from resulting in policyholders' claims not being paid. Considering also the extensive disclosures on the subject in insurance companies' financial reports, an analyst might perceive insurers' risks to be readily quantifiable in addition to being carefully controlled.

In actuality, however, many insurance companies tend not to move, over time, toward extinguishing risk, but rather to seek additional risk in spite of all the constraints placed on them. The underlying reason for such behavior is that insurance is for the most part a service that is difficult to differentiate. A company may design a new type of policy, but competitors can usually copy it. Nor is it easy for an insurer to provide superior yields to policyholders, since the types of asset in which it is permitted to invest offer essentially the same returns to all companies. As a result, the path frequently chosen by companies that hope to achieve above-average profits or growth is to take above-average risks. The opportunities for doing so are numerous, given the insurance business's multifaceted character.

Generally speaking, the potential for stepping up risk on the underwriting side is limited for life (as opposed to property and casualty) companies. Insurance regulators require actuarially sound reserving, so company-wrecking claim experience is unlikely unless fraud has occurred.

On the investment side, however, a company can raise its riskiness substantially while staying well within the law. For instance, an insurer can buy bonds of lesser quality than its peers or invest more heavily in equities, which tend to be more volatile than fixed-income investments. Another strategy that offers potentially superior returns but entails considerable risk is to bet aggressively on the future direction of interest rates. If, for example, the insurance company's investment committee expects a decline in interest rates, it can load the portfolio with bonds of very long maturities. These issues will ordinarily produce the largest capital gains if rates in fact fall, but will likewise result in the biggest losses if the company's forecast proves wrong and rates instead rise.

The marketing arena provides additional opportunities for companies to pursue high growth and profitability while also taking on greater risk. An innovative type of policy—particularly one that emphasizes the tax-advantaged investment aspects of insurance—can suddenly and dramatically accelerate a company's sales growth. Past examples of successful new products have included universal life, single-premium deferred annuities, and single-premium whole life insurance. Excessive concentration in this sort of line can be hazardous, however, since a change in the tax code or in the investment climate may cause sales to decline as sharply as they rose. Another risky marketing strategy involves reliance on a non-captive distribution system such as a stockbrokerage. If the brokerage ever shifts its business to another insurance underwriter, it may precipitate a major wave of surrenders by policyholders, potentially even creating a liquidity crisis. This is a particularly serious threat if the broker's change of loyalty creates opportunities for the salespeople to earn new commissions by "switching" customers out of their old policies and into policies underwritten by the new carrier. An underwriter can minimize this risk by not paying too much of the commission up front, that is, by rewarding the salesperson for selling policies that remain on the books for a long time. A growth-oriented company, however, may accept the risk of surrenders, reckoning that it can grab market share from competitors by assuring salespeople a full and rapid payout.

In addition to assessing the extent to which a company has deliberately left itself exposed both to investment and marketing risk, the insurance analyst must deal with another set of risks related to the industry's dual accounting system. The financial statements that publicly held insurance holding companies disseminate to their shareholders are generally prepared in accordance with GAAP. Their operating subsidiaries—the entities that actually underwrite policies—report on a fundamentally different basis, known as statutory accounting.[7] By studying only the more readily available GAAP statements of a holding company, an analyst may seriously misjudge the total enterprise's financial condition and prospects. Obtaining the statutory statements, which are usually available either from the holding company itself or from the regulatory commissions of the various states in which the company operates, is well worth the additional effort required.

---

[7]Mutual insurance companies ordinarily report to their policyholder/owners on a statutory basis.

A basic difference between GAAP and statutory accounting involves the recognition of revenues and expenses. Following the principle of matching, GAAP statements capitalize costs associated with selling insurance policies, and expense the result intangible asset ("Deferred policy acquisition costs") as premiums are collected. Statutory statements, in sharp contrast, expense up-front costs immediately and recognize premiums when due. In essence, statutory accounting emphasizes solvency, with an eye toward preventing a company from underwriting more business than its capital and surplus[8] can support and thereby putting policyholders at risk.

A consequence of this fundamental difference between the two accounting methods is that an insurance company may appear to be thriving under GAAP while, on a statutory basis, it is simultaneously facing a financial squeeze that could prove debilitating. Consider what happens when a holding company's operating subsidiaries dramatically increase their sales of an insurance product that entails heavy front-end marketing costs. On the parent's books, revenues accelerate sharply and expenses rise only by the amount of the acquisition costs attributable to the current period. Operating profits consequently surge, indicating a strong financial profile. Down at the subsidiaries, on the other hand, the immediate expensing of acquisition costs depletes statutory surplus. If this "surplus strain" becomes severe enough, the state insurance commissioners may impose restrictions on the subsidiaries' ability to underwrite additional business. In that case, the rapid revenue growth reported to public shareholders through the GAAP statements will not be sustainable.

Analysts who extrapolate from current holding company statements to forecast sales, relying heavily on demonstrated market success of the subsidiaries' insurance products, will overestimate both future earnings and present share value. To avoid such an error, it is necessary to construct a statutorylike financial picture of the operating subsidiaries.

Insurance companies and state insurance commissions are generally cooperative in providing copies of statutory statements, but learning to use them requires considerably more effort than obtaining them. Exhibit 8–4 illustrates the unique character of statutory statements. The

---

[8]A stock life insurance company's capital consists primarily of the par value of its outstanding capital stock. (Additional capital may exist in the form of bonds, debentures, guaranty capital notes, or contribution certificates.) "Surplus," simply defined, is the excess of "admitted" assets over liabilities and capital. ("Admitted" assets generally exclude furniture and equipment, as well as doubtful accrued items that appear to provide little liquidation value, such as furniture and equipment, as well as defaulted bonds and accrued income that may prove uncollectible.)

EXHIBIT 8–4   Annual Statement for the Year 1993 of the John Hancock Mutual Life Insurance Company

SUMMARY OF OPERATIONS (Excluding Unrealized Capital Gains and Losses	1 1993	2 1992
1. Premiums and annuity considerations (Exhibit 1, Part 1, Line 20d, Col. 1, less Col. 22)	2,767,189,554	2,126,164,204
1A. Deposit-type funds	5,647,787,284	5,178,492,646
2. Considerations for supplementary contracts with life contingencies (Exhibit 12, Line 3)	28,019,614	21,748,425
3. Considerations for supplementary contracts without life contingencies and dividend accumulations (Exhibit 12, Lines 4 and 5)	136,364,727	151,400,595
3A. Coupons left to accumulate at interest (Exhibit 12, Line 5A)		
4. Net investment income (includes $_____ equity in undistributed income or loss of subsidiaries) (Exhibit 2, Line 16)	2,519,986,649	2,506,746,600
4A. Amortization of Interest Maintenance Reserve (IMR) (Page 47, Line 5)	12,672,657	4,534,392
5. Commissions and expense allowances on reinsurance cased (Exhibit 1, Part 2, Line 26a, Col. 1)	23,771,072	16,543,668
5A. Reserve adjustments on reinsurance coded (Exhibit 12, Line 9A)	2,696,175	(4,322,666)
6. Aggregate write-ins for miscellaneous income	28,855,011	23,381,196
7. Totals (Lines 1 to 6)	11,167,342,743	10,024,689,060
8. Death benefits	777,415,232	759,119,019
9. Matured endowments (excluding guaranteed annual pure endowments)	20,619,286	20,655,696
10. Annuity benefits (Exhibit 11, Part 2, Line 6d, Cols. 4 & 8)	1,152,411,330	1,078,177,032
11. Disability benefits and benefits under accident and health policies	405,664,857	396,747,710
11A. Coupons, guaranteed annual pure endowments and similar benefits (Exhibit 7, Line 15, Cols. 3 + 4)		
12. Survivor benefits and other fund withdrawals	4,157,911,831	3,936,083,482
13. Group conversions	79,388	181,257
14. Interest on policy or contract funds	995,477,556	1,007,127,516
15. Payments on supplementary contracts with life contingencies (Exhibit 32, Line 20.1)	26,017,189	25,223,321
16. Payments on supplementary contracts without life contingencies and of dividend accumulations (Exhibit 12, Lines 20.2 + 21)	178,690,630	196,210,105
16A. Accumulated coupon payments (Exhibit 12, Line 21A)		
17. Increase in aggregate reserves for life and accident and health policies and contracts	935,629,327	424,060,446
17A. Increase in liability for premium and other deposit funds	(614,521,606)	(270,182,168)
18. Increase in reserve for supplementary contracts without life contingencies and for dividend and coupon accumulation	17,335,243	22,364,607
19. Totals (Lines 8 to 18)	8,052,734,263	7,595,768,023

(Continued)

EXHIBIT 8–4   *(Continued)*

	1993	1992
20. Commissions on premiums and annuity considerations (direct business only) (Exhibit 1, Part 2, Line 30, Col. 1)	144,879,775	134,948,494
21. Commissions and expense allowances on reinsurance assumed (Exhibit 1, Part 2, Line 26b, Col. 1, less Col. 11)	13,111,556	13,692,858
22. General insurance expenses (Exhibit 5, Line 30, Cols. 1 + 2 + 3)	531,094,217	487,861,184
23. Insurance taxes, licenses and fees, excluding federal income taxes (Exhibit 6, Line 7, Cols. 1 + 2 + 3)	68,948,563	65,873,695
24. Increase in loading on and cost of collection in excess of loading on deferred and uncollected premiums	(4,180,996)	(3,610,366)
24A. Net transfers to or (from) Separate Accounts	1,533,814,474	1,022,856,787
25. Aggregate write-ins for deductions	80,640,436	94,500,707
26. Totals (Lines 19 to 25)	10,421,042,288	9,401,891,382
27. Net gain from operations before dividends to policyholders and federal income taxes (Line 7 minus Line 26)	746,300,455	622,797,678
28. Dividends to policyholders (Exhibit 7, Line 15, Cols. 1 and 2)	366,109,495	346,951,924
29. Net gain from operations after dividends to policyholders and before federal income taxes (Line 27 minus Line 28)	380,190,960	275,845,754
30. Federal income taxes incurred (excluding tax on capital gains)	51,770,447	31,964,764
31. Net gain from operations after dividends to policyholders and federal income taxes and before realized capital gains or (losses) (Line 29 minus Line 30)	328,420,513	243,880,990
32. Net realized capital gains or (losses) less capital gains tax of $43,888,587 (excluding $61,155,246 transferred to the IMR)	(128,250,543)	(119,235,012)
33. Net income (Line 31 plus Line 32)	200,169,970	124,645,978

CAPITAL AND SURPLUS ACCOUNT

	1993	1992
34. Capital and surplus, December 31, previous year (Page 3, Line 37, Col. 2)	1,727,744,151	1,580,092,889
35. Net income (Line 33)	200,169,970	124,645,978
36. Change in net unrealized capital gains or (losses)	(39,528,511)	51,160,183
37. Change in non-admitted assets and related items (Exhibit 34, Line 13, Col. 3)	(130,349)	1,986,559
38. Change in liability for reinsurance in unauthorized companies (Page 3, Line 24.2, Col. 2 minus 1)		
39. Change in reserve on account of change in valuation basis (increase) or decrease (Exh. 8A, Line D. Col. 4)	42,220,725	19,391,727
40. Change in Asset Valuation Reserve (Page 48, Col. 7, Line 2 plus Line 3 plus Line 11)	(119,285,465)	(39,537,528)
41. Change in treasury stock (Page 3, Lines 35 (1) & (2) Col. 2 minus 1)		
42. Change in surplus in Separate Accounts Statement	5,749,591	4,120,689

(Continued)

EXHIBIT 8–4   *(Continued)*

	1993	1992
43. Capital changes:		
(a) Paid in		
(b) Transferred from surplus (Stock Dividend)		
(c) Transferred to surplus (Exhibit 12, Line 24, capital portion)		
44. Surplus adjustments:		
(a) Paid in		
(b) Transferred to capital (Stock Dividend) (Exhibit 12, Line 25, inside amount for stock $)		
(c) Transferred from capital (Exhibits 12, Line 24, surplus portion)		
45. Dividends to stockholders		
46. Aggregate write-ins for gains and losses in surplus	(2,199,028)	(14,116,346)
47. Net change in capital and surplus for the year (Lines 35 through 46)	86,996,933	147,651,262
48. Capital and surplus, December 31, current year (Lines 34 + 47) (Page 3, Line 37)	1,814,741,084	1,727,744,151
DETAILS OF WRITE-INS AGGREGATED AT LINE 6 FOR MISCELLANEOUS INCOME		
0601. IRS interest receivable	144,855	7,015,050
0602. Profit and loss on insurance	1,261,751	(4,323,889)
0603. Net credit FEGLI conversion	599,184	408,270
0604. Pension investment advisory service fees only	4,352,272	3,501,853
0605. Special service fees	21,296,122	17,330,454
0698. Summary of remaining write-ins for Line 6 from overflow page	1,200,827	(550,542)
0699. Totals (Lines 0601 thru 0605 plus 0698) (Page 4, Line 6)	28,855,011	23,381,196
DETAILS OF WRITE-INS AGGREGATED AT LINE 25 FOR DEDUCTIONS		
2501. Reserve adj. reinsurance assumed	11,308,482	14,504,385
2502. Prov. for future RPA amts.	(3,555,228)	2,734,557
2503. Incr. in annuities certain	52,190,717	43,265,494
2504. Provision for cost restructuring	5,000,000	12,551,789
2505. Reserve adj. for refund provision - IVA	1,157,827	1,365,932
2598. Summary of remaining write-ins for Line 25 from overflow page	14,532,638	20,098,570
2599. Totals (Lines 2501 thru 2505 plus 2598) (Page 4, Line 25)	80,640,436	94,500,707
DETAILS OF WRITE-INS AGGREGATED AT LINE 46 FOR GAINS AND LOSSES IN SURPLUS		
4601. Surplus transfers	24,500,972	0
4602. Additional provision for federal income taxes	(26,700,000)	(24,399,999)
4603. Other surplus charges	0	10,083,653
4604.		
4605.		
4698. Summary of remaining write-ins for Line 46 from overflow page		
4699. Totals (Lines 4601 thru 4605 plus 4698) (Page 4, Line 46)	(2,199,028)	(14,116,346)

"Summary of Operations" combines elements of standard financial reporting's income statement, changes in shareholders' equity, and notes to financial statements.

Although a significant investment of time is required to gain a facility with statutory statements, the payoff in terms of analytical understanding is vast. For example, the operating subsidiaries report reinsurance arrangements in greater detail than the holding company does. The significance is that the liability removed from the balance sheet through a reinsurance contract may not be cleanly shed if the reinsurer is a thinly capitalized offshore company. Examining the statutory statements similarly provides valuable added detail on intercompany investments. It is not uncommon for an insurance holding company to repair the erosion of a subsidiary's surplus by directing another subsidiary to infuse cash into its weak sister, taking preferred stock in exchange. If the faltering subsidiary suffers further financial deterioration, its formerly healthy affiliate may, as a consequence, incur losses and reduction of surplus. Companies that transfer risk in this manner may have, in reality, much less geographic and regulatory diversification than their consolidated reports to shareholders suggest.

Yet another risk that remains hidden to analysts who read only the consolidated statements involves the quality of the company's investment portfolio. While the GAAP statements disclose mainly the dollar amounts held in general asset categories, the statutory statements detail the portfolio security by security, as well as reveal the issues that were bought and sold during the past year. Moreover, under GAAP accounting, a bond that is held as a long-term investment is ordinarily carried at its original purchase price, unless the obligor's ability to pay the interest and principal has become seriously impaired. Without being in imminent danger of default, however, a bond may have a market value far below its original cost to the insurance company. Its trading price may have fallen due to a modest drop in its credit rating, an increased risk premium on bonds in its rating category, or a general rise in interest rates, which affects the prices of bonds in every quality tier. A company's GAAP statements provide only a footnote on the overall portfolio's market valuation. Knowing the specific securities in which the company has invested shows more plainly the portfolio's risks and the potential for future losses. (Losses arising from poor credit decisions, for example, may cause the analyst more concern than fluctuations related to swings in interest rates.) In analogous fashion, the statutory statements define the risks of real estate loans more fully than GAAP disclosures by listing specific properties, along with their respective locations and loan balances. Although up-to-date appraisals are not generally provided, the analyst may be able to make reasonable inferences about current loan-to-value ratios from studying the dates on which the loans were originally booked.

Before leaving the subject of insurance companies' financial statements, a word is in order on the property and casualty sector. Most of the preceding comments apply to P&C companies as well as life insurers, but some additional analytical considerations also apply.

A key consideration is the property and casualty underwriting cycle. Due to the industry's vigorous competition, P&C insurers in aggregate price their product at a loss. That is, claims generally exceed premiums received. The margin of profit derives from income earned on premiums. Profitability, therefore, is sensitive not only to the intensity of competition at a given time but also to the returns available in the capital markets. Both variables are subject to fluctuations—underwriting competition waxes and wanes as capital enters or exits the industry in response to shifts in expected returns, while interest rates and equity prices respond to a variety of economic forces. Exceptionally severe natural disasters (hurricanes and earthquakes) likewise cause industry profitability to vary from year to year by generating extraordinarily large claims.

To track, and possibly forecast, the trend of profitability in the P&C business, insurance company analysts calculate the industry's combined ratio, defined as follows:

$$\text{Combined ratio} = \text{Loss ratio} + \text{Expense ratio} + \text{Dividend ratio}$$

where
$$\text{Loss ratio} = \frac{\text{Incurred losses} + \text{Loss adjustment expenses}}{\text{Earned premiums*}}$$

$$\text{Expense ratio} = \frac{\text{Underwriting and general expenses}}{\text{Net premiums written}}$$

$$\text{Dividend ratio} = \frac{\text{Policyholder dividends}}{\text{Earned premiums*}}$$

*Earned premiums are, in statutory accounting, premiums received in cash.

Combined ratios commonly exceed 100%, meaning that P&C companies generate net losses on insurance operations. Their margin of profit therefore derives entirely from investment earnings. An individual company's combined ratio, utilized in a comparative ratio analysis, may provide a clue that the firm is pursuing overly aggressive strategies in the underwriting or investment area.

Another means of spotting potential problems is to monitor the ratio of reserves to premiums. A decrease in this indicator may suggest that the company is reserving inadequately to maximize its current reported earnings. If this is the case, then the practice will ultimately catch up with the firm in the form of a future penalty to net income.

MUNICIPALITIES

Financial analysis of municipalities, which is ordinarily conducted for the purpose of assessing creditworthiness, presents unique challenges to those more familiar with the statements of business enterprises. For one thing, the statements issued by city governments—which are the main focus of this section—are presented in a very different format from the one that private companies employ. In addition, comparative analysis of municipalities is hampered by a relative lack of standardization in reporting. Finally, the assessment of local economic conditions, an element that is not typically a major factor in analyzing national or multinational corporations, commands top priority in making judgments about municipalities.

Reflecting its importance in the analysis, the study of local economic conditions is the first factor addressed in the following discussion. Next comes a brief guide to evaluating a city government's finances. The section concludes with some comments on quality of management, which while important—as with any issuer of financial statements—tends to be dominated by the other two factors in judging a municipality's fiscal soundness.

Local Economic Conditions

A favorable economic climate is both vibrant and diverse. A prevalence of profitable and expanding industries tends to generate jobs, in turn producing a stable or growing population and thereby supporting property values. If, on the other hand, declining industries represent a large portion of the economic base, revenues derived from payroll or income taxes may decline at the same time that rising unemployment is increasing demands for social services. A predominance of highly cyclical industries is likewise undesirable, since it can result in wide swings in employment and income over periods of a few years. The type of economic mix that is most conducive to long-run financial strength for a municipality is one that is free of concentration in a single sector. Even if an industry is healthy and steady today, it may mature or decline in the future as economic and competitive conditions change. Similar, but more pronounced vulnerability characterizes a locality that relies heavily for employment on a single firm within an industry.

While microeconomic analysis is unfamiliar to some users of financial statements, it utilizes trend assessments and ratio comparisons that are much like those described elsewhere in this book. Municipalities themselves provide raw data for the analysis, with government bodies such as the Commerce Department and the Census Bureau supplying other useful statistics.

Evaluating a Municipality's Finances

Unlike public corporations, municipalities are not bound by financial reporting rules such as those promulgated by the Securities and Exchange Commission. Cities, counties, and states have no obligation, moreover, to file in accordance with GAAP. In fact, some states actually bar the use of GAAP accounting by local governments, instead mandating statutory accounting. An increasing number of municipalities, it is true, have switched to GAAP in recent years, and many also have their statements audited by outside accounting firms. Others, however, are constrained by state laws forbidding external audits—measures perhaps designed to protect the prerogatives of state-employed auditors general. To complicate matters further, each state determines its own filing requirements; rules devised by an entity known as the Government Accounting Standards Board are recommendations only. The net result is that 50 distinct sets of standards exist, greatly impeding comparability. Practices differ on matters as fundamental as the use of cash versus accrual accounting.

Even before addressing the issue of comparability, moreover, the analyst studying a municipality's financial statements must contend with features that distinguish them from most other types of financial statements. The City of Chicago's 1992 financial statements (Exhibit 8–5), for instance, include a "Combined Statement of Revenues, Expenditures, and Expendable Trust Funds," which blends the concepts of the income statement and the statement of cash flows. Observe as well that Chicago provides no truly consolidated statements; the "Totals" shown for the income cash flow statement and for the "Combined Balance Sheet" are memorandum items only.

In lieu of consolidating the financials of its various funds, a municipality reports on them separately. Most important to analysts, as a rule,

EXHIBIT 8–5

City of Chicago, Illinois
(A) Combined Balance Sheet
All Fund Types and Account Groups
($000 omitted)
December 31, 1992

		Governmental Fund	
	General	Special Revenue	Debt Service
ASSETS AND OTHER DEBITS			
Cash and Cash Equivalents	$ 67,912	$161,821	$ 64,901
Investments	95,645	107,471	27,042
Cash with Escrow Agent	3,234	—	83,309
Receivables (Net of Allowances):			
Property Tax	—	294,690	384,305
Accounts	76,811	150,383	836
Due from Other Funds	56,481	50,561	1,392
Due from Other Governments	102,692	214,164	609
Inventories	16,345	—	—
Restricted Assets:			
Cash and Cash Equivalents	—	—	—
Investments	—	—	—
Other Assets	—	19,072	—
Property, Plant and Equipment (Net of Accumulated Depreciation for Proprietary Funds)	—	—	—
Amount Available for Debt Service in Other Funds	—	—	—
Amount to be Provided for Retirement of General Long-Term Obligations	—	—	—
Total Assets and Other Debts	$419,120	$998,162	$562,394
LIABILITIES, EQUITY AND OTHER CREDITS			
LIABILITIES			
Voucher Warrants Payable	$ 83,794	$ 81,328	$ —
Bonds, Notes and Capitalized Lease Obligations Payable-Current	—	—	28,832
Accrued Interest	—	—	34,269
Due to Other Funds	165,704	127,420	381
Accrued and Other Liabilities	64,342	21,969	—
Claims and Judgments	2,000	12,286	—
Deferred Revenue	1,269	582,559	361,061
Current Liabilities Payable from Restricted Assets	—	—	—
Employee Vacation Leave	—	—	—
Bonds, Notes and Capitalized Lease Obligations Payable-Noncurrent	—	—	—
Pension Obligations	—	—	—
Deferred Compensation Plan Obligations	—	—	—
Total Liabilities	$317,109	$825,562	$424,543

See notes to general purpose financial statements.

City of Chicago, Illinois
(A) Combined Balance Sheet
All Fund Types and Account Groups
($000 omitted)
December 31, 1992

Types	Proprietary Fund Type	Fiduciary Fund Types	Account Groups		Totals (Memorandum Only)
Capital Projects	Enterprise	Trust and Agency	General Fixed Assets	General Long-term Debt	1992
$106,520	$ 128,800	$ 402,406	$ —	$ —	$ 932,360
196,506	56,213	5,504,056	—	—	5,986,933
—	—	6,702	—	—	93,245
—	—	—	—	—	678,995
241	120,639	299,541	—	—	648,451
3,392	26,389	246,802	—	—	385,017
8,662	—	—	—	—	326,127
—	15,668	—	—	—	32,013
—	790,324	—	—	—	790,324
—	269,555	—	—	—	269,555
203	34,207	—	—	—	53,482
—	3,395,777	—	880,907	—	4,276,684
—	—	—	—	143,900	143,900
—	—	—	—	2,687,533	2,687,533
$315,524	$4,837,572	$6,459,507	$880,907	$2,831,433	$17,304,619
$ 15,179	$ 70,886	$ 70,410	$ —	$ —	321,597
—	22,010	—	—	—	50,842
—	—	—	—	—	34,269
3,018	42,541	45,953	—	—	385,017
613	72,193	97,811	—	—	256,928
—	—	—	—	163,560	177,846
35	48,453	—	—	—	993,377
—	344,118	—	—	—	344,118
—	—	—	—	53,947	53,947
—	2,748,520	—	—	1,487,338	4,235,858
—	—	—	—	1,126,588	1,126,588
—	—	507,382	—	—	507,382
$ 18,845	$3,348,721	$ 721,556	$ —	$2,831,433	$ 8,487,769

(Continued)

EXHIBIT 8–5   *(Continued)*

City of Chicago, Illinois
(A) Combined Balance Sheet
All Fund Types and Account Groups
($000 omitted)
December 31, 1992

		Governmental Fund	
	General	Special Revenue	Debt Service
EQUITY AND OTHER CREDITS			
Investment in General Fixed Assets	$ —	$ —	$ —
Contributed Capital	—	—	—
Retained Earnings:			
Reserved for Restricted Accounts	—	—	—
Unreserved	—	—	—
Fund Balance			
Reserved for Encumbrances	40,506	24,017	—
Reserved for Resale Property	—	19,072	—
Reserved for Inventory	16,345	—	—
Reserved for Debt Service	—	6,049	137,851
Reserved for Employee Benefit Plans	—	—	—
Unreserved	45,160	123,462	—
Total Equity and Other Credits	102,011	172,600	137,851
Total Liabilities, Equity and Other Credits	$419,120	$998,162	$562,394

See notes to general purpose financial statements.

City of Chicago, Illinois
(A) Combined Balance Sheet
All Fund Types and Account Groups
($000 omitted)
December 31, 1992

Types	Proprietary Fund Type	Fiduciary Fund Types	Account Groups		Totals (Memorandum Only)
Capital Projects	Enterprise	Trust and Agency	General Fixed Assets	General Long-term Debt	1992
$ —	$ —	$ —	$880,907	$ —	$ 880,907
—	577,846	—	—	—	577,846
—	282,990	—	—	—	282,990
—	628,015	—	—	—	628,015
42,531	—	—	—	—	107,054
203	—	—	—	—	19,275
—	—	—	—	—	16,345
—	—	—	—	—	143,900
—	—	5,737,917	—	—	5,737,917
253,945	—	34	—	—	422,601
296,679	1,488,851	5,737,951	880,907	—	8,816,850
$315,524	$4,837,572	$6,459,507	$880,907	$2,831,433	$17,304,619

(Continued)

EXHIBIT 8–5 *(Continued)*

City of Chicago, Illinois
(B) Combined Statement of Revenues, Expenditures and
Changes in Fund Balances
All Governmental Fund Types and Expendable Trust Funds
($000 omitted)
Year Ended December 31, 1992

	Governmental	
	General	Special Revenue
Revenues:		
Property Tax	$ —	$ 245,644
Utility Tax	307,500	15,724
Sales Tax	299,187	403
Transportation Tax	100,689	109,302
State Income Tax	174,558	45,367
Transaction Tax	109,448	—
Other Taxes	112,179	6,191
Federal/State Grants	3,555	504,935
Internal Service	189,119	9,110
Licenses and Permits	36,583	—
Fines	74,729	8,495
Interest	15,459	9,160
Charges for Services	54,724	17,320
Miscellaneous	20,451	2,225
Total Revenues	1,498,181	973,876
Expenditures:		
Current:		
General Government	450,485	434,187
Health	46,409	50,217
Public Safety	929,186	2,484
Streets and Sanitation	206,249	84,278
Transportation	17,261	108,263
Aviation	436	551
Cultural and Recreational	1,838	65,765
Employee Pensions	—	249,703
Other	5,251	868
Capital Projects	—	100,953
Debt Service:		
Principal Retirement	500	4,901
Interest and Other Fiscal Charges	16,745	6,524
Total Expenditures	1,674,360	1,108,694
Revenues Over (Under) Expenditures	(176,179)	(134,818)

See notes to general purpose financial statements.

City of Chicago, Illinois
(B) Combined Statement of Revenues, Expenditures and Changes in Fund Balances
All Governmental Fund Types and Expendable Trust Funds
($000 omitted)
Year Ended December 31, 1992

Fund Types		Fiduciary Fund Type	Totals (Memorandum Only)
Debt Service	Capital Projects	Expendable Trust	1992
$374,102	$ —	$ —	$ 619,746
—	—	—	323,224
376	—	—	299,966
6,665	—	—	216,656
421	—	—	220,346
—	—	—	109,448
174	—	—	118,544
—	—	—	508,490
—	—	—	198,229
—	—	—	36,583
—	—	—	83,224
9,270	7,989	—	41,878
—	—	—	72,044
10,000	804	—	33,480
401,008	8,793	—	2,881,858
—	—	—	884,672
—	—	—	96,626
—	—	—	931,670
—	—	—	290,527
—	—	—	125,524
—	—	—	987
—	—	—	67,603
—	—	—	249,703
—	—	—	6,119
—	114,554	—	215,507
325,951	—	—	331,352
65,913	—	—	89,182
391,864	114,554	—	3,289,472
9,144	(105,761)	—	(407,614)

(Continued)

EXHIBIT 8–5   *(Continued)*

City of Chicago, Illinois
(B) Combined Statement of Revenues, Expenditures and
Changes in Fund Balances
All Governmental Fund Types and Expendable Trust Funds
($000 omitted)
Year Ended December 31, 1992

		Governmental
	General	**Special Revenue**
Other Financing Sources (Uses):		
Proceeds of Debt, Net of Issuance Costs	$184,176	$ 86,577
Operating Transfers In	18,000	3,596
Operating Transfers Out	—	(18,828)
Total Other Financing Sources	202,176	71,345
Revenues and Other Financing Sources Over (Under) Expenditures and Other Financing Uses	25,997	(63,473)
Fund Balance, Beginning of Year, as restated	122,214	189,873
Residual Equity Transfer	(46,200)	46,200
Fund Balance, End of Year	$102,011	$ 172,600

See notes to general purpose financial statements.

are the "General" (or "Corporate") and the "Special Revenue" funds. The latter type includes revenues that are restricted to particular uses. "Proprietary" funds typically involve municipally managed enterprises such as sewer systems, athletic stadiums, electrical power systems, and municipal airports. The City of Chicago includes in its "Combined Balance Sheet" an account group labeled "General Fixed Assets," which includes most property, plant, and equipment not associated with specific enterprises. Note that it is an unaudited element of the financial statements. Accounting for fixed assets is a comparatively recent innovation for most municipalities, with the consequence that for many properties it is not feasible to determine precise historical costs.

Recognizing the limitations of municipal reporting, the analyst can nevertheless apply techniques analogous to those employed in assessing businesses. As in reviewing a company, the analyst should study a municipality's financial statements with emphasis on key ratios. Also like private sector analysis, interpreting a local government's finances requires qualitative, as well as quantitative judgments.

City of Chicago, Illinois
(B) Combined Statement of Revenues, Expenditures and
Changes in Fund Balances
All Governmental Fund Types and Expendable Trust Funds
($000 omitted)
Year Ended December 31, 1992

Fund Types		Fiduciary Fund Type	Totals (Memorandum Only)
Debt Service	Capital Projects	Expendable Trust	1992
$ 21,041	$199,584	$ —	$491,378
13	15,066	—	36,675
(15,047)	(883)	—	(34,758)
6,007	213,767	—	493,295
15,151	108,006	—	85,681
122,700	188,673	34	623,494
—	—	—	—
$137,851	$296,679	$ 34	$709,175

Adapting concepts from company analysis is easiest with the balance sheet. The example in Exhibit 8–5 has a format that is readily recognizable to readers of corporate financial statements.

A prime focus of municipal balance sheet analysis is the "fund balance," which accounts for most of the equity—other than general fixed assets—in Chicago's case. Much like a company's retained earnings, the fund balance represents a cushion against insolvency in the event of a decline in revenues relative to expenditures. In a municipality's case, though, much of the cushion is encumbered, that is, earmarked for specific purposes. Reserves for such items as debt service and employee benefit plans would further reduce access to the fund balance if revenues were ever to fall short. The truest margin of comfort, then, is provided by the unreserved portion of the fund balance. To feel comfortable, municipal finance specialists generally like to see an unreserved fund balance equivalent to at least 5% of revenues.

A caveat to using this particular ratio, however, is that in some municipalities, unreserved fund balances are represented entirely by property tax receivables. If this is the case, the analyst should determine—disclosure practices permitting—what percentage of the total assessed tax bill has actually been collected in past years. If cash represents a significant portion of the unreserved fund balance, it reduces the risk posed by possible delinquencies. Liquidity, in short, is an important balance sheet consideration.

In Chicago's case, the most liquid assets appear fully adequate for satisfying current liabilities. On a consolidated basis, cash and investments total $6.9 billion at year-end 1992. Excluding noncurrent debt, pension and deferred compensation obligations, liabilities aggregate just $2.6 billion.

As for the combined statement of revenues, expenditures, and changes in fund balances, the most basic criterion of soundness is that revenues must, over time, equal or exceed expenditures. Unlike the federal government, a municipality cannot "print money" to pay for deficits.

In political terms, there is always a temptation for a city to live beyond its means by borrowing to finance the gap between revenues and expenditures. Neither a cutback in services nor a tax increase is generally welcomed by voters. Sooner or later, however, the local government must adopt one or both of these unpopular measures, lest the ever-mounting cost of debt service exceed taxpayers' ability to pay. At that point, the municipality faces the even more distasteful choice of defaulting on its debt or drastically reducing expenditures—including outlays for essential services.

A city's income and funds flow accounts can furnish early warning signals that just such a crisis is looming. Revenues, expenditures, and borrowings all provide telltale signs.

Aside from the obvious problem of a prolonged and pronounced decline—which would most likely reflect long-term deterioration in the city's economic base, revenues can also spell trouble if their sources are not sufficiently diversified. For example, it would be unwise for a city to rely almost exclusively on a sales tax, a source of revenues that is highly sensitive to economic cycles. Fluctuations in revenues generated by a general sales tax could be offset by levying a tax on utilities' sales volumes. To a significant extent, the usage of electricity and natural gas varies according to the harshness or mildness of weather during the winter heating and summer cooling seasons. Excessive dependence on a property tax can likewise endanger the stability of a city's revenues, given the demonstrated political appeal of proposals to set statewide caps for levies on homeowners. Note that although the property tax represents Chicago's largest revenue source, it provides only 21.5% of total 1993 revenues, indicating prudent diversification by the city authorities.

While the problem with revenues is most likely to be that they are too low—reflecting either weakness in the local economy or a lack of will in the political sphere—expenditures can cause trouble by being either too high or too low. Profligacy and inefficient procurement can wreak havoc with any budget, whether public or private, but is unfortunately not easy to detect in a city's financials. Comparing per capita expenditures across a number of cities may be misleading, given differences in population age and income profiles (which produce dissimilar needs for services), as well as regional disparities in the cost of providing equivalent services.

The analyst can, however, investigate a municipality's labor contracts, which may indicate a built-in bias toward high-cost operations. As for the problem that arises from underspending, it is primarily based on the fact that deteriorating infrastructure may drive business out of the city. A vicious cycle may develop as rising debt service costs strain the municipality's finances, resulting in a cutback in maintenance of streets and sewers, which in turn causes a shrinkage of the tax base and therefore a worsening of the budgetary troubles. To detect a problem of this sort, the analyst should look for a large jump in expenditures, which could indicate an emergency effort to remediate past neglect. As with most signs of potential danger, another explanation is possible, such as a federally mandated outlay to meet environmental standards. Still, a sharp swing in expenditures warrants further investigation, including, if possible, a physical inspection for obvious signs of infrastructure underspending, such as potholes.

If the vicious cycle of debt incurrence, revenue loss, and further debt incurrence is developing, the municipality's financial statements should furnish fairly explicit evidence of it. First of all, a ratio of debt service (interest plus principal repayment) to total expenditures of greater than 10% raises a red flag. (Note, however, a mitigating circumstance in the case of Chicago. The city relies extensively on tax anticipation notes, short-term financing instruments that increase debt service through a perennially large schedule of debt maturities but do not impair financial strength.) Another warning sign is a surge in borrowings, although the explanation may simply be that a recently elected administration finds it politically attractive to prefund before pressures surrounding reelection efforts begin to build. Finally, the debt burden—unlike expenditures, as previously explained—can be fruitfully analyzed in per capita terms, with a high ratio relative to other municipalities suggesting potential fiscal instability. To get an accurate picture, the analyst should consider the overall debt burden of city residents, including not only the city's direct borrowing, but also the residents' proportionate share of debt incurred by the county, the board of education, and special districts (lighting, fire, etc.). If this total figure exceeds 10% of the estimated market value of the city's taxable property, it is yet one more signal that danger may lie ahead.

Also on the subject of assessing the risk of indebtedness, analysts should remember that municipalities, like corporations, can employ off-balance-sheet leveraging techniques. Lease financing, a common form, has been used for many years but has grown in popularity in recent times. By leasing capital equipment, rather than buying it with borrowed funds, the city may complete the procurement more quickly and with less paperwork, while simultaneously obtaining a lower cost of funds. Even if the municipality's decision to lease reflects sound economic motives, however, and not a desire to disguise its true financial condition, the credit analyst should consider the impact of off-balance-sheet leverage, much as suggested in Chapter 6, under the heading "What Constitutes Total Debt?"

Other significant off-balance-sheet items include pension obligations and potential liabilities arising from litigation. Retirement benefits for city workers may present a sizable financial burden, as a consequence of a past failure to fund the obligations. In addition, municipal labor unions—where legal—have tended to bargain aggressively. Legal contingencies can likewise have a large, adverse impact on a municipality's finances. Environmental and discrimination claims are prominent among the categories of lawsuits that currently threaten to generate massive awards against municipal borrowers.

CONCLUSION

The didactic method utilized in this chapter has been to emphasize the interrelationship between an issuer's accounting practices and the economic and legal environment in which it operates. Adding to this recipe the objectives of management and investors—a theme stressed throughout this book—readers can construct a valid analytical framework for any of the numerous other types of issuers they may come across. As indicated in Chapter 1, the superior analyst looks outside the financial statements to understand more fully what is in them. The special categories of issuers discussed in this chapter should demonstrate that these external explorations can be much more stimulating than the phrase "financial statement analysis" could ever suggest.

GLOSSARY

accelerate To demand immediate repayment of debt in default, exercising thereby a right specified in the loan contract.

Accounting Principles Board (APB) Formerly a rulemaking body of the American Institute of Certified Public Accountants. Predecessor of the Financial Accounting Standards Board (see).

accrual accounting An accounting system in which revenue is recognized during the period in which it is earned and expenses are recognized during the period in which they are incurred, whether or not cash is received or disbursed.

actuarial assumptions Forecasts of the rates of phenomena such as mortality and retirements, used to determine funding requirements for pension funds and insurance policies.

APB Accounting Principles Board (see).

bridge loan A temporary loan made in the expectation that it will subsequently be repaid with the proceeds of permanent financing.

business cycle Periodic fluctuations in economic growth, employment, and price levels. Phases of the classic cycle, in sequence, are peak, recession, trough, and recovery.

capital-intensive Characterized by a comparatively large proportion of plant and equipment in asset base. The heavy depreciation charges that arise from capital intensity create a high level of fixed costs and volatile earnings.

capitalization (of an expenditure) The recording of an expenditure as an asset, to be written off over future periods, on the grounds that the outlay produces benefits beyond the current accounting cycle.

Chapter 11 Under the 1978 Bankruptcy Reform Act, a method of resolving bankruptcy that provides for reorganization of the failed firm as an alternative to liquidating it.

class-action suit A type of lawsuit filed under Federal Rule of Civil Procedure 23, which allows one member of a large group of plaintiffs with similar claims to sue on behalf of the entire class, provided certain conditions are met. Damages awarded in certain class-action suits have been large enough to compromise the solvency of corporate defendants.

comparability In accounting, the objective of facilitating financial comparisons of a group of companies, achieved by requiring them to use similar reporting practices.

consolidation (of an industry) A reduction in the number of competitors in an industry through business combinations.

convertible With reference to bonds or preferred stock, redeemable at the holder's option for common stock of the issuer, based on a specified ratio of bonds or preferred shares to common shares. (See also *exchangeable.*)

cumulative dividend A characteristic of most preferred stocks whereby any preferred dividends in arrears must be paid before dividends may be paid to common shareholders.

default The failure of a debt obligor to make a scheduled interest or principal payment on time. A defaulting issuer becomes subject to claims against its assets, possibly including a demand by creditors for full and immediate repayment of principal.

depreciation A noncash expense meant to represent the amount of capital equipment consumed through wear and tear during the period.

dilution A reduction in present shareholders' proportional claim on earnings. Dilution can occur through the issuance of new shares in an acquisition, if the earnings generated by the acquired assets are insufficient to maintain the level of earnings per share previously recorded by the acquiring company. Existing shareholders' interest is likewise diluted if the company issues new stock at a price below book value. In this circumstance, a dollar invested by a new shareholder purchases a larger percentage of the company than is represented by a dollar of net worth held by an old shareholder.

discounted cash flow A technique for equating future cash flows to a present sum of money, based on an assumed interest rate. For example, $100 compounded annually at 8% over three years will cumulate to a sum of $125.97, ignoring the effect of taxes. This figure can be calculated via the equation

$$P \times (1 + r)^n = F$$

where P = Principal value at beginning of period (Present value)
r = Interest rate
n = Number of periods
F = Principal value at end of period (Future value)

In this case, $\$100 \times (1.08)^3 = \$125.97$. (Note that this formula implicitly assumes reinvestment of cash interest received at the original rate of interest throughout the period.)

If $125.97 three years hence is equivalent to $100 today—given the assumed "discount rate" of 8% per annum—then the ratio $100.00/$125.97, or 0.794, can be used to determine the present value (see) of an any other amount discounted back from the same date and at the same rate.

By using the same general formula, it is possible to assign a value to an asset, based on a series of cash flows it is expected to generate. By way of illustration, suppose the right to distribute a particular product is expected to generate cash flow of $5,000 a year for four years, then expire, leaving no terminal value. At a discount rate of 15%, the distribution rights would be valued at $14,820, derived as follows:

Year	Expected Cash Flow	Discount Factor	Present Value
1	$5,000	.870	$ 4,350
2	$5,000	.756	$ 3,780
3	$5,000	.658	$ 3,290
4	$5,000	.572	$ 2,860
		Total:	$14,280

discretionary cash flow   Cash flow that remains available to a company after it has funded its basic operating requirements. There is no universally accepted, precise definition of discretionary cash flow, but conceptually it includes funds from operations less required new investment in working capital and nondiscretionary capital expenditures. The latter figure is difficult to quantify with precision, but it exceeds the required "maintenance" level required to keep existing plant and equipment in good working order. Ordinarily, some additional expenditures, which may be designated "semi-discretionary," are necessary to keep a company competitive with respect to capacity, costs, and technology. Only a portion of the total capital budget, including expansion-oriented outlays that can be deferred in the event of slower-than-expected growth in demand, can truly be considered discretionary. In a similar vein, mandatory principal repayments of debt, by definition, cannot be regarded as discretionary. Still, a company with strong cash flow and the assurance, as a practical matter, of being able to refinance its maturing debt, has considerable freedom in the disposition even of amounts that would appear to be earmarked for debt retirement.

diversification In portfolio management, the technique of reducing risk by dividing one's assets among a number of different securities or types of investments. Applied to corporate strategy, the term refers to participation in several unrelated businesses. The underlying premise is often countercyclicality, or the stabilization of earnings over time through the tendency of profits in certain business segments to be rising at times when they are falling in others.

double-entry bookkeeping A system of keeping accounts in which each entry requires an offsetting entry. For example, a payment to a trade creditor causes both cash and accounts payable to decline.

Dow Jones Industrial Average A widely followed index of the U.S. stock market composed of the common stocks of 30 major industrial corporations.

EBIT Earnings before deduction of interest expense and income taxes.

EBITDA Earnings before deduction of interest expense, income taxes, depreciation, and amortization. (Also referred to as EBDIT, an acronym for "earnings before depreciation, interest, and taxes.")

economies of scale Reductions in per-unit cost that arise from large-volume production. The reductions result in large measure from the spreading of fixed costs (i.e., those that do not vary directly with production volume) over a larger number of units than is possible for a smaller producer.

exchangeable In reference to a security, subject to mandatory replacement by another type of security, at the issuer's option. (See also *convertible.*)

externally generated funds Cash obtained through financing activities such as borrowing or the flotation of equity. (See also *internally generated funds.*)

FASB Financial Accounting Standards Board (see).

Financial Accounting Standards Board (FASB) A rule-making body for the accounting profession. Its members are appointed by a foundation, the members of which are selected by the directors of the American Institute of Certified Public Accountants.

financial derivative A financial instrument with a return linked to the performance of an underlying asset, such as a bond or a currency.

financial flexibility The ability, achieved through such means as a strong capital structure and a high degree of liquidity, to continue to invest in maintaining growth and competitiveness despite business downturns and other financial strains.

fixed-rate debt A debt obligation on which the interest rate remains at a stated level until the loan has been liquidated. (Compare *floating rate debt.*)

floating-rate debt A debt obligation on which the interest rate fluctuates with changes in market rates of interest, according to a specified formula. (Compare *fixed-rate debt.*)

future value The amount to which a known sum of money will accumulate by a specified future date, given a stated rate of interest. For example, $100 compounded annually at 8% over three years will cumulate to a sum of $125.97, ignoring the effect of taxes. This figure can be calculated via the formula

$$P \times (1 + r)^n$$

where P = Principal at beginning of period.
    r = Interest rate
    n = Number of periods

In this case, $100 \times (1.08)^3 = $125.97. (Note that this formula implicitly assumes that cash interest received will be reinvested at the original rate of interest throughout the period.)
    (See also *discounted cash flow, net present value,* and *present value.*)

GAAP Generally Accepted Accounting Principles (see)

Generally Accepted Accounting Principles Rules that govern the preparation of financial statements, based on pronouncements of authoritative accounting organizations such as the Financial Accounting Standards Board, industry practice, and the accounting literature (including books and articles).

GDP Gross Domestic Product (see)

Gross Domestic Product The value of all goods and services that residents and nonresidents provide in a country.

historical cost accounting An accounting system in which assets are recorded at their original value (less any applicable depreciation or other impairment of value), notwithstanding the fact that the nominal dollar value of the assets may rise as a result of inflation.

hostile takeover An acquisition of a corporation by another corporation or by a group of investors, typically through a tender for outstanding shares, in the face of initial opposition by the acquired corporation's board of directors.

internally generated funds Cash obtained through operations, including net income, depreciation, deferred taxes, and reductions in working capital. (See also *externally generated funds.*)

investor-relations officer An individual designated by a corporation to handle communications with securities analysts.

involuntary inventory accumulation An unintended increase in a company's inventory levels, resulting from a slowdown in sales that is not offset by a reduced rate of production.

leverage (financial) The use of debt financing in hopes of increasing the rate of return on equity. In the example below, the unleveraged company, with no debt in its capital structure, generates operating income of $30 million, pays taxes of $10 million, and nets $19.8 million for a return on equity (net income divided by shareholders' equity) of 13.2%. The leveraged company, with an equivalent amount of operating income, relies on long-term debt (at an interest rate of 12%) for one-third of its capital. Interest expense causes its net income before taxes to be lower ($24 million) than the unleveraged company's ($30 million). After taxes, the leveraged company earns less (15.8 million) than the unleveraged company ($19.8 million), but on a smaller equity base ($100 million versus $150 million) provides shareholders a higher rate of return ($15.8% versus 13.2%).

($ Million)

	Unleveraged Company	Leveraged Company
Operating Income	$ 30.0	$ 30.0
Interest Expense	0.0	6.0
Net Income before Taxes	30.0	24.0
Taxes	10.2	8.2
Net Income	$ 19.8	$ 15.8
Long-Term Debt	0	$ 50
Shareholders' Equity	150	100
Total Capital	$150	$150
$\dfrac{\text{Net Income}}{\text{Shareholders' Equity}}$	13.2%	15.8%

Note, however, that leverage works in reverse as well. In the scenario shown below, operating income declines by two-thirds (to $10 million) at both companies. With no interest expense, the unleveraged company manages to net $6.6 million for a 4.4% return on equity. The leveraged company, obliged to pay out 60% of its operating income in interest expense, suffers a sharper decline in return on equity (to 2.6%). Clearly, incurring financial leverage increases the risk to equity holders, whose returns become more subject to fluctuations. The greater the percentage of the capital structure that consists of debt, the greater is the potential for such fluctuations.

($ Millions)

	Unleveraged Company	Leveraged Company
Operating Income	$ 10.0	$ 10.0
Interest Expense	0.0	6.0
Net Income before Taxes	10.0	4.0
Taxes	3.4	1.4
Net Income	$ 6.6	$ 2.6
Long-Term Debt	$ 0	$ 50
Shareholders' Equity	150	100
Total Capital	$150	$150
$\dfrac{\text{Net Income}}{\text{Shareholders' Equity}}$	4.4%	2.6%

LBO   Leveraged buyout (see)

leveraged buyout (LBO)   An acquisition of a company or a division, financed primarily with borrowed funds. Equity investors typically hope to profit by repaying debt through cash generated by operations (and possibly from proceeds of asset sales), thereby increasing the net value of their stake.

liquidity   The ability of a company to meet its near-term obligations when due.

macroeconomic   Pertaining to the economy as a whole or its major subdivisions, e.g., the manufacturing sector, the agricultural sector, the government. (See also *microeconomic.*)

market capitalization   The aggregate market value of all outstanding shares of a corporation.

mature   With respect to a product, firm, or industry, at a stage of development at which the rate of sales growth remains positive but no longer exceeds the general growth rate of the economy.

microeconomic   Pertaining to a small segment of the economy, e.g., an individual industry, a particular firm. (See also *macroeconomic.*)

multiple   With respect to a common stock, the ratio of the share price to earnings per share. Similarly, the price paid in an acquisition can be viewed as multiple of the acquired company's earnings, cash flow, or EBDIT.

mutual fund   An investment vehicle consisting of a portfolio of securities, shares of which are sold to investors. The firm that organizes the fund collects a fee for managing the portfolio, while shareholders enjoy a diversification benefit that would be more costly to obtain via direct purchase of individual securities.

net present value The present value (see) of a stream of future cash inflows, less the present value of an associated stream of current or future cash outflows. This calculation is useful for comparing the attractiveness of alternative investments, as shown in the example below. Both proposed capital projects require an expenditure of $60 million during the first year. Project A generates a higher cash flow, without trailing off in the latter years as Project B is projected to do. Residual value in year 10 is likewise superior in Project A. Even so, Project B is the more profitable investment, based on a higher net present value ($17.7 million versus $14.3 million for Project A).

Net Present Value Illustration
(Presumed discount rate = 20%)
($000,000 omitted)

	Year											Net Present Value
	0	**1**	**2**	**3**	**4**	**5**	**6**	**7**	**8**	**9**	**10**	
Project A												
Cash flow*	(40)	(20)	16	18	21	24	24	26	26	26	20	
Discount factor	1.000	.833	.694	.579	.482	.402	.335	.279	.233	.194	.162	
Present value	(40.00) + (16.66) + 11.10 + 10.42 + 10.12 + 9.65 +											
			8.04 + 7.25 + 6.06 + 5.04 + 3.24									= 14.26
Project B												
Cash flow*	(10)	(50)	17	20	22	23	23	23	22	21	17	
Discount factor	1.000	.833	.694	.579	.482	.402	.335	.279	.233	.194	.162	
Present value	(10.00) + (41.65) + 11.80 + 11.58 + 10.60 + 9.25 +											
			7.71 + 6.42 + 5.13 + 4.07 + 2.75									= 17.66

*Figures in parentheses represent projected outflows, i.e., construction costs. Figures for years 2–9 represent projected inflows, i.e., net income plus noncash expenses. Year 10 figure represents expected residual value of equipment.

(See also *discounted cash flow, future value,* and *present value.*)

nominal dollar A monetary sum expressed in terms of its currency face amount, unadjusted for changes in purchasing power from a designated base period. (See also *real dollar.*)

payment-in-kind security (PIK) A security (generally a bond or preferred stock) that gives the issuer an option to pay interest or dividends in the form of additional fractional bonds or shares, in lieu of cash.

payout ratio Dividends per share divided by earnings per share. In financial theory, a low payout ratio (other than as a result of a dividend reduction forced upon the company by financial distress) is generally viewed as a sign that the company has many opportunities to reinvest in its business at attractive returns. A high payout ratio, in contrast, is appropriate for a company with limited internal reinvestment opportunities. By distributing a large percentage of earnings to shareholders, the company enables them to seek more attractive returns by investing elsewhere.

PIK Payment-in-kind security (see).

portfolio A group of securities. Barring the unlikely circumstance that all securities contained in it produce identical returns in all periods, a portfolio generally produces a steadier return than a single security. The comparative stability arises from the tendency of declines in the prices of certain securities to be offset by rises in the prices of others during the same period. (See *diversification.*)

present value The sum that, if compounded at a specified rate of interest (or "discount rate"), will accumulate to a particular value at a stated future date. For example: To calculate the present value of $500, five years hence at a discount rate of 7%, solve the equation

$$F/(1 + r)^n$$

where F = Future value
    r = Interest rate
    n = Number of periods
    p = Present value

In this case $500/(1.07)^5 = $356.49.
    (See also *discounted cash flow, future value,* and *net present value.*)

pro forma Describes a financial statement constructed on the basis of specified assumptions. For example, if a company made an acquisition halfway through its fiscal year, it might present an income statement intended to show what the combined companies' full-year sales, costs, and net income would have been, assuming that the acquisition had been in effect when the year began.

rationalization In reference to a business or an industry, the process of eliminating excess capacity and other inefficiencies in production.

real dollar A monetary sum expressed in terms of its purchasing-power equivalent, relative to a designated base period. For example, at the end of the first quarter of 1990, $500 (face amount) had only 77.6% of the purchasing power that $500 had in the base period 1982–84. The erosion reflected price inflation during the intervening years. The real value of $500 in January 1990 was therefore $388 in 1982–84 dollars.

reinsurance   A transaction whereby one insurance company takes over the risk of a policy originally issued by another company.

reorganization proceedings   A procedure under Chapter 11 of the Bankruptcy Reform Act that permits a bankrupt company to continue in operation, instead of liquidating, while restructuring its liabilities with an aim toward ensuring its future financial viability.

reported earnings   A company's profit or loss for a specified period, as stated in its income statement. The figure may differ from the company's true economic gain or loss for the period for such reasons as delayed recognition of items affecting income, changes in accounting practices, and discrepancies between accruals and actual changes in asset values.

   Disparities between reported and economic earnings can also arise from certain nuances of inventory accounting. For example, under the last-in, first-out (LIFO) method, a company's inventory account may include the historical acquisition costs of goods purchased several years earlier and unaffected (for book purposes) by inflation in the interim period. To the extent that a surge in sales causes a company to recognize the liquidation of older inventories during the current period, revenues will reflect post-inflation (i.e., higher) values but expenses will not. The mismatch will produce unusually wide reported profit margins in the current period, even though the nominal dollar (see) gains arising from inflation are in reality benefits that accumulated over several preceding periods.

scale economies   (See *economies of scale.*)

SEC   Securities and Exchange Commission (see).

Securities and Exchange Commission (SEC)   An agency of the federal government that regulates the issuance and trading of securities, the activities of investment companies and investment advisers, and standards for financial reporting by securities issuers.

senior debt   Borrowings that have preference in liquidation over other, subordinated, debt (see). In the event of a bankruptcy, senior lenders' claims must be satisfied before consideration can be given to subordinated lenders or equity investors.

sensitivity analysis   The testing of "what-if" scenarios in financial statement analysis. Typically, sensitivity analysis measures the potential impact (on earnings, cash flow, etc.) of a change of a stated amount in another variable (sales, profit margins, etc.). In connection with financial forecasting, sensitivity analysis may be used to gauge the variation in projected figures that will occur if a particular assumption proves either too optimistic or too pessimistic by a given amount.

SFAS   Statement of Financial Accounting Standards. Designation for a numbered series of statements of accounting rules promulgated by the Financial Accounting Standards Board (see).

shakeout   A reduction in the number of competitors (through failures or through mergers) that typically occurs as a rapidly growing industry begins to mature. Factors that may contribute to a firm's survival during a shakeout include advantages in raising new capital, economies of scale (see), and superior management.

standard error of estimate   A measure of the scatter of the observations in a regression analysis. In statistical terms, the standard error of the estimate is equivalent to the standard deviation of the vertical deviations from the least-squares line.

statement of stockholders' equity   A financial statement that details changes in components of stockholders' equity, including capital stock, paid-in capital, retained earnings, treasury stock, unrealized loss on long-term investments, and gains and losses on foreign-currency translation. The basic problem addressed by the statement of stockholders' equity is that it may not be possible to reconcile one year's equity account with the next year's using only the income statement and statement of cash flows, since certain adjustments to equity are included neither in earnings nor in cash flows from financing activities.

statutory tax rate   The percentage of pretax income that would be recorded as income tax if all of a company's reported income were subject to the corporate tax rate specified by federal law. Disparities between the statutory rate and the effective rate (that which is actually recorded) arise from such reasons as tax credits, differences between U.S. and foreign tax rates and the presence of expenses (such as amortization of goodwill) that generate no tax shelter.

straight-line method   A depreciation method that charges off an equivalent portion of the asset in each period. During inflationary periods, straight-line depreciation may understate the true economic impact of capital consumption. That is, as the replacement cost of the asset rises in nominal terms, the dollar amount required to offset wear-and-tear during a period grows to exceed a pro rate write-off based on the original acquisition cost. In these circumstances, accelerated methods of depreciation—which result in larger amounts being written off in earlier than in later years—represent more conservative reporting of expenses.

subordinated debt   Borrowings that have a lesser preference in liquidation vis-à-vis other, senior, debt (see). In the event of a bankruptcy, subordinated lenders' claims cannot be provided for until senior claims have been satisfied.

units-of-production method   A depreciation method that is based on the estimated total output of an asset over its entire life. The asset's cost is divided by the estimated number of units to be produced. Depreciation for the period is then calculated by multiplying the cost per unit by the number of units produced during the period. The units-of-production method appears, on its face, to match revenues and expenses rather precisely. While a piece of equipment sits idle, however, it generates no depreciation expense—even though its value may be decreasing as a result of the introduction of technologically more advanced, lower-cost equipment by competing firms. In this light, adoption of the units-of-production method by a firm that formerly employed a straight-line or accelerated method should generally be viewed as a switch to a more liberal accounting practice.

working capital   Current assets minus current liabilities. Working capital is commonly employed as an indicator of liquidity, but care must be taken in interpreting the number. The balance sheets of some corporations that are strong credits by all other methods ordinarily have little (or even negative) working capital. These companies manage inventories closely and extract generous terms from creditors—including long payment periods, which result in chronically high trade payable balances. In such cases, no threat of illiquidity is implied by the fact that more liabilities than assets will be liquidated during the current operating cycle.

BIBLIOGRAPHY

Books

Browne, Lynn E., and Eric S. Rosengren (Editors), *The Merger Boom: Proceedings of a Conference Held in October 1987* (Boston: Federal Reserve Bank of Boston, 1988)

Dirks, Raymond L., and Leonard Gross, *The Great Wall Street Scandal* (New York: McGraw-Hill Book Company, 1974)

Fabozzi, Frank J., and T. Dessa Fabozzi (Editors), *The Handbook of Fixed Income Securities,* Fourth Edition (Burr Ridge, Illinois: Irwin Professional Publishing, 1995)

Fridson, Martin S., *High Yield Bonds: Identifying Value and Assessing Risk of Speculative-Grade Securities* (Chicago: Probus Publishing, 1989)

Hale, Roger H., *Credit Analysis: A Complete Guide* (New York: John Wiley & Sons, 1983)

Levine, Sumner N. (Editor), *Handbook of Turnaround & Bankruptcy Investing* (New York: Harper & Row Publishers, 1991)

Maginn, John L., and Donald L. Tuttle (Editors), *Managing Investment Portfolios: A Dynamic Process,* Second Edition (Boston: Warren, Gorham & Lamont, 1989)

McConnell, Campbell R., *Economics: Principles, Problems and Policies,* Tenth Edition (New York: McGraw-Hill Book Company, 1987)

Mosteller, Frederick, Robert K.E. Rourke, and George B. Thomas, Jr., *Probability with Statistical Applications,* Second Edition (Reading, Mass.: Addison-Wesley Publishing Company, 1970)

Pass, Christopher, Bryan Lowes, Leslie Davis, and Sidney J. Kronish (Editors), *The HarperCollins Dictionary of Economics* (New York: HarperCollins Publishers, 1991)

Prochnow, Herbert V. (Editor), *Bank Credit* (New York: Harper & Row Publishers, 1981)

Siegel, Joel G., and Jae K. Shim, *Dictionary of Accounting Terms* (New York: Barron's Educational Series, 1987)

Standard & Poor's Municipal Finance Criteria (New York: Standard & Poor's Corporation, 1989)

White, Gerald I., and Ashwinpaul C. Sondhi (Editors), *CFA Readings in Financial Statement Analysis* (Charlottesville, Virginia: The Institute of Chartered Financial Analysts, 1985)

Periodicals

CreditWeek (New York: Standard & Poor's, Weekly)

Moody's Bond Record (New York: Moody's Investors Service, Monthly)

Moody's Bond Survey (New York: Moody's Investors Service, Weekly)

Schilit's Shenanigan Busters (Rockville, Maryland: Center for Financial Research and Analysis)

Standard & Poor's Bond Guide (New York: Standard & Poor's, Monthly)

Articles

Altman, Edward I., Robert G. Haldeman, and Paul Narayanan, "Zeta Analysis: A New Model to Identify Bankruptcy Risk of Corporations," *Journal of Banking and Finance* (June 1977), 29–54.

Beneish, Messod D., "The Detection of Earnings Manipulation," Working Paper, Duke University, Fuqua School of Business.

"British Accounting Standards: Bean-Counters Fight Back." (December 14, 1991).

"Cincinnati Milacron Overstated Earnings by $300,000 for Half," *The Wall Street Journal* (August 4, 1993).

Helene and Emory Thomas, Jr., "Physician-Investors Get Cold Shoulder from T2 Medical," *The Wall Street Journal* (August 13, 1993).

Dorfman, John R., and William M. Bulkeley, "Supercomputer Maker Kendall Square's Effort to Crack Business Market Has Some Skeptics," *The Wall Street Journal* (October 11, 1993).

"Eljer Industries Unit Files for Chapter 11 to Resolve Litigation," *The Wall Street Journal* (May 25, 1994).

Exton, Lynn, "Ratings for Latin American Banks Shaped by Volatility and Risk," *Moody's Speculative Grade* Commentary (May 1994), 4–5.

Fielding, Nick, Richard Thomson, and Larry Black, "Undisclosed Debt Worries Hang over O&Y," *The Independent* (May 10, 1992).

Fridson, Martin S., "The Transformation of Credit Research," *Bondweek* (October 29, 1984), 6.

Gallese, Liz Roman, "Kendall Square Fires Founder Burkhardt, Two Demoted Executives," *Bloomberg Business News* (December 14, 1993).

――――, "Kendall Square Stock Closes Down 32%," *Bloomberg Business News* (October 29, 1993).

Goldstein-Jackson, Kevin, "Finding Profit from a Loss," *Financial Times* (February 24, 1990).

Holland, Kelley, William Glasgal, Maria Mallory, Rick Melcher, and Greg Burns, "A Black Hole in the Balance Sheet; A Spate of Big Losses from Derivatives Sparks a Call for Disclosure," *Business Week* (May 16, 1994), 80–82.

Jensen, Michael C., and William H. Meckling, "Theory of the Firm: Management Behavior, Agency Costs and Ownership Structure," *Journal of Financial Economics* (1976:4), 305–60.

Krensavage, Mike, "T2 Medical 3rd-Quarter Net Falls 40%; Company Restates 1st Half," *Bloomberg Business News* (August 23, 1993).

Lipin, Steven, "Citicorp Unit's Top Officials Are Dismissed," *The Wall Street Journal* (November 11, 1991).

Meyer, Priscilla S., "Equity Funding Scandal Grows; Involves $120 Million in Nonexistent Assets," *The Wall Street Journal* (April 24, 1973).

Miller, Michael W., and Lee Berton, "Softer Numbers: As IBM's Woes Grew, Its Accounting Tactics Got Less Conservative," *The Wall Street Journal* (April 7, 1993).

"Net of First Financial Management Corp. Restated for 3 Periods," *The Wall Street Journal* (December 30, 1991).

Pauly, David, "Ways of Wall Street: T2 Medical's Numbers Aren't Right," *Bloomberg Business News* (August 13, 1993).

Pouschine, Tatiana, "Reel Assets," *Forbes* (December 29, 1986), 64.

Quinson, Tim, "T2 Medical Says Management Group May Make Buyout Offer," *Bloomberg Business News* (May 25, 1993).

Schwartz, Jerry, "T2 Medical Stock Plunges; Two Executives Step Down," *New York Times* (August 13, 1993).

"T2 Medical Net Fell 40% in 3rd Period; Company Restates Profit for First Half," *New York Times* (August 24, 1993).

Tinker, John, "Orion Pictures Corporation," Research report published by Balis & Zorn, Inc. (December 2, 1985).

Urry, Maggie, "When a Niche Becomes a Tomb," *Financial Times* (February 24, 1990).

Wang, Penelope, "Dictionary, Please," *Forbes* (March 7, 1988), 88–89.

Zeckhauser, Richard, Jayendu Patel, Francois Degeorge, and John Pratt, "Reported and Predicted Earnings: An Empirical Investigation Using Prospect Theory," Project for David Dreman Foundation (1994).

Zielenziger, David, "Kendall Square Drops 21% after Auditors Withdraw Backing," *Bloomberg Business News* (November 29, 1993).

INDEX